S0-AYH-507

What are Chinese intentions toward the West? Russia? Africa? Tibet? Mongolia? Southeast Asia? The UN?

What is the current state of Chinese agriculture? Industry? Science? Education?

What have been Red China's greatest successes? Her most painful setbacks? What is the mood of the different strata of her population?

After the Great Cultural Revolution what? After Mao what?

These are some of the questions examined in

ANATOMY OF CHINA

ABOUT THE AUTHOR: DICK WILSON was educated at Oxford and at Berkley. As correspondent for the *Financial Times* and as Editor of the *Far Eastern Economic Review*, he has traveled widely through Africa and Asia during the past fourteen years. Mr. Wilson has been a regular contributor to such leading journals as *The Guardian, The London Times* and *The Daily Telegraph*, and in 1964 won the Ramon Magsaysay Award for Journalism and Literature. He recently completed a tour as guest lecturer in the United States. For this Mentor edition, the author has revised ANATOMY OF CHINA to bring it completely up to date.

Other SIGNET and MENTOR Books
of Related Interest

☐ **LOVE AND HATE IN CHINA, by Hans Koningsberger.** A unique and multi-faceted view of a land shrouded in mystery, by an author who traveled through Red China, opening his eyes, ears, and heart to its people. "A stunning, perceptive account . . . a beautiful book."—**New York Times**
(#T3154—75¢)

☐ **HO CHI MINH ON REVOLUTION, edited by Bernard B. Fall.** A book of vital importance to every American who wishes to understand the man who holds the key to peace in Vietnam. Ranging over four decades, a collection of the writings and speeches of the North Vietnamese leader.
(#Y3389—$1.25)

☐ **REPORT FROM A CHINESE VILLAGE, by Jan Myrdal.** "For the first time, contemporary China becomes credible and alive," commented **The New York Times** on Jan Myrdal's intimate portrait of life in Red China today.
(#Q3024—95¢)

☐ **ASIA IN THE MODERN WORLD, Helen G. Matthew, ed.** Prominent authorities study the people, culture, and political history of Asia and provide the background for understanding its current role in world events. Illustrated with maps.
(#MQ762—95¢)

☐ **THE NATURE OF THE NON-WESTERN WORLD, by Vera Micheles Dean.** A noted expert on foreign affairs throws new light on the conflict between East and West as she probes the beliefs, traditions and emotions that motivate the people of the non-Western nations.
(#MY862—95¢)

THE NEW AMERICAN LIBRARY, INC., P. O. Box 2310, Grand Central Station, New York, New York 10017

Please send me the SIGNET and MENTOR BOOKS I have checked above. I am enclosing $＿＿＿＿＿＿＿(check or money order—no currency or C.O.D.'s). Please include the list price plus 10¢ a copy to cover mailing costs. (New York City residents add 6% Sales Tax. Other New York State residents add 2% plus any local sales or use taxes.)

Name＿＿＿＿＿＿＿＿＿＿＿＿＿＿＿＿＿＿＿＿＿＿＿

Address＿＿＿＿＿＿＿＿＿＿＿＿＿＿＿＿＿＿＿＿＿＿

City＿＿＿＿＿＿＿＿＿＿State＿＿＿＿＿Zip Code＿＿＿＿＿
Allow at least 3 weeks for delivery

ANATOMY OF CHINA:

*An Introduction to
One Quarter of Mankind*

SECOND REVISED EDITION

DICK WILSON

Originally published in England under the title
A QUARTER OF MANKIND

LIBRARY
COLBY-SAWYER COLLEGE
NEW LONDON, NH 03257

A MENTOR BOOK

Published by THE NEW AMERICAN LIBRARY

DS 777.55 .W46 1969
OCLC 04770785
Anatomy of China /
Wilson, Dick.

© 1966, 1968, 1969 BY DICK WILSON

All rights reserved. For information address
Weybright and Talley, Inc., 3 East 54th Street,
New York, New York 10022.

Library of Congress Catalog Card Number: 68-14095

This is an authorized reprint of a hardcover edition
published by Weybright and Talley, Inc.

MENTOR TRADEMARK REG. U.S. PAT. OFF. AND FOREIGN COUNTRIES
REGISTERED TRADEMARK—MARCA REGISTRADA
HECHO EN CHICAGO, U.S.A.

MENTOR BOOKS are published by
The New American Library, Inc.,
1301 Avenue of the Americas, New York, New York 10019

FIRST PRINTING, JUNE, 1969

PRINTED IN THE UNITED STATES OF AMERICA

*To my father and to
the memory of my mother*

PREFACE

BOTH NAPOLEON, WHO CHANGED HISTORY FOR THE NINE-teenth century, and Lenin, who changed it for the twentieth, foresaw the resurgence of China in world affairs. In September 1949, when his conquest of China was assured, Mao Tse-tung declared: "Today the Chinese people stood up." Since then the Communist government has restored China's national unity and stability, begun the drastic social changes which modernization requires, and taken the first steps towards economic development. China has also served notice of her intention to assert herself in the international arena on terms of equality with the other powers.

As Borodin remarked in the 1920s, it is almost academic to talk of Communism in such a poor country as China. Much of what Mao has done in the past twenty years is what any vigorous administration would have attempted. In domestic as well as in international affairs, the Communists have often trod the same path that Chiang Kai-shek would have taken. We in the West might more often sympathize with the aims of China's leaders, if we were not alarmed by their profession of Communism. They have not given up their ideological dreams of remoulding the minds of men and creating a socialist utopia in which an enforced selflessness prevails. Many of the difficulties which the Chinese face today stem from the intellectual rigidity, which, for example, persuades their leaders to renounce Russian economic aid lest it subvert China's march to pure socialism, and to divert some of their meagre resources to the promotion of world-wide revolt.

The outside world is awed and frightened by the spectacle

of a country which contains a quarter of mankind flexing her muscles for the first time in centuries. China counted for so little in recent history that we have grown used to ignoring her, and fail to understand the unique complex of cultural and ideological differences which make our relationship with her so difficult. How far is Mao a nationalist patriot, seeking, like any founder of an imperial dynasty, to put the foreign barbarians in their place: how far is he a zealot set on converting us all to his particular interpretation of the old-fashioned Marxist idea? How well-informed about our world are he and his likely successors? Will Chinese civilization absorb and transform Marxism as it did Buddhism, or will it give up its soul to the Communist philosophy? Will the Chinese change their character in the process of reforming their society? What are the outstanding problems within Chinese national life today? Will China expand? Will China cooperate?

These are the questions which outsiders ask themselves when they consider the face, both belligerent and self-righteous, which China now turns to the world. This book sets out the minimum factual background necessary to debate these questions, and suggests some tentative answers. It is the product of six years' study of current Chinese affairs from Hongkong, deepened by frequent travels in Asia, Africa, Europe and America (in each of which very different appraisals are made of the Chinese question), and culminating in a visit to several parts of China in 1964.

The book draws principally on the Chinese sources themselves, though supplemented by the testimony of visitors, and the work of foreign scholars, and it seeks to convey the mood and texture of contemporary China by quoting actual examples and cases. It begins by considering the main elements and tensions within Chinese cultural, social and political life: the second part of the book discusses the national economy and the third deals with China's international relations.

"Whoever understands China . . . holds the key to world politics during the next five centuries," said an American statesman sixty years ago. China's power is going to increase, relative to the West's, in the coming decades, and our dealings with her will become more difficult. Yet every possible barrier stands in the way of our understanding. Language, culture, religion, geography, history and political ideology combine to ensure that Americans and Europeans misunderstand China more profoundly than they do any other part of the non-Western world. Indians and Japanese, Africans and Arabs are all now to some extent incorporated within a European-initiated world system. Only China resists. But the forces of the contemporary Chinese revolution can be made to yield to analysis and comprehension in Western terms, and that is what this book attempts.

ACKNOWLEDGEMENTS

I have been helped by many people in searching for the truth about China. I wish most of all to thank all my former colleagues with the Far Eastern Economic Review in Hongkong who gave so freely of their time and knowledge, and especially P. H. M. Jones, Colina MacDougall, Kayser Sung and Robert Tung. It would be ungracious not to record also my debt to such other Chinese friends in Hongkong as Nelson Chow, Fei Yi-ming, Han Suyin, Choh-ming Li and Li Tsung-ying. I have learned so much from them, although none of them would agree with all that I have said in this book. Finally, parts of my manuscript were read and criticized by Ian Adie, Sally Backhouse, Jerome Ch'en, Audrey Donnithorne, C. H. G. Oldham and George Patterson, and I am most grateful for the trouble they took.

DICK WILSON

CONTENTS

Introduction

The Past

"AND THESE WERE THE UNIFORMS WORN BY THE BRITISH IM-
perialist aggressors against the Chinese people in the Opium
War. . . ."

Miss Hsu, the young interpreter, looked reproachful as she
spoke. There was an accusing glint in the eye of the guide
whose sentences she was translating, and the visiting peasants
and schoolgirls stared curiously as if I were a part of the exhibits. This was the Museum of the Chinese Revolution, one
of the new showpieces in Peking. With its sister, the adjoining
Museum of Chinese History, it is one of the first places to
which a foreign visitor is taken. It is probably the best,
though not the most comfortable, introduction to contemporary China. In this vast, modern, massively austere building "constructed by the Chinese people in only ten months," a
picture is painted of the Chinese past as China's present rul-
ers see it. It is a China of beauty and invention, home of a
civilisation which enjoyed cast iron, paper, printing, gunpowder and the mechanical clock long before Europe, and which
produced perhaps the richest language and the most delicate
painting and poetry the world has known. It is also the China
of sorrows, where floods in the Yellow River basin could destroy two or three million people: a whole Los Angeles, as it
were, washed away or starved. Famine in the single province
of Szechuan only thirty years ago took the lives of over a
million human beings. Finally, this is a China made weak by
an unkind history during the century just past, in which first
Europe and then America reached the apex of their power.
The humiliations which the Chinese have experienced at the
hand of foreigners are well remembered, and, in the Museum
of the Chinese Revolution, scrupulously documented and de-

picted. As a schoolboy in England in the 1940s I had learnt practically nothing about China, and it was an effort of memory to recall the events of the Opium War in 1840. But only a decade ago a film of this embarrassing contest, showing British merchants surrendering their opium stocks to the Chinese officials and Cantonese peasants organising a "put-down-the-British" corps, was voted the second most popular on the Peking and Shanghai cinema screens.[1]

"Today," Mao Tse-tung declared on 21 September 1949, "the Chinese people stood up." Chiang Kai-shek would not agree with his old foe's choice of date, but the Generalissimo's book *China's Destiny* leaves one in no doubt that reactions to foreign insults (and to foreign kindnesses misinterpreted as insults) are similar in Chinese breasts no matter what ideology beats beneath the skin. Long after the Communist Government had established itself, Liu Shao-chi, then Chairman of the People's Republic, could complain:

> Our country has been oppressed for over a hundred years by foreign nations. Today although we are liberated, although we progress rapidly in every field, there are still found people who retain the mental attitude and the imprint of the oppressed and in their hearts keep their . . . inferiority complex.[2]

Only a year or two ago a well-known Chinese Marxist historian [3] was attacked because he believed that "the centre of History is Europe." Chu Chien-chih, a courageous scholar specialising in Sino-European relations of the sixteenth, seventeenth and eighteenth centuries, had a running battle in the late 1950s with the philistines of the Chinese Communist Party over his assessment of the role of the early Jesuits at Peking.* It was an insult, they said, to portray these European clerics as bringing true science to China; only in very recent times, since the Opium War, had China become backward (because of the ravages of foreign imperialism), and

---

* Matteo Ricci established himself in Peking in 1601, in spite of the sixteenth-century Law Against Heresies, by wearing the robes of a Buddhist monk and teaching mathematics and science. His humility and usefulness gained the Court's favour, and he later introduced Jesuit astronomers, physicians, diplomats and gunfounders into the Emperor's service. He argued to the Catholics of Europe that Confucius, not being divine, should be honoured in his own country and that Chinese ancestor-worship was really a civil, not a religious, matter. But Ricci's successors in China took a less accommodating doctrinal line, and in 1704 Pope Clement XI insisted that Chinese Christians reject Confucius and the tending of graves, thus dooming Christianity as a popular movement in China. See Hudson, Chapter 10.

besides the Jesuits were opposed by such good Chinese scholars at the time as Yang Kuang Hsien. Professor Chu retorted that Yang was in fact a reactionary who taught that the earth was not round; that the progressive intellectuals of the time had absorbed new Western developments in natural science from the Jesuits; that Matteo Ricci had disobeyed the Vatican in implementing Catholic policy towards China (unlike modern Jesuits, who submit to the Pope's order); that all this is quite another thing from defending religion; and that "the mutual influence of cultures cannot be judged merely from the point of view of nationalism, it must be looked at from an international point of view, too." [4]

This kind of debate goes on in other fields of scholarship and will take many years to resolve: Mao wants the Chinese to become modern people as quickly as possible, and yet he also wants them not to feel emotionally obligated to the foreign sources of modern technology.

The dilemma appears most clearly in the official attitude towards that generation of intellectuals which, in the early part of this century, revolted completely against the apparently effete past. Hu Shih, the great Chinese scholar of this century, who defied the Nationalists and the Communists equally, was appalled that patriotic Chinese should regard the rude Boxer rebels of 1900 as heroes and denigrate Western culture as mere imperialism. "We cannot," he said, "stand comparison with outsiders in any line; not in material techniques, in political organisation, in morals, in learning, in literature, in music, in arts, not even in our physical make-up." [5] This exaggerated depreciation of the Chinese heritage is compared by the Communist press to the ideas of Lin Yutang, the Chinese writer who is perhaps best known to the West, to whom the Communists attribute a belief that "even the moon shines more brightly" outside China. Such cultural betrayal is incompatible with national pride, Peking believes, and yet a proper respect for the Chinese past must not stand in the way of absorbing certain necessary technical skills from foreign cultures.

A similar debate goes on about the Chinese cultural tradition itself. In 1938 Mao spoke as a Chinese: "We must not cut off our whole historical past. We must make a summing up from Confucius to Sun Yat-sen, and enter into this precious heritage." But on another occasion he declared: "The problem is quite plain. We wish to eradicate the old Chinese culture; it is inseparable from the old Chinese government and the old Chinese economic system. We intend to establish a new kind of Chinese national culture. . . ." A barometer of this contradiction is the official status of *Dream of the Red Chamber*. This eighteenth-century novel satirising the decadent aristocracy of the day was elegantly reprinted by the Communist presses in 1953, and an old literary professor, Yu Ping-po, republished a critique in praise of the book's calm spirit. At first the official periodicals approved, but in the following year two young Marxists challenged Yu. *Dream of the Red Chamber* represented the writer's revolt against the vanity of the time and was thus a social phenomenon. Professor Yu had based his appreciation not on an analysis of social struggle but on individual taste, and had thus betrayed himself as an idealist rather than a materialist. "This problem," the two critics warned, "has come before the people now, and it must be discussed. Essentially it is a severe struggle on the ideological front between the worker and the bourgeois class. . . ." [6]

Professor Yu stood for a refusal to import contemporary political ideas into the literature of the past. For the last fifteen years he and others have played the Communists' sense of national pride against their contempt for traditional values and have thus secured a reprieve for much of their common literary heritage. Despite pressure from the younger, semi-educated Marxists, few of the great writers of the past have been definitively labelled as unprogressive. But the classics are being expurgated so that the students will not be misled.[7] The elevation of Taoist-tinted emptiness and internal solitude, which Professor Yu so much admired in *Dream of the Red Chamber*, offers too easy an escape for the young man or woman being pressed to maintain a constant political awareness and social concern. If life is like a dream, what point is there in trying to improve it? The full texts, therefore, are to be available only to scholars, and the classics are thus to be retained as museum-pieces. As Professor Levenson has put it: "They are subject to scrutiny from a mental world beyond them; they do not govern the mental world (as they once did) themselves." [8] Even the edited texts are regarded with ambivalence, and young people are still criticised if they show a taste for reading "much ancient, little modern."

If anyone doubted the personal opinion of Mao himself, he was enlightened when the Chairman published some of his own poems in the classical style (that is to say, in the traditional way of expression, which the Government nowadays discourages in favour of the rougher, more direct and idiomatic style of current speech). "For a long time," Mao explained, "I did not want to publish these things because they are in the old form, and I was afraid that this disreputable seed might spread and be misunderstood by young people." [9] The insult to the classics was softened by the Chairman's breach of his own self-imposed rules.

The old theatre also came under the cloud. The *People's Daily* stated in 1951:

> Historically the theatre is the product of Chinese feudal culture and is deeply impregnated with Confucian and Taoist philosophies; it bears the indelible stigma of its origin. Its plays have spread the feudal concepts of hero, filial piety, loyalty to master and family above loyalty to the country, as well as a fundamentally fatalistic conception of life. With the establishment of the New Democracy, such ideas must be totally rejected as incompatible with the new social conditions. [10]

Many old favourites were banned from the boards, but later a less restrictive policy was adopted (perhaps because popular demand was so strong), and the authorities even revived certain forms of provincial folk drama which had almost died of neglect. This was more out of shrewd appraisal of the propaganda potential of the local drama form than concern to preserve the content of the nation's folklore. As a senior official has said, "We mean . . . not merely to edit the old heritage, but to create something new." New social attitudes are easier to promote from behind the footlights than on the school blackboard.

As for classical philosophy, it was assumed in 1949 that the corpus of Chinese thought through the millennia would now be regarded as an aberration from which Marxism had rescued China. But some brave souls insisted that China's ancient philosophers ought not to be pigeonholed into the European categories invented by European Marxists; they did, after all, produce a commendable degree of rational and scientific thought, and it could be argued that over the centuries a steady progression is discernible away from idealism and towards the materialism so dear to the Marxist. [11]

From time to time the philistine wing of the Communist Party calls for more orthodox analysis, but so far the tentativeness of the scholars, whether feigned or not, has kept the matter open. As an article in a philosophic magazine [12] urged in 1963:

> To write up ancient figures today as fighters for democracy and the proletariat . . . is bound to be harmful. . . . It may create a muddled picture among the masses concerning the meaning of the revolution, it may guide them towards the worship of ancient things and may turn their attention towards the past.

It will be noted that this reasoning, of such appeal to the Party man, is also an argument against condemning historical figures as enemies of the people and thus saves them for future study by scholars.

Above all, this relates to the Master himself. Confucius has neither been claimed nor rejected outright by the Communists, though most of the social institutions popularly (but in historical truth, wrongly) linked with his name were denounced and dismantled by them. In 1956 the respected scholar Fung Yu-lan began a skilful defence of Confucius before the court of the Chinese Marxists. The *Tien* of which Confucius spoke is Nature, not a personal god (the Peking Jesuits had argued similarly in their debate with the Pope three hundred years before). The Master should not be regarded, therefore, as a theist. Furthermore his eagerness for knowledge deserves praise. "The feudalist system which has set up his name as a symbol has gone for good; but the name of Confucius himself is, and always will be, respected and cherished by the Chinese people." [13] In the following year, under Fung's guidance, the Philosophy Department of Peking University drafted a textbook on ancient philosophy which credited Confucius as an early pioneer in the struggle for reason and democracy, a reformer and educationalist who kept pace with the development of history. The Communist Government indeed honoured the sage by having his temple at Sian and his tomb at Chu-fu repainted and regilded,* but the Party philosophers were soon at Fung's throat. Confucius was, they argued, a supporter of the ruling class who did not disguise his contempt for the common people. [14] More recently, another writer [15] was severely criticised by the authorities for arguing that Confucian ethics were above Marxism-Leninism

---

* Despite the good intentions and instructions of the Peking leaders, local Communist officials are often indifferent to cultural relics. Perhaps the worst case was the consignment of priceless Sung Dynasty books as pulp in the Nanchang papermill. Archeology understandably has low priority in the present state of the Chinese economy, and there are too few trained specialists for the work involved. A typical way of thinking is expressed in the following remark by a local official in defence of the destruction of pagodas for road-building purposes: "To be frank, what is the value of culture? Production is what counts. Ancient curios cannot be used as food. Building roads is an important task. It is no harm to remove some ancient relics and to use some old Buddhas as scrap." (*People's Daily*, 17 March 1957). The remark is cited in an article which ends by defending the preservation of cultural monuments, and it should not be thought that work on antiquities and archeology has stopped, although the Red Guard movement in 1966-8 set it back heavily.

and trying to "replace the Marxist theory of class struggle with the bourgeois doctrine of humanism."

The classic statement by Mao Tse-tung on the whole problem of the cultural heritage remains his closing speech [16] at the Forum on Literature and Art, held in Yenan during the guerrilla days in 1942:

> We must assimilate all the magnificent literary and artistic heritage from the past, we must critically borrow from it everything useful it contains so as to use it as a basis for the creation of new works taking their themes from the people's life in our time and in our country.
>
> We must not refuse to take over the legacy of the ancients and the foreigners and to learn from such examples, whether feudal or bourgeois. But succession to a legacy and learning from examples should never take the place of the creation of our own work, for nothing can take its place. In art and literature, the uncritical appropriation and imitation of the ancients and foreigners represent the most sterile and harmful artistic and literary doctrinairism.

More precisely, if less modestly, a Shanghai newspaper article [17] remarked in 1961 that "the beauty which the socialist system can create will greatly transcend everything people of the past could dream of."

The Government nevertheless takes meticulous care of the principal national monuments, the Imperial Palaces within the former Forbidden City, the charming Summer Palace outside Peking replacing that which British and French troops had sacked in 1860, the recently-excavated Ming Tombs near Peking, the Great Wall and many others. Miss Hsu, my interpreter in Peking, said that the former Emperor Pu Yi, who had been toppled from the throne as a boy in 1911 and was later "re-educated" as a citizen of the new People's Republic, had recently revisited the Imperial Palaces where once he reigned supreme. "They are much better kept than in my day," he is said to have remarked.

But the scars of foreign wounds are retained. Here is an urn from which British soldiers had scraped the gold plating; there is a display case of mediaeval art works with a small card reading: "This is a copy of the original, which was taken by foreign troops at the time of the such-and-such intervention and is now in the so-and-so museum in New York [or Pittsburgh]. . . ." When the East German Prime Minister, Mr. Grotewohl, visited China in 1955, he ceremonially returned one of the ten Boxer rebel flags seized by German troops during the eight-power intervention of 1900. The Chinese were deeply moved; any restoration of this kind releases deep emotions. Meanwhile small amounts of precious foreign exchange are allocated for a purchasing programme of Chinese works of art from abroad. The Government hopes to fill some of the major gaps in its own collections, but the feelings aroused by the necessity of buying Chinese treasures back from the foreigners who now possess them may be imagined.*

If the Communist leaders have generally followed an ambivalent policy towards their cultural heritage, there is one notable exception: the language reform. The Chinese language presents a unique problem for any modern administration. The spoken language varies immensely from province to province, and the differences are not merely ones of dialect —as one should expect, after all, in a country larger than the whole of Western Europe. The Pekinese does not necessarily understand very much of what is spoken in Canton, no more than a Parisian would understand Portuguese. It is a famous unpublished fact that Chairman Mao himself does not inflict his heavy provincial accent on the Chinese radio,† presumably because it would detract from his image as an all-China leader. The so-called Mandarin speech, the northern language as spoken in Peking itself, is accepted as the national spoken language.

Three or four hundred years ago Mandarin was widely understood even in the South, but under the Manchu emperors its use declined. Now the Communist Government seeks to spread again the use of Mandarin as the national language, rather as Latin was the *lingua franca* in old Europe, and you can hear taxi-drivers and schoolchildren in Canton speaking to each other in Mandarin. People from different provinces are deliberately mixed together in the civil administration, in all kinds of government service and in the armed forces, so that the use of Mandarin as the common spoken language is promoted (along with national unity). Schools everywhere teach in Mandarin, or at least teach it early as the first non-

---

* It is against this background that the total ban on export of objects more than eighty years old should be understood. Foreign residents in Peking affect amusement at a rule which prevents their taking home with them, at the end of their stay, small dishes and bowls picked up for the equivalent of a dollar or so in the Tung An market, but the Chinese sentiment is not without grounds.

† There was one exception, when Peking relayed a speech made by Mao in Moscow on one of his two visits. Even then Chinese listeners heard only the first few sentences of the original, and the rest was re-spoken in standard Pekinese tones by the radio announcer.

native language to be learnt. The younger generation in the South is becoming fluently bilingual.

So far so good. The difficulty comes with the written language, which comprises no fewer than 40,000 different ideographs or characters, each of which would be immediately understood but quite differently *pronounced* by a northerner and a southerner. Because the character pictures the word, its meaning is universal: thus a foreigner can learn the written characters and write fluent Chinese without necessarily being able to understand any single word spoken by a Chinese! In one sense this common written language holds China together. You can often see two Chinese from different birthplaces supplementing their spoken dialogue by a quick "drawing" of a character, with a finger only, no pen or pencil, either on the tablecloth or the table surface or even in the air. But a written language based on meaning instead of sound—ideographic rather than phonetic—has certain disadvantages. You cannot tell how to pronounce a word, and this makes it difficult not only for foreigners who wish to learn the speech but also for the Chinese themselves when it comes to compiling indices (there being no alphabetic order to follow) or translating foreign names and terms. There are six ways, for example, of writing "Dostoyevsky" in Chinese, and eight ways of writing "chocolate." Furthermore the Chinese script is quite unsuitable as a vehicle for writing Mongolian, Tibetan and the other languages of the so-called minority nationalities within China.

One way of simplifying the problem is to simplify the Chinese characters themselves. When the young James Yen volunteered to interpret for the Chinese labourers employed behind the allied lines in the First World War, he found that a thousand characters were sufficient for ordinary purposes of peasant life, and he launched the "Thousand Character Mass Education Movement." The number was later reduced to 800. It is usually said that of the 40,000 characters (no single man, however learned, can remember all of them), a scholar knows 10,000, a university entrant 5,000 or 6,000, and an average newspaper-reader 3,500. The Communists have all along favoured the more direct and colloquial style of writing which ignores the old high-faluting variations. There is now only one way of writing "I" or "you," the simple, direct way, and this even when addressing the Chairman of the Republic himself. These are obvious simplifications of what before had been an almost feudal system riddled with verbal class distinctions. But in addition, several hundred difficult characters have been officially abbreviated, abolished or simplified.

This is only tinkering with the problem, however. Even the shorter list of slightly simplified characters represents a greater burden on the learner than a truly phonetic script. When calculating the number of years needed to transform illiterate peasants into literates able to absorb the first elements of modern agricultural technology, or the number of teachers needed for this laborious task, the Chinese Communists have had to ask themselves: "Can we justify retaining a language which takes twice as long to learn as any other?" So the pressure to move towards a phonetic language has strong, practical, economic and social origins.

The Japanese, Koreans and Vietnamese have all had the same problem. The Japanese continue to use the old Chinese characters but supplement them with a specially invented set of phonetic signs used for foreign terms or names and instead of difficult characters: ultimately Japan may adopt *Romaji*, the Latin alphabet. Korea invented its own alphabet five centuries ago and has now dropped the Chinese characters altogether. Vietnam has taken over the romanisation of her language invented by European missionaries three centuries ago. What should China do? In 1956, after much debate, the Cabinet adopted a plan for a thirty-letter Latin alphabet for "discussion and trial" side by side with the Chinese ideograms.[18] In the following year many scholars, taking advantage of the free speech of the "Hundred Flowers" campaign, attacked this romanisation scheme as a programme foisted on the Communist Party by a small clique of radicals willing to sacrifice everything for the promotion of scientific progress.[19] An official newspaper article commented sternly that "the phonetic reform is a necessity for the masses, and the Party will not yield to the sentimental feelings of the five million intellectuals."[20] The linguist Tang Lan proposed a rival plan for a Chinese phonetic script of one thousand signs. But the leaders stood firm, reducing the Latin letters to the twenty-six corresponding to the alphabet used in England or France. Prime Minister Chou En-lai defended the policy, recalling that the Latin alphabet has 350 years of history in China (referring to Matteo Ricci's work in 1605) and remarking that it was as universal as the Western calendar or Arab numerals: he expressed the hope that in some future time the whole world would be united and speak the same language. Meanwhile, he calmed the traditionalists by affirming that "the adoption of this alphabet does not make Chinese a phonetic language. Whether the Chinese ideographs . . . should be replaced by a latinised or other phonetic language is a question we are not in a hurry to decide." [21]

There the matter stands. A standard romanisation is now in sight for Chinese, and this will simplify foreign intercourse immensely. As in other fields of life, the Communists want to move quickly. The Korean and Vietnamese reforms were successful partly because they were allowed to take natural root over centuries, but the Chinese are hoping to achieve faster results by legislation and propaganda. In so doing, they alienate a section of the more traditional intellectuals (who have, after all, a vested interest in their knowledge of ten times as many characters as the average literate peasant) and run the risk of loosening the national cohesiveness which the common ideographic script provides. The ideographs do not carry with them the *sound* of the Mandarin speech, but the phonetic written language is unmistakably Mandarin, intelligible only to people familiar with the Mandarin pronunciation. For the time being romanisation is a parallel system, but when the Government decides to make it compulsory, there will be considerable resistance from the southern provinces and China may face difficulties comparable to those in India. The most striking feature of the language reform, however, is the willingness of the Communist leaders to make such a sharp break in the cultural tradition and to move towards a language system that will bring China closer to the Western world.

The official interpretation of Chinese history also presents the Peking leadership with intellectual dilemmas. Some embarrassment has been caused in Sino-Soviet academic circles because the Maoist view sees feudalism surviving much later in China than orthodox Soviet Marxists had supposed. Undertones of nationalism are detectable in the debate [22] on Chinese nationhood: one Soviet view holds that China did not become a nation in the Marxist sense until 1840 or thereabouts, whereas Chinese views range from the third century BC to the seventeenth century AD. Most Chinese would prefer to suppose that their nation is a very ancient one. It is also difficult for Chinese Marxists to accept or explain the fact that capitalism did not evolve out of Chinese feudalism but had to wait for the penetration of the West. National sensitivities inhibit a full Marxist analysis of Chinese economic history. Mao and his followers cling with one hand to the past which made them Chinese, but with the other they reject those aspects of the Chinese tradition which hinder the drastic social and economic reforms needed to restore China's greatness.

ONE: *SOCIETY*

1: *THE PEASANTRY*

Life in the Communes

THE OVERWHELMING PREPONDERANCE OF THE 650 MILLION peasants who form more than four fifths of Chinese society makes Mao Tse-tung's Communist revolution different from its Leninist precedents in Europe. The peasant, not the urban proletarian, is the central character in China's drama.

The first step of the Communists in 1949 was land reform, as they had promised. Well over a hundred million acres of farmland were taken from four million landlords and given to fifty million previously landless tenant cultivators, within the first three years of the Communist administration. To each village came a team of Communist-led enthusiasts who investigated the land ownership, spread propaganda about its inequity, promoted discussion and organized those peasants who were most responsive—the "positive elements"—into a task force. To break the power image in the peasants' minds, the cadres held meetings, iconoclastic events at which increasingly articulate and voluble poor peasants "spoke bitterness" and "settled accounts" for the past misdeeds of the petty tyrants of the village. The campaign was often helped by the use of folk-drama, especially the *yangko*, which has been developed into a kind of village opera with dance and music. Perhaps the most famous of these is *The White-Haired Girl*,[1] in which the heroine is abducted and raped by an unscrupulous landlord, after her tenant father has been driven to suicide by his demands. She escapes to the mountains to avoid being pressed into prostitution, and years later is brought back by Communist officials to add her denunciation at the meeting where the newly-liberated peasants arraign the landlord. It is said to be based on a true story.

In real life the landlords were often publicly humiliated, sometimes beaten up and in extreme cases summarily executed, depending on the degree of hatred they had aroused, the mood of the villagers and the amount of control exercised by the sometimes inexperienced Communist cadres; but the great majority were punished by being made to work in the fields.* After these dramatic scenes, the cadres determined the class status of each villager, formally confiscated the land, farm tools, equipment and draught animals of the landlords, including those of religious and Government institutions, and redistributed them. The old title deeds were burnt and new landholding certificates issued. Landlords who actually farmed kept enough land to maintain their families. The local authority took over responsibility for the upkeep of the schools and hospitals formerly run by religious bodies from the produce or rent of their land. All peasants farming their own land, either by themselves or with hired labour, were guaranteed the continued possession of their holdings.

Many died in this land reform, probably several hundreds of thousands.[2] Mao Tse-tung had said as early as in 1927, of his experience in organizing peasant rebellions in Hunan province, that "A revolution is not the same as inviting people to dinner, or writing an essay, or painting a picture, or doing fancy needlework; it cannot be anything so refined, so calm and gentle, or so mild, kind, courteous, restrained and magnanimous. . . . To put it bluntly, it was necessary to bring about a brief reign of terror in every rural area; otherwise one could never suppress the activities of the counter-revolutionaries in the countryside or overthrow the authority of the

---

* When a British editor visited the Hua Dong People's Commune in Kwangtung province at the end of 1964, he was told that most of the ex-landlords had become "new men" living by their own labour: "Only about ten in the whole Commune had remained stubborn." One of these, hearing rifleshots one day in 1962, and not knowing that the People's Liberation Army was practising rifle fire nearby, ran through the village street shouting "Good! Good! The Kuomintang is coming!" (Derek Davies, "A Kwangtung Commune," in the *Far Eastern Economic Review*, 17 December 1964, p. 566). *Hurricane*, Chou Li-po's Stalin Prize-winning novel (Peking, 1949), describes the lynching of a landlord after the Communist cadres have worked the villagers into a mob fury. One oppressive landlord who was punished was the father-in-law of Chou En-lai, the Prime Minister: his distinguished relative did not intercede for him (Snow, p. 298). See William Hinton's *Fanshen* (New York, Monthly Review Press, 1966) for a close and revealing eye-witness account of the land reform.

gentry." [3] But the Chinese land reform was less bloody than the Russian one had been, partly because of a difference in temperament and partly because it was better prepared and supervised by leaders familiar with the villages.

The Communist Party never claimed that its agrarian revolution would stop at this point, indeed some commentators have wondered why it bothered to go through this stage of distributing land to the peasants when it knew that the ultimate goal was collectivization. Why give little pieces of land to peasants only to take them back again a few years later? Surely this stage of individual landholding could have been bypassed on China's road to Communism? Apart from the fact that redistribution had been pledged, and had become an important basis for the popularity of the Party in its struggle for power, there were good reasons for the reform. As a purely practical matter, the Communists needed to retain the rich-peasant economy during the few years which they required for preparations to substitute a state-directed agriculture. If they had proceeded directly to collectivization, the dislocation of production would have been extremely damaging to the economy, whereas the land reform in fact confirmed the efficient, go-ahead richer peasants in the profitability of their work. When collectivization did come, however, it would succeed only if the poorer peasants had already been aroused to assert their interests and if the hold of the rich gentry had already been broken. Both these conditions were met by the land redistribution. "The basic aim of agrarian reform," said Liu Shao-chi, then Mao's chief lieutenant, in the summer of 1950, "is not purely one of relieving peasants. It is designed to set free the rural productive forces from the shackles of the feudal landownership system of the landlord class, so as to develop agricultural production and thus pave the way for New China's industrialization." [4]

At the end of 1951, only eighteen months after the agrarian reform, the Government felt secure enough to press on with its first measures of collectivization. The peasants were encouraged first to form Mutual Aid Teams for the sharing of tools and equipment, and then to plunge into a simple form of cooperation by pooling their labour, their draught animals and even their land in order to wrest collectively a better return from their small holdings. The leaders made it clear that this was intended to be a voluntary process. It was "perfectly legal" for a peasant stubbornly to insist on working his land on his own, and "no one has the right to encroach on the individual peasant." Local cadres were exhorted to show "patience in helping and educating individual peasants." [5] But the fine edge between voluntary persuasion by "education" and compulsion by the social pressures so readily available in Chinese society was often blurred, and local cadres were tempted by the short cut of authority. Then, at the end of 1953, the Government launched its crucial campaign to transform all the cooperatives into fully-fledged collective farms in which the land was held in common by the group. This was to be implemented only gradually, the new measures were to be made "understandable to the peasant masses," and the cadres were sternly told to avoid "precipitate haste and adventurism at all costs." The model rules for the Agricultural Producers' Cooperative, as the new institution was called, provided for members to leave freely at the end of any production-year if they wished, taking with them their land and any capital contribution they had made to the Cooperative; disabled landowners who had depended on rent for their living should be maintained out of the Cooperative's welfare fund; graves and houses were not to be collectivized; and the Cooperative's production must follow the state plan.[6] A Cooperative usually extended over several villages to include about a hundred households.

As in Russia, the ones to suffer from the new arrangement were the "kulaks" or better-off peasants who now had to share the fruits of their work with their lazier or more stupid neighbours. The kulak did not live off rents like a landlord, but his landholding was usually twice as big as the average poor peasant's, he sometimes hired labour to help farm it, he maximized his profits by entering into commerce where possible and he lent out money at interest. This "upper crust" of the peasantry was officially estimated to number only about two per cent of the total,[7] and its strength was reduced first by the thoroughness of the land reform, in which the cadres had tried to promote poor peasants into positions of leadership, and then by the state monopoly of trade in the principal crops (complete by 1953). A newspaper article explained that the land reform had annihilated only "feudalistic exploitation, not capitalist exploitation . . . we struck at feudal exploiters by expropriating the land let out at rent by the rich farmers, but we preserved the rich peasantry economy." Now the attack must be directed against "rich farmers who are an extremely wicked exploiting class." [8]

Collectivization was resisted. In some places, the *People's Daily* complained in an editorial at the end of 1954, rich peasants "wreck the agricultural implements, owned by the Cooperatives, and the water irrigation equipment, destroy the grain, kill their animals and murder Party cadres, . . . thus spreading chaos and terror, in order to induce the people to quit the Cooperatives." [9]

In Chou Li-po's celebrated novel *Great Changes in a Mountain Village,* published in Peking in 1958, the feelings of an old peasant on the eve of collectivization are poignantly described. "No matter how you look at it, I cannot bear to give up the few pieces of hill land," he confides to his wife. "Everyone," she says, "is handing it over; public horses are for the public to ride. We shall be spared a lot of worries; in the future we shall only have to work and eat." The old peasant reluctantly agrees, but falls silent, and early next morning at daybreak he goes out alone to his fields and weeps.

Early in 1956 a Twelve-Year Plan for Agriculture was introduced. The *People's Daily* cartoonist let his imagination run in sketching "just a normal village in twelve years' time" with doctors telling patients to "eat less meat," lorries carrying the cotton bales, buses taking children on picnics, a basketball ground, recreation club, radios and telephones.[10] Mao declared that almost every peasant should receive a higher income as the result of collectivization. The Communist Party was by now well spread on the ground, with a cell in nine-tenths of the villages, and its members took pains to gauge personal relationships and class consciousness in every village, in the drive to achieve a 100 per cent voluntary adhesion to the collectives. Soldiers in the People's Liberation Army wrote letters to their relatives at home urging them to overcome their hesitations, and in some cases troops were seconded as cadres to promote the movement. Unfortunately 1956 turned out to be a bad year for weather, and the promise of more income could not be kept. One Cooperative in Hopei province secretly disbanded itself by unanimous vote one night, telling the village Communist Party secretary next morning that "we do not work in a collective now, do not try to teach us any more" (its members were presumably persuaded to try again).[11] The Kwangtung province Party Committee admitted that during the winter of 1956–7 about half a million people withdrew from the Cooperatives, though the majority of them rejoined.[12] And active resistance continued: in one county (Shantai county in Szechuan province) the Public Security Department reported a hundred cases in the first seven months of 1957 "involving unlawful landlords, rich peasants and counter-revolutionary elements, reckoning old scores with the peasants, wresting or attempting to wrest from the peasants lands, houses and other items of property, revenging themselves on and beating up peasants and cadres, poisoning livestock, destroying water conservancy works and crops, alienating relations between cadres and the masses and spreading rumours." [13] One survey showed that a mere forty per cent of the peasants in a district joined spontaneously, thirty-two per cent hesitantly and only after "encouragement," twenty per cent out of fear of the consequences.[14] Some cadres said at village meetings that no one was to leave until he had made up his mind to join the collective.

The Communists were wise enough to exempt the pig, the supreme standby of the Chinese farmer, from collectivization,[15] and although this period did see a decline in livestock (partly from neglect after the ending of individual responsibility, partly from kulak destruction, partly from shortage of feed) there was no repetition of the Soviet debacle in the early 1930s, when half of Russia's animals were lost in the course of collectivization.

By 1957 collectivization was complete, and the final step came in the following year. The merger of collectives into People's Communes began in the spring of 1958 in Honan province, where a larger-scale deployment of labour was badly needed to counter the Yellow river floods: it quickly spread over the country. In December, the Central Committee declared that "In 1958 a new social organization appeared fresh as the morning sun above the broad horizon of East Asia . . .": the commune would now be "the basic unit of the socialist social structure of our country." *

Some cadres, and possibly some in the higher echelons of leadership, genuinely believed that they were on the threshold of true Communism, and did away with wages and individual property overnight, even collectivizing pots and pans, pins and needles. Some cadres who had been on the Long March with Mao reverted to the guerrilla system of free supply of goods,

---

* The Russians had experimented with the communalization of all property in the 1920s, but their communes concerned only farming, and did not include militia, local government and industrial activity as do the Chinese communes. They did not last, and to this day the Russian collective farm or Cooperative has not fundamentally changed since its inauguration thirty-five years ago: no wonder the Russians were sceptical about the Chinese communes. The *Washington Post* reported on 17 December 1958, that Khrushchev had told Hubert Humphrey that the Chinese communes were "reactionary." Mr. Gomulka, the Polish Leader, described the commune as "a certain specific phenomenon arising from the historic development of China, . . . absolutely impossible to transfer mechanically . . . to our country" (Keesing, p. 16599). Marshal Tito said, less diplomatically, that the commune had "nothing in common with Marxism" though "such a military type of Socialist development" might suit the Chinese (*ibid*). In Bulgaria a commune was formed at Botevgrad but nothing more was heard of it (CQ 3, 1960, p. 81).

irrespective of work, as if the trust and camaraderie of the People's Liberation Army could be re-created in the vast morass of China's peasantry. In an excess of ideological zeal some of them constructed not only communal mess halls, creches and nurseries for children, but even separate dormitories for men and women, assuming that the peasants' enthusiasm for increasing their output and promoting national construction would make it easy for them to forgo their family life. These arrangements allowed the cadres to organize large-scale irrigation works for the first time, but they also aroused considerable popular resentment.

It was the extreme examples which were publicized by the foreign press, both Communist and capitalist, and which shocked opinion in Moscow and Warsaw as well as in New York. In fact such experiments represented a tiny fraction, not more than a few per cent of the total communes, and they were discouraged by Peking; none of them lasted more than a few months.

The commune is an organization of about a hundred villages, containing about 50,000 people. It is the highest unit of agriculture and the lowest unit of government all in one, and it includes military, security, judicial, fiscal and industrial functions in addition to farming. There are three tiers in the commune: the Production Team, which is a unit often based roughly on the old village; the Production Brigade, sometimes equivalent to the old Cooperative; and the commune itself.

At first labour was deployed on a commune-wide basis. Although women were not normally forced to work, the provision of institutions where their children could be cared for enabled more of them to participate in farming and bring additional income to the household. In the old days peasants had been over-worked during the sowing or harvesting seasons and relatively idle the rest of the year. Now the commune undertakes public works, industry and handicrafts to keep people occupied all the time. But within a year or two it had been a common experience that the high ideals and dedication of the Communist cadres were not fully shared by the general population, and the emphasis accordingly shifted between 1960 and 1962 from the commune first to its constituent Brigades and then to the Teams.[16] The Team was accorded more recognition and stability by the so-called "four fixes," by which it obtained a semipermanent allocation (a Roman lawyer might have called it *usus,* as distinct from *dominium*) of land, labour, animals and tools.

It was recognized, in effect, that team spirit and trust can only be built up among peasants at this level of education in a group small enough for everyone to know each other. In Kwangtung province recognition was given even to the "small Team" comprising a mere two families.[17] The principle of work incentives was also fully restored. The element of "free supply" of goods in total rural remuneration had been gradually reduced since 1958, and the element of money wage increased. By 1961 cash accounted for two thirds and the proportion by now is probably higher. Tao Chu, then leader of the Kwangtung Province Communist Party, wrote in 1964 of the importance of "avoiding equalitarianism" and propounded the slogans "From each according to his ability, to each according to his work" and "He who works more shall receive more, and he who does not work neither shall he eat."[18] The material basis for the creation of Communism, in which rewards are equal, has not yet been constructed, and meanwhile production must come first.

A 1958 HUMAN VILLAGE FAMILY BUDGET [19]

| | ANNUAL AMOUNT | | |
	PER HEAD	FOR THE FAMILY OF SIX	COST IN *yuan*
Rice	424 lb	2,541 lb	175
Sweet potatoes	147 lb	880 lb	11
Cooking oil	4 lb	26 lb	13
Salt	11 lb	66 lb	9
Pork	7 lb	44 lb	18
Sugar		2 lb	1
Cloth	13 feet	79 feet	29
Socks	1 pair	6 pairs	3
Shoes		1 pair	4
Other items*			38
		Total	301

* Vegetables, beancurd, beanflour, spices, hemp for weaving, production expenses for winter handicrafts (costing twelve *yuan*) and drugs (twelve *yuan*).

Before examining the rural wage system, one should have a clear idea of the low level of farmers' incomes. The accompanying table has often been published in Peking: it is an official estimate of the annual consumption of a typical farming family, a couple and four children, in a Hunan village at the beginning of 1958. A Western reader unfamiliar with China or with Asia might find this table disturbing, even unbelievable. The *yuan* is exchanged, officially, at two and a half to the US dollar, which means a weekly spending per head of about forty cents. Even if this is trebled or quadrupled to allow for price differences when compared with the USA, it is still a meagre life. It is not a starvation income by any means, and if any Westerner doubts it he should try consuming eighteen and a half ounces of rice in one day. But it is a poor life, barely raised above subsistence; such rich foods as vegetables, fish and meat are still rarely taken by the Chinese peasant, and, when they are available, they are eaten almost as a condiment.

At the end of the main harvest each year the Production Team (i.e., the village) calculates its gross proceeds, either in cash, from the sale of crops to the state, or in kind. Roughly two fifths [20] of this is allocated to meet the Team's costs, to pay its Land Tax and to keep up its own Welfare and Accumulation Funds. The remaining three fifths is divided among the Team members according to the number of work units they have each earned during the year. The work point system [21] is based on the principle that a reasonably good worker should expect to earn about ten work points a day. Time-rates are used only when there is no other way of reckoning the work; tending a bullock, for example, earns ten points a day, but cutting stalks of ripe grain in the field and bringing them to the threshing machine merits three points per 110 pounds, and threshing earns 1.2 points per 110 pounds. Some work is measured by area, as for instance muckspreading or sugarcane planting. Thus one man was paid an advance of twenty *yuan* in July; in December his work points had aggregated 3,200 for the year, and the value of each point was calculated at 0.022 *yuan*. His annual earnings were thus seventy *yuan*, and he promptly received the balance of fifty *yuan* in cash. But a peasant also receives foodstuffs in kind. This man was entitled to 290 pounds of rice, and he was given this in two equal instalments in July and December, along with ration coupons for monthly amounts of sugar, salt, oil and cloth.

A farmer also derives income from the produce of his private plot, which supplements his collective earnings by perhaps thirty to forty per cent. The old Model Regulations for Cooperatives had provided for an amount of land up to one twentieth of the whole to be set aside for individuals or families to raise their own vegetables. In 1958 these little side-line plots of a few square yards each, which sugar the collective pill for the average peasant, were absorbed into the com-

LIBRARY
COLBY-SAWYER COL
LONDON NH 0

munes, and the local ideological fanatics who raced ahead of the Central Committee in that year took satisfaction in suppressing them. The Government restored them in the following year, however.*

The products of these side-line plots may be sold through rural fairs, and the income kept by the individual household. Such sales have been estimated at about one tenth of total national supply.[22] It is in this little private sector of the rural economy that "king pig" still reigns. About half of China's pigs are privately reared and since 1962 official policy has favoured the private pig. It was decided, after agonizing debate, that the private pig-rearer could sell his animal for cash at the rural fairs.[23]

All this seems a far cry from the purity of Communism, but it is certainly practical at China's present stage of economic development. The private plot and the private pig are, however, ideological inroads made into the communes during a period of exceptional food shortage and peasant demoralization (because of the technical errors committed on the soil during 1957–9 and the natural calamities of 1959–61, both described in Chapter Ten below), and they may yet be reintegrated into collective life once agrarian development resumes its upward thrust. The magazine *Youth of China* did, however, promise in 1961 that the "means of subsistence" (defined as one's house, furniture, bedding, clothing and small private plot) would not be encroached on "at any time, whether in a socialist society or a communist society." [24] Elsewhere the official press refers to the plots as "remnants of capitalism," surviving only because of the low level of production.

The crop failures in the three successive years 1959, 1960 and 1961 plunged the peasants into their worst plight for decades, and provided the regime with the sternest test it could have faced. Food was desperately short, especially during the rockbottom winter of 1960–1. The authorities encouraged people to go into the hills and find wild plants, herbs, bark and anything edible to supplement their rations. The newspapers praised the austerity of people who "alternated liquid meals with solid meals." [25] Joseph Alsop, the American columnist, claimed after interviewing refugees in Hongkong in 1962 that the Chinese economy was on a "descending spiral"

---

* Theatregoers in Peking recently saw a one-act opera called *A Basket of Manure*, in which a husband and wife argue whether the basketful (which sat in the centre of the stage throughout) should be spread on their own side-line plot or on the collective fields (*China Reconstructs*, Peking, No. 8, August 1964, p. 4).

OLBY-SAWYER COL
NOW AU C

and that the average daily food intake was between 1,300 and 1,600 calories, "so low that one cannot imagine the Chinese masses surviving, at this wretched diet level, for three years on end." [26] They did survive, as they had survived worse disasters before. Malnutrition was, however, widespread. Every locality had bodies swollen with dropsy (oedema), liver enlargements were common and so were intestinal parasites, nightblindness and beri-beri. Pregnancies became less frequent, and some women temporarily ceased to ovulate.[27]

There is no documented evidence of large-scale deaths from starvation in 1959–61* and the comment of most thoughtful Chinese with personal experience of previous famines is that this time the government did better than any of its predecessors, in ensuring as equitable a distribution of food as was organizationally possible, and in providing relief. Indeed the argument has been advanced that if the government had been more cynical and less scrupulous of human life it might have localized the famine by withholding relief from the worst-off areas, thus keeping a large proportion of the country adequately nourished for production purposes at the expense of a small section of it which would have been decimated (as happened in most previous famines). The result of the government's efforts was a spreading of the available food so thinly all over the ground that virtually no one had any energy for work of any kind, and the immediate setback to the national economy was, for this reason, probably worse than if the disaster had been confined to two or three provinces.

During the disaster years ideology was forgotten and every priority was given to relief, survival and production. One consequence of this was the resurgence, in the almost laissez-faire conditions of the early 1960s, of the enterprising peasant who was able to achieve some degree of economic independence by manipulating the small work teams and exploiting the private plots and rural fairs. And so class struggle is now waged fiercely in the communes. Students are mobilized to tour the villages as storytellers, showing magic lantern

---

* There are, however, one or two reported cases of those horrific incidents which are the authentic mark of a famine. A man who had killed six children and either eaten or sold their flesh was driven through the streets of Tsinan to the accompaniment of loudspeaker denunciations, and summarily shot in the back of the head on a hillside (*Saturday Evening Post*, 16 November 1963, p. 106). An almost identical news report, retailed by a refugee in Hongkong, is given in CNA 364, 17 March 1961, p. 2 (this issue, headed "What do people eat?," provides a saddening selection of testimony from refugees).

slides, projecting movies, and organizing village libraries and programmes to remind everyone how the rich peasants abused their position in the past, how the activities they want to resume are exactly those things which led in the old society to the poorer peasants' coming under the control of rich, grasping landlords, continually in their debt and power.[28] The problem is serious enough for such a highly practical measure as instructing the thousands of rural credit cooperatives to make loans not to the collectives but to the individual poor and lower-middle peasant households to help them in their struggle against the richer peasants! [29] And poorer peasants are encouraged to form special associations to watch over their interests within the collective groups, the Production Team and the commune. Even the village cadres are to be supervised by the Poor and Lower-Middle Peasant Associations, whose members are usually the least enterprising, least diligent and least intelligent people in the village.[30]

The cadre worker is the lynch-pin of the whole Communist rural campaign. If he is conscientious then he is by definition overworked. As one explained in a newspaper report, "I am accountant, tax-collector, statistician and public health officer all in one; I worked in the fields for 214 days last year and did my office work in the evenings. . . ." [31] The other side of the coin is revealed in a complaint by an officer of the Central Committee's Organization Department in 1953 that some bureaucratic Party members "terrorize the population, using the village militia to force the farmers to labour on public works; farmers are often beaten up if they do not obey; similarly they arrest people arbitrarily; under the cover of the marriage reforms they violate women and cause the deaths of many people." [32] There were cases of cadres over-assessing their own work points, choosing easy work, favouring their relatives or friends and overpaying themselves. In six districts of Hunan province no fewer than eleven per cent of all the Cooperative officials were embezzling funds in 1956 [33] and a Peking newspaper protested: "Many village cadres are still acting illegally, searching houses, arresting, torturing, forcing people to marry and embezzling common property." [34]

The principal answer of the Central Committee to these abuses is to ensure that the cadres take part in physical work and avoid becoming divorced from the ordinary people. Many junior cadres, the *People's Daily* said in 1963, were "still peasants not long ago, but became infected by the traditional idea of despising labour." [35] Even eight-day indoctrination courses failed to convince some of them, and the higher echelons were faced with the arguments that administrative work left no time for manual labour, that physical work caused the cadre worker to lose the peasants' respect and forfeit his authority over them, and that manual work was a waste of his talents. But now the cadres are under instruction to observe the "four togethernesses" (eating, living, working and discussing with the people), especially during the annual "Love the People" month, and to carry out their work at fixed places at fixed hours under the watchful eye of the local Poor and Lower-Middle Peasant Association.[36] No one has really answered the *cri de coeur* of an official in Hupei province at the end of 1964: "(If) the people criticize the cadres, the cadres will not be able to lead them at all. It is all right for the upper levels of government to criticize the cadres, but if the people do, then things will become chaotic." [37] This rural dialectic was brought to a new pitch of intensity during the Great Proletarian Cultural Revolution of 1966–7, when many village cadres became quite demoralized by criticism, and it still goes on.

How should one assess the People's Communes? This is how one commune director, Teh Hung-hwa of the Ma Lo Commune near Shanghai, described the advantages of the new institution when I visited it in 1964:

Under the Cooperatives we were still hampered in our drive to develop agriculture by inadequate labour power, material and financial support. The commune has solved these problems. Since its establishment, six years ago, we have dug irrigation canals which required 100,000 labour-days, moving ten million square metres of earth. . . . People said "during the period of the Cooperatives we thought of this but could not achieve it." Now we have good irrigation equipment, a water gate and fifteen irrigation pumping stations aggregating more than 700 horse-power. We also have thirteen mobile electric pumps on boats, using either the grid or diesel engines. So we irrigate now all of the 5,450 acres of cultivated land in our commune. Even in the 1960 drought we still had a good harvest here. When the rice needed water that year there were seventy-two days without rain. But we mobilized all the peasants, took out all the irrigation pumps and as a result we produced sixty-two kilograms from each acre, which is still a harvest. We also now have sixteen large tractors and seventy per cent of the fields are worked by tractor. We have built fifty-two concrete bridges for the tractors, and six miles of road. We do our rice threshing by machine and have three 60-horsepower boats to transport the rice. All these things were wanted under the Cooperatives but couldn't be organized.

It is not only agricultural improvement which the commune facilitates. The peasant's introduction to industry and to the idea of self-help in many fields of manufacturing is also a feature of the new system. The so-called "backyard steel" drive in which innumerable village furnaces attempted to forge steel is described in Chapter Twelve below. Anna Louise Strong, the veteran American authoress who resides in Peking, visited Liangko commune in Kwangtung province in 1959 and made the following report:

I was surprised to learn that it had eight "paper mills". Paper mills to me implied fairly large enterprise: that a single commune should erect eight of them meant to me either an unusual demand for paper or an economic waste. I visited one of the paper mills and ceased to be surprised.

At one end of a large rice-field on a rise of land against a hill stood a wooden structure, a shed with walls shoulder-high and the upper part open, topped by an overhanging roof. Inside there was a brick stove with a metal boiler, and a dipping vat with a wire netting for lifting and draining pulp. Outside the building a large pool had been made of boulders with the chinks filled in by cement. This was the total equipment needed to turn rice straw into paper of several kinds and colours. The manager explained that the seven other paper mills were of even simpler construction, and were in the hills where there were wastes from bamboo.

Why did they have eight paper mills instead of one? I asked. He explained that all eight cost less than 10,000 yuan * and it was much cheaper and more convenient to make eight near the various sources of rice straw and bamboo waste than to haul the bulky refuse to the mill. The purpose of these mills, he said, was not to make a lot of paper, but to use up all their wastes and make all the paper they needed as well as make some income by selling paper. They expected, on the investment of 10,000 yuan and by the labour of some eighty-five people, to make about 250,000 yuan during the year. In the present state of China's transport, paper supply and wage scale, eight small paper mills were an efficient means of meeting a local problem. In the future they might not always be. . . .

I saw the power plant. A small irrigation ditch had been diverted to send a stream some twenty inches in cross-section through a wooden flume where it turned continually a home-made wooden turbine. From this a belt of woven hemp connected with a motor and a switchboard. . . . The cost of the project, including motor, switchboard and wiring to four hundred houses, was less than 10,000 yuan. It furnished only about fifty watts of light bulb per house, but this was brighter than kerosene and also cheaper.

* $4,000 at the official rate.

"We can pay for it by one year's kerosene bills," the manager said.[38]

I quote this at length because it shows, better than any abstract analysis, how the present organization in the Chinese countryside can lead, under optimum conditions and wise local leadership, to a release of new economic and social forces of the kind needed to transform this vast peasantry into an educated body of advanced farmers. As the *Manchester Guardian* commented on 11 September 1958: "Mao's own and entirely original contribution to the theory and practice of Communism is that he proposes to turn the peasantry into an industrial proletariat without urbanizing it, as both the West and Russia had to do in their own industrial revolutions."

It would be wrong to ignore the difficulties. There are some Western scholars who doubt whether very many communes ever existed at all outside the "showpiece" examples visited by the Peking leadership and foreign dignitaries. These sceptics point to the August 1958 resolution of the Central Committee which said that "in the early period of the mergers [of Cooperatives into communes] the method of 'changing the upper structure, while keeping the lower structure unchanged' may be adopted. . . . The original organization of production and system of administration may for the time being remain unchanged and continue as before." How many of the 70,000 communes exist except on paper? Such critics go on to argue that the reversion of power to the Production Team and the retention of the private plot represent in substance a retreat from the high aims of 1958, whether a tactical retreat dictated by the accident of bad weather or a strategic one based on a more realistic, less sanguine appraisal of the pace at which the peasant is willing to change. *Pravda* claimed on 24 August 1963 that, "Time has shown that the propaganda about the communes being a ladder to paradise was premature; the communes did not justify themselves."

The official Chinese line is, naturally, a very different one. It paints the commune as an extremely flexible institution, able now to accommodate the concessions to petty capitalism which the primitive state of Chinese agriculture demands, but ready also in the future to provide the framework for full Communism. The commune, argues Peking, avoids the wasteful duplication of political and economic apparatus which the Soviet system involves and provides a convenient basis for the introduction of rural industry. Eventually, after the rural economy becomes mechanized one or two decades hence, the communes may federate into larger groupings.

The Chinese took the risk of collectivizing the land before they could afford to mechanize agriculture.[39] It is probably true that what a peasant yearns for is not his own field as such, but the security and prosperity which that field brings him. The collective, if it is to succeed, must also fill its members with a sense of being secure and prosperous. The Communist experiment will not stand a chance unless the state can ensure a reasonably steady rise in the flow of consumer goods to the communes and in the standard of living.

The Chinese peasant will gradually become a more rational, educated, sophisticated and scientific farmer. His Rubicon is crossed when he genuinely realizes that material progress comes from human acts rather than from the whims of heaven. Mao made a village speech in his early days in which he declared:

> The gods, they may quite deserve our worship, but if we had no Peasant Association, . . . could we have knocked down the local bullies and bad gentry? . . . Now you want to have your rent reduced. I would like to ask: How did you go about it? By faith in the gods or faith in the Peasant Association?[40]

This is the kind of propaganda which Mao hoped every cadre would successfully put over. Unfortunately not every cadre worker is a Mao. Mao's explicit advice to his followers is that "The idols were set up by the peasants, and in time they will pull them down with their own hands; there is no need for anybody else prematurely to pull down the idols for them." Many cadres tried to force the pace, however. One wonders what was the ultimate effect of the action of some cadres in Swatow who led the peasants to clear a large graveyard (traditionally sacred and inviolable in China) for the plough, and used the wood of the uprooted coffins to make open-air lavatories and night-soil (human manure) buckets.[41] Did this ruin the Communists' chances of gaining acceptance in that community, or did the shock to custom reinforce their appeal to reason, especially among the younger generation? During the Cultural Revolution of 1966–7, it was the younger generation of "Revolutionary Rebels" which went to even further extremes in this kind of rural iconoclasm.

These are the stirring times in which the average Chinese peasant lives today, in a wattle-and-daub hut with his wife and three small children, in a district where the rain is always too much or too little. Thin and reed-like from the famines and droughts of his youth, he lives on a daily ration of just over a pound of rice and one teaspoonful of meat,* and grows his own cabbage and beans in his backyard. Depending on the harvest, his monthly cash wage is about $3 and he can buy enough cloth to have a new pair of overalls or a cotton suit every New Year (his ordinary working clothes are a loving amalgamation of large patches). He usually walks to work, which is organized by a committee of the natural leaders in his village and occasionally inspected by officials from the county town. He ploughs in bare feet behind a buffalo, saves his own night-soil carefully to use on the fields for fertilizer, and harvests by hand without a tractor. Once a week he must go to a political "pep talk" meeting, and once a month he can see, in a makeshift village hall, a government film, exalting the collective life, or recalling the worse aspects of the old life before 1949, or exposing the inefficacy of the village gods and spirits, or urging birth control, or explaining elementary science or illustrating the enormities of American imperialism.

Gradually his life is becoming better: it is certainly steadier and fuller than in the old days. Mao Tse-tung promised to free him from three fetters; from political authority, from the power of the clan, and from the authority of gods and ghosts. From the latter two and also from the cruelties of the weather he is perceptibly more free. The political authority, on the other hand, is even stronger than before. Who can know what he really feels, how in his heart he weighs the good against the bad consequences of Communist rule? All one can say with certainty is that he is nearer to becoming a modern, twentieth-century man than were any of his ancestors.

* But meat is invariably saved for wedding feasts, festivals and other special occasions.

2: THE PROLETARIAT

Reluctant Revolutionaries

"THE SPECIAL CHARACTERISTIC OF THE CHINESE REVOLUTION," one of its leaders remarked in 1949, "is that the cities were not occupied because of any revolt of the urban workers, but by the armed forces of the People's Liberation Army." [1] Mao realized, as Stalin and the other European Marxists who took it on themselves to advise him in the 'thirties and 'forties never realized, that the peasants constituted a more important revolutionary force in China than the two million industrial workers. There were, of course, strikes and sporadic risings in Shanghai and the other big cities where Japanese and Western entrepreneurs had started manufacturing. But none of these proved crucial in the Communist Party's rise to power. Chinese industry was, after all, small and extremely new. Only since the end of the nineteenth century and the early years of the twentieth had industrial enterprises begun to appear, first in the mineral-rich provinces of the Northeast, the former Manchuria, and later in Shanghai. Even today, after fifteen years of Communist industrialization, the factory proletariat is a relatively small, though highly favoured, part of Chinese society. Its sense of cohesion and antipathy to the arrogant bookishness of the young student (traditional standard-bearer of political change) provided the material for one of the sharpest tensions in the Cultural Revolution.

It is favoured, firstly, in its wage levels. The average factory worker receives about seventy *yuan* (almost $30) a month, whereas the peasant's average cash income is only about twenty *yuan* a month. Prices tend to be higher, sometimes twice as high, in the towns, and the peasant has additional income or consumption goods from his own sideline occupation or private vegetable plot, so the comparison must not be pressed too strictly. Nevertheless the factory worker is better off than his country cousin, and his income does not compare too unfavourably with that of the technicians and directors under whose orders he works. At the Shanghai Ma-

chine Tool Factory, for example, manual workers receive between forty-four and 124 *yuan* monthly, technicians up to
250 *yuan,* and directors between 140 and 220 *yuan.* The director starts where the manual worker's scale ends, and the
qualified engineer, who usually draws only fifteen–twenty per
cent more than the manual worker, can earn more than the
director himself. The average wage for all three groups in
this factory is seventy-three *yuan,* and these scales are fairly
typical (except for heavy industries, such as steel and mining,
where wages are markedly higher). Bonuses and prizes for
over-fulfilling targets are a common supplement to wages,
which usually contain an element of piece-work as well as of
time-rates.[2]

A second area of privilege is in housing. Workers often
live in factory housing, on or off the premises, and it is
usually estimated that rent, including power and water supply, does not exceed ten per cent of a man's wages. In both
Anshan and Fushun, the steel and mining centres of the
Northeast, with almost a million inhabitants each, the authorities claim to have constructed almost two and a half million
square metres of new housing since 1949: Shanghai has put
up seven million square metres, enough to house a million
people anew, since 1949. Housing is extremely short in
Chinese cities, the average floor space available in the mid-
fifties being not much more than three or four square metres
per head.[3] Some of the new industrial housing estates are, in
this context, luxurious. The Ming Hang estate, for example,
about an hour's drive from the centre of Shanghai, is a new
satellite town built around a cluster of factories making
electrical equipment. After six years it has a population of
70,000, and its residents enjoy a hospital, cinema, swim-
ming-pool, shopping arcades, schools, clinics, bus services, a
hotel and most of the other amenities of a Western industrial
satellite town. Its red-brick blocks of flats with brave, new-
looking trees dotted about are little different, though more
barely furnished and lacking TV aerials, from similar estates
in Europe or the USA.

Thirdly, the urban proletariat is favoured by the provision
of social services. Since the best propaganda for the Communist Party in its early days came from the way in which capitalist, and especially foreign, managements treated their men,
it is understandable that the government has made every
effort to improve the life of the worker. The comparison is
constantly brought home, both to the worker himself and to
the visitor: in the Shanghai Machine Tool Factory I was told
the old story of a former manager (in the capitalist days,

when the plant was American-owned) who refused to lend money for a worker to buy his dead mother a coffin, but who offered a reward of $100 for the discovery of his lost pet dog. In the city where the Europeans maintained their notorious park, forbidden to dogs and to Chinese, this tale has a special meaning. The present government introduced a social insurance scheme for industrial workers in 1951, providing for managements to pay the equivalent of three per cent of their wage bill into funds controlled by the trade unions for the use of workers' medical and funeral expenses and disablement and retirement pensions. Nowadays the factory itself usually gives pensions, ranging from fifty to seventy per cent of the final wage, after the age of sixty (fifty for women). A textile mill in Shanghai provides fifty-six paid maternity days for its female workers, who constitute sixty per cent of the total labour force there. Few rural communes can afford such luxuries.

Public health services have been improved to the point where almost every urban baby is born in a hospital or maternity home, and given BCG injections against tuberculosis as well as smallpox vaccinations within three days of birth.[4] Most factories provide free medical treatment for their workers, with treatment at half-fee for their families: the Shenyang Cable Factory, to cite one example, boasts a sixty-bed hospital, a kindergarten catering for 400 children, a club, a library and bathrooms all for the benefit of its labour force.

Education is also stressed. Factory workers are regarded as the best breeding ground for future engineers, directors and Communist Party cadre workers, and at the Shanghai Machine Tool Factory, for example, I was told that 600 men and women had come up from the factory's ranks to fill such posts, either in the factory itself or elsewhere. At the Shenyang Cable Factory the Superintendent explained that sixty per cent of its workers participated in spare-time studies, and that sixty of them were even enrolled in the factory's "spare-time university," set up with the help of the local university. This factory had 800 illiterate workers on its books in 1956, but has now eliminated illiteracy.

But learning brings its burdens, in the form of the political studies to which such strong importance is attached in Chinese industry. The worker's life is full of slogans and campaigns. Giant posters are displayed depicting international workers' solidarity (a Chinese worker, all muscle and fibre, shoulder-to-shoulder with a European, an Arab, an African under the scarlet banners of world socialism) or the struggle against racial discrimination (a Negro brandishing the flaming torch of freedom in front of the Capitol in Washington) or the leadership of Mao (a fat, fatherly, benignant face smiling out of a faded-khaki uniform) or such more mundane messages as factory safety and over-fulfilment of targets. The Shanghai Machine Tool Factory, its engineer told me, religiously impressed on its labour force the importance of the "Five-Goods": good political ideas, good over-fulfilment of tasks, good solidarity and help to others, good study of culture and technique and good adherence to all the requirements. Most factories follow the system of the technicians' and directors' spending one day a week in manual work alongside the other manual workers, "to improve ideas and knowledge, and to help settle problems," as one of them explained to me.

Minimum food rations for town-dwellers were laid down in 1955, providing for twenty-nine ounces of rice a day for workers in very heavy industry, twenty-three ounces for those in heavy industry, eighteen ounces for those engaged in light physical work, sixteen ounces for white-collar workers, eighteen ounces for students, fourteen ounces for those not working and for young teenage children, and smaller quantities for even younger children.[5] For northern Chinese who prefer bread to rice, the flour ration is ten per cent heavier than the rice ration. After a good harvest people can usually buy more than the ration, though sometimes at a higher price; conversely the ration dips when times are bad. During the years of crop failures, 1959 to 1961, Shanghai rations were reduced to twenty ounces for workers, and sixteen ounces for other adults; only about one tenth of the ration could be supplied in rice or flour, and people had to make do with low-grade maize and potatoes for the balance. Other cities fared no better. It was common in the cities at that time to hear of quarrels and even murders on account of ration tickets and of people going out at night to steal food from the fields.[6] But in the years since then the conditions of city life have gradually recovered.

The principal additions to the staple grain—cooking oil, meat, fish and sugar—have also been rationed in the cities during the past fifteen years. But in Shanghai only three foodstuffs are still rationed: grain, cooking oil (one ounce per head per week) and sugar (one and a half ounces), and even these can be obtained in larger quantities for a higher price. Cotton cloth is also rationed (ten feet a year in Shanghai, thirteen in Peking).

Working conditions in the factories are extremely variable, depending on the political and economic campaigns of the day. Periodically workers are urged to fantastic feats of endurance and exertion in the interests of fulfilling production targets. In the 1953 production drive there were factories where a formal guarantee of eight hours daily rest had to be issued.[7] At the Anshan steelworks, according to the *People's Daily,* "many workers collapsed through sheer fatigue," and the newspaper commented: "forced labour competitions must be restricted." [8] In 1956 the Ministry of Forestry complained that its staff members worked so hard at their jobs that they had no energy to spare for the morning gymnastics which were then being introduced in all enterprises and institutions. This plea met with no sympathy, and the *People's Daily* publicly denounced the Ministry for sabotaging the plan to build up the people's health.[9]

Another competitor for a worker's time is the political meeting. During the first eighteen days of 1956 the workers at the No. 4 Textile Mill in Tientsin had to go to eleven meetings lasting an aggregate twenty-six hours, all in their own spare time. Some had no time even to eat, and managed to squeeze in only five or six hours sleep on some days.[10] During the Great Leap Forward in 1958–9 and the Cultural Revolution of 1967–8 similar stories were told of heroism and hard work, but such periods are usually followed by lulls in which work returns to more normal proportions.

The trade unions have taken second place to the Communist Party as in other Communist states. During the period of freedom of expression in 1957, when "a Hundred Flowers bloomed," the unions spoke out a little less timidly. They welcomed the wage increases which the Government had authorized in 1956, but noted that they had been overdue. Lai Jo-yu, then Chairman of the General Federation of Labour, went on a long tour of the country and came back with many criticisms of the unions' position. The *Daily Worker* of Peking published his conclusions, that the trade unions were losing prestige because they were unable to solve the workers' problems, and that the union elections had become empty formalities. "If the unions truly reflect the interests of the masses, some friction between the unions and the administration is unavoidable. One should not be afraid of friction and dispute. . . ." [11] Another young trade union official came out in support of the university lecturer who had, during the Hundred Flowers period, "well said that the life of the people has not improved, it is your life only that has improved, you*

* i.e. the Communist Party cadres and leaders.

who in the past wore worn-out clothes and tattered shoes today wear nylon and travel in cars." [12]

Such sentiments were unacceptable, and the official was denounced as a rightist. Lai himself died in 1958, and some of his colleagues in the General Federation of Labour were removed. The docile role of the unions was reaffirmed at a conference in the summer of 1958 where it was laid down that "The Party is the highest representative and expression of the working class. The view that 'only the trade unions care for the life of the worker' is a complete error. The main work of the trade unions must be, at all times, production." [13]

The industrial worker is organized in his leisure as well as in his work. At first this was done by the street committees or city residents' committees, each embracing anything from a hundred to six hundred households. Their main purpose, a 1954 Regulation declared, was to "promote observance of Government regulations, take the lead in ensuring public security, look after public welfare and compose disputes." [14] In practice it was the Party's principal means of compiling dossiers on everyone and keeping an eye on their activities. Then, in 1958, some northern cities experimented with urban versions of the People's Commune. The December resolution of the Central Committee declared that "In the future, the urban People's Communes, in a form suited to the specific features of cities, will also become instruments for the transformation of the old cities and construction of the new, socialist cities. . . ." By mid-1960 China claimed over a thousand urban communes with over fifty million members. [15]

Some were based on an enterprise (such as a large factory), some on a government department or school or similar institution, others on residential street zones. Communal dining halls were established, along with nurseries, kindergartens and community service centres which organized laundry, house cleaning, repairs, errands and odd jobs. These arrangements allowed many housewives to give up their domestic chores and increase the family income by going out to work. The communes organized their own simple industries, making bicycle parts, telephones, dresses, pharmaceuticals and a whole range of city necessities, sometimes with the help of local factories.

This new institution took some root in the northern and inland cities, but proved far from popular in westernized Shanghai and Canton, in spite of assurances that "all personal belongings of the Commune members, including houses, clothing, furniture and other household goods, bank and credit deposits, remain the property of the individual." [16]

From late 1960 onwards, little publicity was given to the urban communes. The question caused some embarrassment when I asked about it in China in 1964. In Shanghai I had been told, in answer to a casual question, that there were only rural communes, and so none were to be found in Shanghai city. In Shenyang, the Northeastern city, I asked if there were urban communes and my informant said doubtfully that he did not think so. At the Lung Fung coalmine in Fushun I was told quite definitely, in answer to a question, that the mine did *not* form an urban commune. Going back to the city centre afterwards by car I asked my official guide if there were *any* urban communes in Fushun and this provoked a *sotto voce* discussion between the guide and the interpreter (who had also been present when I had asked the same question in Shenyang) culminating in the statement to me that the government was now summing up the people's experience of urban communes with a view to deciding how better to organize them.

In my western way, I felt that my specific question had been dodged, but rather than crudely repeat it I explained that I had read a good deal in the official Chinese publications about the urban communes when they first started but had not seen any reference to them for quite a long time. My companions smiled understandingly and said that I should not conclude that an institution had ceased merely because it was not referred to in news items. Did I read Chinese characters? No. Then I was not perhaps aware that in every city one could see the name-signs above the various commune headquarters (apparently some of these do survive). By this time, rightly or wrongly, I had formed the conclusion that my question was being evaded. I asked my two companions whether they themselves belonged to an urban commune. This once more led to a low exchange between them, the only outcome of which was the question addressed to me, "What do you think?" I replied that my thoughts were irrelevant, that I did not know what to think and merely sought information. I asked the question again, and had my attention drawn to the fact that it was raining, a change of subject being the Chinese way of indicating that a line of conversation has come to an end. This was the only occasion on which I found the official interpreters and guides vague or confused about the Party line. Since the foreign speculation in 1959 about the imminent demise of the urban communes had been denounced by the Chinese as the "vile slanders" of the Yugoslav revisionists, one can understand the official sensitivity on the issue. I cite this experience not because of any light it sheds on the urban communes but because it illustrates the conflict that sometimes occurs between Western and Chinese attitudes, the difficulty of getting information on controversial matters and the naiveté with which foreign visitors are sometimes treated.

Presumably the urban communes were then discontinued, perhaps to be reintroduced or revivified during the next period of sustained enthusiasm. How permanent they could ever become seems questionable. The Cultural Revolution produced in 1967 some attempts to establish urban communes on the model of the Paris Commune of 1870, with stress on the subjection of officials and administrators to regular popular elections. Shanghai was a notable example. But, as Premier Chou En-lai was reported to have told a group of young "rebels" early in 1967, the left-wing forces were still in a minority in China and a premature insistence on fully democratic procedures might cause their defeat.[17]

3: THE BOURGEOISIE

Captive Collaborators

ALMOST ALL THAT THE BOURGEOISIE STANDS FOR IS ANATHEMA to the Marxist, and yet in China it possessed all the secrets of modernization, of technology and culture and management, which the Communists needed. So the middle class has become a captive collaborator with the Communist Party, having to work for its own downfall in the interests of a reconstructed, proletarianized nation. As Prime Minister Chou En-lai put it in his report to the National People's Congress in December 1964: "As a class, the bourgeoisie must be eliminated, but the individuals belonging to it have a bright future provided they are willing to remould themselves and successfully pass the test of the Socialist Revolution. . . ."[1]

It was naturally to the business community that the Communists' attention was initially directed. Just before their entry into Shanghai, the Mecca not only of the Chinese middle class but of many bourgeois families of other nations as well, thousands of businessmen fled south, to Hongkong, with their wives and children, their foremen and engineers, their money and prize possessions, even their machinery and industrial secrets. It was they who, over the ensuing decade, put the British colony of Hongkong on the map as an important manufacturing centre. But the majority of businessmen, especially the smaller ones, remained, either because they thought they could work with a Communist administration or because lack of funds or sentimental ties inhibited their flight. To a western reader it may sound improbable for a businessman to welcome Communist rule, but then enterprise had been far from free even under the former Kuomintang authorities. Some businessmen actually returned from their exile in Hongkong after 1949, and Professor C. P. Fitzgerald * quotes the explanation of one of them:

> I am coming back, not because I expect that I shall be allowed to make a fortune out of my business, but because I am told that as I was not a hard employer the Communists have no complaint against me. I shall be able to make a living, my work interests me, and although my son will never be allowed to inherit the business, he is a good engineer and will always be acceptable as a technical expert. Under the late regime I tried to operate my business for more than twenty years. Sometimes I made big money; then all would be taken from me by some military figure, or some monopolist would be granted rights which destroyed my chance of profit. I never knew from year to year what would happen to me. Now I know; I can run the factory, more or less for the state, but making a secure livelihood, and that will go on until I die.

But in 1951 the business community was shaken by the first of many national campaigns to find victims within its ranks, the so-called *sanfan* or "three-antis" campaign against corruption, waste and excessively bureaucratic behaviour. Many businessmen were denounced for offences within these three categories and some were obliged to confess their misdeeds at mass meetings. Within a few months the second campaign followed, this time the *wufan* or "five-antis" movement to root out bribery, tax evasion, theft of state property, theft of state economic secrets and embezzlement in carrying out state contracts. These campaigns were not exclusively directed against the private businessman, and a number of civil servants and Communist Party cadre workers were also found guilty of the offences. But the business community bore the main brunt. In February 1952, the Party organized

* In his book, *The Birth of Communist China* (London, Penguin, 1964), p. 176.

a Patriotic Denunciation Campaign in which workers were encouraged to accuse their employers. There were many suicides in Shanghai and other cities during this period.[2]

The pressure was relaxed after a while, but in 1955 the government strengthened its control over the funds of private business by the issue of new banknotes: the *yuan* was revalued (one new *yuan* to replace 10,000 old *yuan*) and the last visible reminder of the post-war inflation thus removed. The notes had to be exchanged personally at the bank, however, and in this way the Party was able to find out how much money each businessman had and also to exert maximum pressure on them to put their money into state bonds. The Chinese tradition abhors the crudity of a direct order, but if you go to your bank to change your old currency notes into new ones and happen to meet the local Communist Party branch secretary there, and if he remarks how wonderful it is that in a Communist state a man like you can legitimately own such a large amount of money and make profit from it, and how lucky you ought to consider yourself, and how even happier you would be if you knew that the working people around you regarded you as a patriotic man with a social conscience who does not care only for himself and his family, and how So-and-so, the former chairman of the old Chamber of Commerce, had already put 100,000 *yuan* into state bonds—how can you resist, especially if your teenage son, fresh from political lectures at his school, adds his voice to the clamour? It is no wonder that the Confederation of Industry and Commerce, which officially represents the interests of private business under the Communists, complained in an internal circular [3] that the currency revaluation was "a serious trial of our patriotism."

This was quickly followed by the complete socialization of all private businesses, the majority of which were transformed into joint state-private enterprises with their former owners serving as salaried managers and drawing a fixed interest on the value of the business (the interest was sometimes as low as one per cent in the beginning, but was raised to a minimum of five per cent in 1956). This drastic change was consummated in an astonishingly short period amid extraordinary public scenes in January 1956. The larger firms had mostly been taken over already, often because of the inexorable pressure of the very stringent tax laws. Companies were put in a position where they gratefully accepted nationalization as the way out of a tax mess which might otherwise have led their owners into legal and political tribulations stretching over years: the prospect of a safe, salaried managership seemed appealing by contrast.

Now thousands of young workers in the private sector, following the instructions of the Party, organized themselves into brigades in every city to persuade *all* their employers first to sign petitions asking to be taken into joint public ownership and then to join in "joy" processions through the streets to celebrate the event. The traditional Double-Joy character was displayed on the factories, newspapers went into one of their rare splurges of red ink for the occasion, and the finale came when a crowd of 200,000 watched representatives of private business offer their "joy announcement" and their "surrender of hearts" to Chairman Mao himself in Peking.[4]

Those who had never been popular or fair became little more than despised subordinates in their own factories. Almost their only salvation was the knowledge they possessed as former entrepreneurs, and which the Party cadres were slow to acquire. It was hoped that the "capitalists will teach the Party workers the technique of business management,"[5] but no doubt many retained their secrets as an insurance for the future. One embarrassing feature of the socialization campaign in 1956 was the lack of enthusiasm on the part of some of the workers involved. The *People's Daily* found it necessary to remind them that "their former high wages were unreasonable . . . a remnant of the out-moded capitalist system and a strategic manoeuvre of the capitalists."[6] It was hard to explain why nationalization should involve a cut in pay.

Towards the end of 1956, a special College of Socialism was founded for the education of former capitalists, the majority of whom, declared Liu Shao-chi at the September 1956 Party Congress, had been "remoulded into working people worthy of the name." But people's minds do not change so easily. A prolonged conference of ex-capitalists was held in the winter of 1959–60 when the failure of the Great Leap Forward had become widely, though not officially, recognized. "A majority of the industrialists and merchants," the *People's Daily* concluded, "are, in various degrees, sceptical and unsure in their acceptance of the Chinese Communist Party's leadership and in the attitude towards . . . the Great Leap Forward and the People's Communes; some of them are . . . opposed to these things."[7]

One of the instruments by which the Communists maintain some kind of control over the bourgeoisie is the United Front. Eight small political parties, left of centre but not Marxist, agreed to cooperate with Mao Tse-tung in 1949, and in theory the Chinese Government is a coalition of these nine parties. The China Democratic League is a group of intellectuals who in the early 1940s looked towards the Communists rather than the Kuomintang (the only two serious contenders for power); the Revolutionary Committee of the Kuomintang is a splinter group of the latter body, formed in 1948; the China Chih Kung Tang is the long-established organization of the Overseas Chinese; the other five represent similar small liberal democratic interests. The Communists use the first to control the intellectuals, the second to control the ex-Kuomintang members who remain on the mainland, the third to control the returned Overseas Chinese. The small parties act as safety valve and buffer; through them the Communist Party knows what these sections of opinion are thinking before having itself to take an attitude about it, and conversely it can have its policies put over to these sections of opinion in a way which would appeal to them best but which a Communist himself could not, perhaps, adopt. Each Party is dependent on the government financially, and although they participate in the government (providing a handful of Cabinet Ministers as well as senior civil servants and advisers) and in the National People's Congress, they wield no power of their own. A Communist Party member once argued that his wife's having joined one of the small democratic parties was a valid ground for divorce! [8]

This impotence of the only political organizations able to represent the interests of the middle class was abundantly proved in 1957 when their leaders took advantage of the freedom of speech offered in the Hundred Flowers period to criticize the Communists openly and advocate constitutional changes (such as a second chamber in which the democratic parties would have a stronger voice). Some of them apparently thought that the Chinese Communists, having observed the unpopularity of the Polish and Hungarian Communist Governments and the risings which were provoked in those countries at the end of 1956, were prepared to step down and share their power with social democrats. But as the leading democrat, Chang Po-chun, the Minister of Communications, said just before the end of the Hundred Flowers, the democratic parties had not bargained for so many Communist errors coming to light. The wave of criticism which the democrats had done so much to encourage became finally a flood which the Communist Party had to stem by force if it were not to risk losing its authority. In the process Chang Po-chun and others were charged with "rightism" and dismissed from their posts (some years later, however, they were mostly reinstated, and are obviously not now regarded as a serious threat to the Communists).[9]

Politically and economically, then, the middle class is restricted to a humiliating minor role. It is only when one visits Shanghai that one realizes the extent of its inner resistance to the Communist kiss of death. Shanghai was one of the wonders of the capitalist world, an enormous metropolis (its population numbers ten million people if the outskirts be included) teeming with life, with squalor and splendour in equal proportion. It was cosmopolitan, it was largely run by foreigners, and it exuded the reckless gaiety of a city without responsibility. As the symbol of foreign intervention and the nursery of Chinese capitalism, Shanghai was a prime target for Communist hatred, and in the first years of Mao's government it was expected that the city would be allowed to run down, both to prevent the capitalists from regaining power and to prove that they were not omnipotent. Plans for industry in those days involved the concentration of new investment in the interior regions, away from the militarily vulnerable sea coast. But gradually it was realized that the national production effort needed all the help it could get from the existing plant, and there was a certain reinstatement of Shanghai's considerable body of light industry. The natural advantages of the city as an industrial centre, notably its good port and facilities for transportation and storage, even led the government to sink money into new heavy industry there. The supreme compliment came in 1963 when a national campaign to "emulate Shanghai" was launched throughout Chinese industry, and delegations from other cities came to see the technical innovations and diligence of the quick-witted, industrious workers of Shanghai.

But the city has not been dragooned into a dull uniformity. It is still the main centre of whatever little vice and frivolity escape the heavy hand of the puritanical authorities. In 1954, five years after Liberation, the *People's Daily* [10] announced with horror that there were still 2,500 "yellow" bookshops * in Shanghai, and that thirty-eight amusement centres were still attracting 20,000 young customers every day. I went to the Great World Amusement Centre in 1964, and saw eager audiences informally watching a dozen different operas and dramas, all with an official theme. "This place used to be a centre of prostitution and a haunt of petty despots," the young official interpreter told me, "so that many people were

* Bookshops specializing in "feudalistic, superstitious, robber and sex stories."

afraid to come. Now it is quite different." But as a good product of Shanghai ("I am really interested in literature and music," he had said on our first day at the factories, "and do not understand these technical industrial terms") he sniffed about him as if there might be something lively and amusing going on, and I noted that the only empty rooms were those where the hopeful authorities had arranged posters and propaganda about birth control, hygiene, factory safety and similar topics. The interpreter looked slightly guilty, but also secretly sympathetic when I drew attention to this: "Of course," he commented, "people come here during the intervals of the operas," but he said it half-heartedly, and even if this were so it still betrayed a sense of priorities which would never have been allowed in high-minded Peking.

The contagion of the foreigner remains; about six hundred Norwegian, British, Dutch, Polish, Japanese and other ocean-going ships normally call at Shanghai every year, and their crews enjoy the hospitality of the Social Club for Chinese and Foreign Seamen, where the famous Long Bar used to stand. There is still a handful of resident British businessmen.

Now Shanghai has a new jet runway to receive the *Pakistan International Airways* Boeing liners, and busloads of East and West European tourists are shuttled about to see the sights.

The Party still complains occasionally that there is more illegal private enterprise in Shanghai than anywhere else, although it is only a shadow of its former self. Speculators and private businessmen came into their own in the anarchic conditions of 1967–8. Superficially the Shanghai middle class has submitted dutifully to the egalitarian, idealistic direction of the Communist Party, but in the struggle of the mind it is not so clear which force is the stronger. This will be again apparent when we consider the position of the educated bourgeoisie, the intelligentsia.

4: THE INTELLIGENTSIA

Fragrant Flowers or Poisonous Weeds

"NEVER TREAT A PERSON AS IF HE WERE WORSE THAN DOG shit one moment and worth ten thousand ounces of gold the next. The intellectuals cannot stomach the ice cold, nor can they swallow the piping hot." [1] This candid comment on the Communist Party's policy towards the Chinese intelligentsia was offered by the Shanghai Professor, Hsu Chung-yu, during the brief part of 1957 when free speech reigned under the slogan "Let a Hundred Flowers Bloom and Schools of Thought Contend." Only a minority of the highly educated give whole-hearted support to the Communists: Chou En-lai estimated in 1956 that of the 100,000 "high intellectuals," about two fifths actively supported the government, an equal number passively obeyed and the remaining one fifth actively or stubbornly resisted the leadership of the Communist Party.[2] Most of the intellectuals are either Chinese traditionalists, looking principally to China's past, or western-educated people looking vaguely to some sort of western democracy as the ideal. The fact that the Communist Party is both foreign in its inspiration and authoritarian in its methods leaves it with few true friends among the scholars, artists and professional men.

The Politburo itself is, by most political standards, an exceptionally cultivated group. Mao Tse-tung, his old comrade in arms Chu Teh and Foreign Minister Chen Yi are all poetically inclined as well as being seasoned generals, and can produce classical verse rather as politicians in Elizabethan England wrote sonnets. Chou En-lai is the darling of the intellectuals, however, since he combines the Communist sense of social justice with the impeccable manners and grace of his mandarin ancestors. It was Chou who, soon after the Communists took power, wrote letters to many of the talented exiles in Hongkong and elsewhere inviting them to return and help rebuild China into a powerful, modern nation, appealing to their patriotism even if they felt reservations about the

Communist Party itself. Many responded, though a few of these, like the scientist Mu Fu-sheng,* chose to become exiled again because of the frustrations they faced in China.

Unhappily for Mao and Chou, the vast majority of the seventeen million Communist Party members through whom they have to work are men of action rather than intellectuals, unsympathetic to the intelligentsia and probably not a little envious of it. As Mao himself publicly admitted in 1957: "Many of the comrades are not good at getting along with intellectuals. They are stiff with them, lack respect for their work, and interfere in scientific and cultural matters in an uncalled-for way." [3]

Life for many intellectuals became a perpetual battle of wits against the Communist branch secretaries and their satellites with whom they had to work. At a meeting where members of the democratic parties formulated criticism of the government during the Hundred Flowers period in 1957, one Hsu I-kuan summed it up:

> Since 1952, campaign has succeeded campaign, each one leaving a great wall in its wake, a wall which estranges one man from another. In such circumstances, no one dares to let off steam even privately in the company of intimate friends, let alone speak his mind in public. Everyone has now learnt the technique of double-talk; what one says is one thing, what one thinks is another. . . . [4]

The running was mostly made by the old scholars who were too dignified to flee from the Communists, too venerable for the Communists to humiliate or remove, too clever for the Communists to trap in subversive attitudes. In the Chinese scholastic tradition recantations made under public pressure are not despised, as they would be in the West, but regarded as an inevitable though unpalatable feature of living under new governments. It is a part of their resilience that Chinese scholars are willing to make confessions of non-Communist behaviour and declarations of intent to change their thoughts, and then carry on just as before. Almost all the non-Communist scholars of international reputation issued confessions or announcements of mental adjustment in terms similar to Ho Lin's: "After the Liberation, the clemency of the people and my own young friends saved me . . . and I started a new life. My philosophical reform was based on the writings of Mao Tse-tung. . . ." [5] The political scientist, Professor Kung Hsiang-jui, publicly regretted that on returning from the Lon-

* Whose book, *The Wilting of the Hundred Flowers* (London, Heinemann, 1962), gives a fair and interesting account of his experiences.

don School of Economics he had tried to spread the ideas of "that running-dog of Imperialism," Harold Laski.[6]

The most famous of the resisting scholars are the philosopher Fung Yu-lan and the economist Ma Yin-chu. Fung is the subtler of the two, constantly apologizing for his indiscretions, such as the remark that "in teaching questions, not even Chairman Mao can be a guide," and issuing confessions containing such phrases as "my egoism is terrifying." In 1958, he said, with unmistakable irony, that "since the Liberation I have set forth 135 self-examinations, but I did not delve deeply enough."[7] In 1961, in the course of an article on Confucius, in a learned journal, he quoted Marx and Engels in their essay on the French bourgeois revisionist, Feuerbach: "A new class, when it desires to replace the old ruling class in order to reach its aim, cannot but present its own interest as the common interest of the totality of society. To put this in abstract terms, the presentation of their own ideas as a universal formula attributes to these ideas exclusive rational truth of universal validity." Fung then adds his own elaboration of this dictum from such unimpeachable authorities, in the words: "This universal character is a fraud perpetrated against the labouring people."[8] He hastens to remind his readers that he is referring to the French bourgeoisie, but it is difficult not to agree with the suggestion that another, very contemporary parallel would occur to many a Chinese reader, and that Fung has his tongue in his cheek here.[9] But the old man was nevertheless to be seen in a *People's Daily* photograph in 1963 shaking hands with the Chairman of the Republic, in spite of his having proved, from dicta of Mao's, that Communist philosophy is utilitarian (which the cadres felt to be a slur, but had to accept) and in spite of his becoming involved in further controversy with the Marxists over his excessive defence of Confucius' position in the class struggle.[10]

Ma Yin-chu, the celebrated President of Peking University until 1960, had been imprisoned by Chiang Kai-shek in 1940–2, and no one ever doubted either his patriotism or his integrity. Since 1939 he had identified himself with the Communists, having, in his own words, "renounced my class and denied my old ego" by deeds, just as Marx himself had done.[11] But he had never followed the Party line slavishly and was renowned for his unorthodox exposition of Communist policies. He was one of the scholars who returned from Hongkong at the express invitation of the Communist leadership, but gradually he ran foul of the more conventional Party economists, who accused him of only pretending to re-

fute Keynes and Malthus and of being half-hearted in his dia-
lectical materialism. He irritated the young Party nominees
freshly returned from economic studies in the Soviet Union
by drawing attention to the economic differences between the
Russia of 1917 and the China of 1949 and arguing that these
made it absurd automatically to choose Russian-type solu-
tions for China's problems. He made himself unpopular in
official circles by frankly admitting that the Chinese population growth was excessive, and that it could cause unemployment (a phenomenon which the more ostrich-like of the
Party hacks insisted could not exist in a socialist society).[12]
In the November 1959 issue of the magazine *New Construction,* Ma defended himself from the destructive criticism of
his antagonists. "It is not enough," he wrote, "to destroy; one
must build." It is true, he admitted, he might be bourgeois in
his thinking, and if a properly scientific proletarian explanation of these phenomena in the Chinese economy could be
advanced then he would humbly yield to it. Until then, his
principles required him to stand his ground, in spite of the
well-intentioned advice of some of his friends to retract and
thus preserve his political standing: on scientific questions, "if
one is sure of the truth, then one must face all consequences,
even if they do not serve one's own interest or even one's
life." Professor Ma ended this unusual article with a word to
the "friend" (widely assumed to be Chou En-lai himself)
whose cable had brought him from Hongkong in 1949: "I
would be glad to know that he will not take my refusal to
confess as resistance to order." [13] The editor of *New Construction* was well aware of the risk he ran in publishing such
an article; he introduced it with a note to say that it was included at the "demand" of the Professor. A few months later
Ma was replaced as President of Peking University and little
more has been heard of him.

It was with men of the calibre of Ma Yin-chu and Fung
Yu-lan active in the leadership of the academic world that
the Chinese intellectuals went through the dramatic sequence
of events known as the Hundred Flowers. On 25 January
1956 Mao Tse-tung, in the course of an address on agrarian
policy, first quoted the couplet that was to become so famous:

> Let a hundred flowers blossom together,
> And let a hundred schools of thought contend.

The Party had decided on a new policy towards the intellectuals; there was henceforth to be freedom of scientific debate
and an end to forced confession. Chou En-lai addressed a

meeting of intellectuals in humble and almost apologetic vein. The Party, explained Lu Ting-yi, its propaganda chief, to a meeting of writers and artists, wanted "freedom of independent thinking in literature, art and scientific research; freedom of debate; freedom of creative work and freedom to criticize." [14] He stressed, for the benefit of scientists, that "natural sciences have no class character" and may therefore be discussed apart from considerations of class struggle.* But the response was cautious.

In the following year the leaders tried again. Mao spoke explicitly on the topic in his famous 27 February 1957 speech "On the correct handling of contradictions":

> Our intellectuals have made some progress, but they should not be complacent. They must continue to remould themselves, gradually shed their bourgeois world outlook and acquire a proletarian, communist world outlook, so that they can fully meet the needs of the new society and closely unite with the workers and peasants. . . . But a thorough change in world outlook takes quite a long time, and we should go about it patiently and not be impetuous. Actually, there are bound to be some who are all along reluctant, ideologically, to accept Marxist-Leninism and Communism. We should not be too exacting in what we expect of them; as long as they comply with the requirements of the state and engage in legitimate pursuits, we should give them opportunities for suitable work. . . . Ideological struggle is not like other forms of struggle. Crude, coercive methods should not be used in this struggle, but only the method of painstaking reasoning. . . . People may ask: Since Marxism is accepted by the majority of the people in our country as the guiding ideology, can it be criticized? Certainly it can. As a scientific truth, Marxism fears no criticism. If it did and could be defeated in argument, it would be worthless. . . . Marxists should not be afraid of criticism from any quarter. . . . Plants raised in hot-houses are not likely to be robust. . . .

* This concession was subsequently withdrawn, and the relationship between natural science and the class struggle continues to perplex the Party. In a discussion about psychology, for instance, in 1959, Chang Chi-chang wrote that "class differences will be extinguished only in the Communist society, and only then will a common nature for the human race be formed" (*Kuang Ming Daily*, Peking, 26 March 1959). The psychologists replied that this confused psychological with ethical evaluation of the human mind, and asked whether a working man perceived the colour red any differently from a bourgeois. The Party was constantly rebuking those intellectuals who ignored the class element in their work. "In this world where class opposition between exploiters and exploited, oppressors and oppressed, exists, there can be no talk of some all-embracing 'love of humanity,' " Chou Yang told a writers' and artists' congress in 1960.

But still the flowers hung shyly back, afraid of being nipped in the bud, and local Party cadres were uncertain how to apply the new policy. As the historian Chien Po-tsan remarked, intellectuals wondered "if the loosening of the grip is genuine or fake; whether it is an honestly sought goal or only a trap; whether it is meant to enrich culture and science, or only investigate minds." [15] A librarian at Shanghai University said: "We were full of joy when Chairman Mao . . . took up once more the theme of the advance towards free expression of opinions. But a doubt remains. Today I may speak as I will; but after a period, after a year or two, will not a written record of my words be brought up against me?" [16]

Then, in May, the Party launched a Rectification campaign, in which it was to cleanse itself from the three evils in its style of work—bureaucratism, sectarianism and subjectivism—with the help of criticism from the public. At last the dykes broke and the criticism poured in. From about the middle of May 1957 words were spoken in public places in China that no one had ever dared to use in any Communist country before. The public began with the innumerable administrative complaints which the authorities had doubtless expected. Employment grievances ("there are returned students from Britain who earn their living as cart-pullers and returned students from the US who run cigarette stalls . . ."),[17] press grievances (reporters and photographers being pushed aside at public events by loud-mouthed officials),[18] politicians' grievances (the democratic parties having no worthwhile function to perform)[19]—all were given their first real airing in eight years.

But the traditionally restive students of Peking University (known familiarly as Peita) soon began to attack the Communist Party itself and its political premises. They had a speakers' corner "like Hyde Park," as one newspaper described it,[20] and specialized in dramatic posters. Tan Tienjung, a physics student who gained national fame during this period, wrote a poster which quoted Heraclitus: "In Ephesus all adult men should die, and the government of the city should be handed over to beardless young men." The *People's Daily,* Tan said, was "the Great Wall sealing off the truth," but he regarded himself as a good Marxist and expressed his disappointment that "Marxism has transformed itself into its own negation, into revisionism and dogmatism." [21] Four physics students privately translated (from the English version printed in the *Daily Worker* of New York) the secret speech of Khrushchev denouncing Stalin at the Soviet Party's Twentieth Congress. The Chinese Party called them "unconscious agents of Allen Dulles" and branded them as counter-revolutionaries, a charge which they vigorously denied.[22]

The teachers joined in. Professor Ko Pei-chi said:

> Some say that the standard of living has risen. Whose standard of living? The standard of those who ride in cars and dress in wool, Party members or cadres. When the Communists entered the cities in 1949 they were welcomed by the people. Today these same people keep at a respectful distance from the Party. . . . Therefore you Party members say to yourselves: "we are the State." If you act wrongly the masses can overthrow you; they may kill the Communists. This should not be called unpatriotic, for the Communist Party is not serving the people.[23]

Friends and enemies cautioned this fierce young man, but he would not be silenced. A few days later he took the rostrum again to say:

> I will say it again: the masses want to overthrow the Communist Party and kill the Communists. If you do not change, if you continue to degenerate, they will some day do so. This is the law of socialist development. It is no use shouting "Live for Ten Thousand Years." [24]

These sentiments were quickly taken up at other universities and colleges throughout the country. At Kweilin Teachers' Training College in South China a group concluded from its "Hundred Flowers" discussions that "the Communist Party has changed qualitatively since it seized power, is going downhill and will one day topple down"; one of the students proposed a "new society" comprising "Eastern Communism plus Western democracy." [25] Meanwhile the democratic politicians were advocating constitutional reforms designed to give themselves more power.[26]

The Party's authority was directly and unequivocally challenged, and having proved its inability to retain people's hearts by persuasion it had to resort to force or else bow out. After only a few eventful weeks, the *People's Daily* on 9 June announced that the time had come to "counter-criticize," and those who had gone too far for the Party's liking were branded as "counter-revolutionaries." * A few days after this turning-point, there were ugly scenes at Wuhan, the central Chinese city, where students rioted and attacked first the Communist Party office and then the local government offices

---

* It was in vain that such people as the writer Lao She argued that "a genuine counter-revolutionary wouldn't dare" to express unorthodox views (*Wen Hui Pao*, Shanghai, 28 May 1957)—the same argument used against McCarthy by American liberals.

in what the press called "the petty Hungarian incident." [27] Subsequently the three student ring-leaders were executed befor an audience of 10,000 [28]—the only ones in the whole of the Hundred Flowers affair to lose their lives.

Three of the Ministers nominated by the small democratic parties were dismissed, Chou En-lai meticulously answered most of the criticisms which had been made of the government (he made heavy weather of the well-aimed ones), a thousand high-level Party officials were quickly transferred to universities and colleges all over the country to restore discipline, and the full text of Mao's 27 February speech was at last published, but with the important addition of six new criteria for distinguishing "fragrant flowers from weeds." Words or actions which went against the socialist path or the leadership of the Communist Party were to be considered poisonous weeds rather than fragrant flowers, a postscript presumably added by Mao to clarify the doubts his original speech had created.[29] One of the last posters to appear on the Peita walls expressed the bitter disappointment of "A group of first-year students in the Department of History":

> Intelligent friends! Everyone has been cheated! The goal of the Rectification Campaign of the Communist Party was not the removal of the three evils, the solution of the contradictions among the people or the improvement of the style of work, but the acquisition of even greater power, to be able better to rule over the "stupid" Chinese people. Isn't that clear? Even after the Emperor has ordered the Party to mend its ways, the mandarins of all degrees are nevertheless still in place, everything remains just as before. Lately, the Emperor has discovered some "right-wing elements" and he now uses them to frighten the "stupid" Chinese people.[30]

And so the "mandarins" won, as perhaps Mao knew they would. There had been a curious encounter in mid-May when a group of journalists asked Mao whether they should report on the antagonisms within the people. He thought for a moment, and then replied: "Try it. Then let us see." [31] Impressed by the hornet's nest which Khrushchev had aroused by the revelations of Party excesses under Stalin, Mao no doubt thought that a safety valve could be arranged for the periodical venting of grievances against the Chinese Party. But he clearly underestimated the discontent.

The Peking leaders still aim at the total conversion of the intelligentsia to Communism by a gradual process of persuasion and discipline. The Third Writers' and Artists' Conference in Peking in 1960 reaffirmed Mao's earlier dictum that "all revolutionary artists and writers of China . . . must, for long periods of time, unreservedly and wholeheartedly go into the midst of the masses . . . before they can proceed to creation." Year after year the novelists and the philosophers, the biochemists and the painters, go to live for weeks at a time with peasants or factory workers, sharing their lives.

These experiences affect the intellectuals in varying ways. Some are hardened in their dislike of both the *lumpenproletariat* and the Communist Party, and regard their days in the country or the factory as a form of penance or punishment, to be endured merely. Others, with a better social conscience, are impressed by the reminder of the hard life which the average Chinese has and even by the spirit and dynamism which he sometimes exhibits in the first flush of emancipation from his feudalistic backwater; some writers and scientists are warmly touched by the genuine, if naïve first expressions of appreciation of art and science by the new peasant and worker whom Communist China is gradually breeding. A few intellectuals become more or less permanently enthusiastic about the possibilities of this relationship with a new and highly impressionable audience.

This is not the atmosphere in which great art is born. But it is the atmosphere in which the gulf between the city and village, a gulf which one intellectual, enabled by these policies to measure it for the first time for himself, estimated at two thousand years, can begin to be bridged. During the Great Leap Forward of 1958 the authorities launched a "million poem" movement to encourage the peasants to express themselves in a medium previously thought to be the preserve of the *literati*. One of these mass productions reads:

In Heaven there is no Jade Emperor,
Nor is there a Dragon King in the sea.
I am the Jade Emperor,
I am the Dragon King.
Hey, you Three Sacred Mountains and Five Holy Peaks,
Make Way!
Here I come.

This will not be remembered in the treasuries of world literature, but it and thousands like it mark the perceptible liberation of a suppressed class from a social tradition which denied all culture to its members. "Of course we dare," a character in a recent story exclaims, "under Party guidance I can get the moon!"

The traditional intellectual's contempt for manual labour is also to be undermined by this policy. Chairman Liu Shao-chi, when he met the famous night-soil collector Shih Chuanhsiang (who was admitted to the Communist Party and elected to the Peking Consultative Committee, but who was reportedly a victim of the subsequent Cultural Revolution in 1966–7), said: "You collect night-soil; you are a people's worker. I am the Chairman; I am also a people's worker. The difference between us lies in the division of our revolutionary work, but each is doing an indispensable part of the work for our revolutionary cause." [32] In this way the leaders attempt to break down the old hierarchies of occupational status. The Ming Tombs reservoir outside Peking is an example of a project executed mostly by "volunteers" from all walks of life, from Chairman Mao and his colleagues and even friendly members of the diplomatic corps down to the students and workers of the city. But the fact that one has to put the word "volunteers" in inverted commas indicates the price of this necessary, but contrived change in outlook. There is a chance of persuading very young children to begin their lives with a proper, healthy respect for the dignity of labour,* but it is quite another thing to convert people whose ideas are already fixed. One of the principal reasons given by trained doctors taking refuge in Hongkong for refusing to return to China is their reluctance to work for periods of up to five years in poor and remote villages. [33]

The task of promoting a Chinese proletarian art taxes all the talents of the Party. The creative literature of the early days of the Communist government, such as the novels of Chou Li-po about the land reform, was far more free and more convincing than the entirely propagandistic work of to-day's writers. Literature must today be subordinated to politics, the Party must direct its course and its explicit purpose must be to educate workers and peasants in the Party's policies. It is small wonder that a survey of Shanghai students in 1958 revealed their preference for Romain Rolland and *Dream of the Red Chamber* over contemporary fiction. [34]

Writers are in the dilemma that the Communists want them at the same time to turn their backs on the bad old forms and yet also retain the conservative-minded peasant's

---

* Even this is far from easy. An Chi, a pedicurist of the Peking Ching Hua Chih Bathhouse and a bathhouse worker of thirty-seven years' standing, told the *Daily Worker* of Peking on 9 January 1964, that he was glad that nowadays "graduates from secondary and primary schools are continually sent to work in the bathhouses," but that unfortunately some of them were critical, saying "there is no future in the service occupations . . . we have wasted our time spent at school." Like the night-soil collector Mr Shih, An Chi became a Party member and deputy to the Peking Municipal People's Congress, and since 1949 he has found his work "glorious and dignified." (See Henry Lethbridge's "Augean Equality," in FEER, 7 May 1964, p. 297.)

interest and engage his imagination. Poetry has been allowed some licence since Chairman Mao has come out with so many poems in the purely classical style. "We should not construct a narrow cage for ourselves," wrote Kuo Mo-jo thankfully in 1962 in a poetry magazine.[35] But opera and drama have had to struggle most uncomfortably with the new criteria. "It is inconceivable," the Party magazine *Red Flag* laid down in 1964, "that a stage dominated by emperors and kings, generals and prime ministers, talented scholars and beauties, can serve the militant task of 'fostering proletarian ideology and eliminating bourgeois ideology'. . . ."[36] But what talent, dedication and persistence it requires to entrance the peasant, used to the wicked generals, foppish courtiers and magical princesses of the old folk operas, with such contemporary figures as the Party branch secretary, the unrepentant ex-landlord and the chairman of the Poor and Lower-Middle Peasant Association!

In the visual arts the uncertainty of the official attitude towards the Chinese past and the foreign present has been particularly perplexing. On the one hand China's sculptors are rapped on the knuckles for adoring Rodin and setting up Greek-European bourgeois sculpture as their ideal,[37] while on the other hand Professor Liang Ssu-cheng, the architect, is rebuked for giving the new Peking Police Office an excessively decorative Chinese-style roof.*

The musicians have had an especially difficult time under

---

* In the end the building was completed minus one storey, since Professor Liang refused to economize on his roof and the budget could not support both the roof and the final storey. The outstanding example of early extravagance in copying the old style was the Government Hall and Guesthouse at Chungking, completed in 1954 with a lavish triple dome modelled on the Temple of Heaven in Peking. A *People's Daily* cartoon of 5 April 1955, showed the Dowager Empress Tzu Hsi telling a Communist official as they gazed at one of these new buildings: "You certainly have a gift for spending money. When I built the Summer Palace, I never thought of using glazed tiles on the kitchen" (a million square metres of expensive glazed-tile roofing had been used in the early years of the Communist administration). Liang argued that steel-and-concrete suited the Chinese tradition, allowing the old wooden skeleton to be embodied in a modern building, but the authorities persisted with massive brick-walled structures. Liang described the new building of the Peking City Communist Party Committee as "like a bathroom turned inside out," which was hardly tactful. Eventually he was criticized for rightist tendencies, and in 1959 was obliged to confess: "In 1953 the correct policy of 'utility, economy, and, if conditions allow, beauty' was announced. At the time I interpreted this as ignorance of architecture and for many years I ceaselessly disputed it." At the age of sixty he publicly affected joy at becoming, to please his Party-member daughter, a candidate member of the Communist Party. (See CNA 87, 10 June 1955, and 377, 23 June 1961.)

Communist rule. The Party has consistently accused them of failing to produce music that was politically highly-charged and revolutionarily stimulating. Instead the composers tended to follow the well-worn paths of the western classical composers. "Bach, Beethoven, Schubert, Schumann, Berlioz, Liszt and Chopin lifted high the banner of reform," declared the Party's magazine, *People's Music,* "and they made an indelible contribution to the development of music," but their music did after all belong to the bourgeois class and should be accepted therefore with discimination.[38] Debussy, whose delicacy and suggestiveness seems to have a strong appeal to the Chinese ear, was singled out for special criticism: his work was steeped in bourgeois class ideology and his impressionism was a wild weed to be rejected by healthy revolutionaries. Some Chinese composers were asked to rewrite their Debussy-esque passages.[39] The authorities insisted that the "superstitious belief in Western music and technique" [40] must be broken down, stating categorically that "worship of Western music means worship of capitalism." [41] The teachers at the Central Musical College in Peking were asked to abandon the teaching of Western classical music; they refused, and so all 400 teachers and students were sent down to the villages for manual work and ideological remoulding.[42] This was early in 1964. A few months later Chou Yang, the architect of the Party's cultural policies, proudly inaugurated a new Chinese Musical College which would cultivate a national music.[43]

The trouble had been that the Western-educated teachers despised the sounds of the traditional Chinese instruments and refused to sully what they considered to be the main stream of world music by introducing them into the conventional European orchestra. But as an official said in 1949, "one cannot carry a piano about and one cannot have a piano in every village. In our world the piano is not required." [44] One can begin to picture the background against which the Chopin Prize-winner, Fou Ts'ong, defected while on a foreign tour (he subsequently married Yehudi Menuhin's daughter and settled down in Europe). All compositions have to go to the Musicians' Association for criticism and acceptance before being published, just as all novels, plays, poems and other works of art require an official *imprimatur* before being offered to the public. In 1961 the musicians protested against their being sent, along with other artists and intellectuals, to do regular manual work on the farms. "By manual labour," they complained, "the talent of an artist is destroyed and his technique will fall off." But the Party insisted that digging with a spade keeps one's hands supple, and helps to convince one of the urgency of producing works which the masses want.[45]

Perhaps the high point of official denigration of Western music came in 1964 when *People's Music* recounted how the conductor Li Ling had said, after the Chinese Central Philharmonic Orchestra had performed Beethoven's Ninth Symphony in 1959, that all of the older musicians in China had looked forward to the day when a Chinese orchestra could perform this crown of classical music. "How," remarked *People's Music*, "could the Ninth Symphony express the ideas of the oppressed peoples in the world of today?" [46] Such is the world of the Chinese writer and artist.

China differs from Russia in that the Communist Party faces no organized religious threat to its leadership. Of a total population of about 550 million in 1949, fewer than two per cent were Muslim and fewer than one per cent Christians. None of the older religious persuasions (if Confucianism, Taoism and Buddhism may all be so described) had anything like an organized church, save for the Lamaist Buddhists of Tibet and Mongolia on the outer fringe of China proper. Mao's policy towards religion was thus able to be more optimistic and less brutal than the Soviet; he concluded that no intensive propaganda struggle was needed to spread atheism, because the eradication of the exploiting classes together with general economic improvements would solve the problem. In the Chinese tradition, after all, ethics count for far more than faith. The Communists did conduct persecution, but not against religion as such, only against those who were unwilling to reconcile their faith with loyalty to the Chinese Communist Government. Such people were regarded as counterrevolutionaries, "acting under the cloak of religion," and the attacks directed against them were political, not ideological in motivation. As Mao said, "we cannot force people not to believe, and we cannot force people to give up their idealism."

The Taoists, Muslims,* Buddhists* and Christians were all organized into national associations and obliged to demonstrate their patriotism as well as submit to the leadership of the Communist Party. Chairman Yueh Chun-tai announced, at the inauguration of the Chinese Taoist Association in 1957, the astonishing transformation of these highly individ-

---

* Since Islam and Buddhism primarily concern the national minority peoples of Tibet, Inner Mongolia and other autonomous regions in the interior of China, their fate under the new Government is discussed in Chapter Seven below.

ualistic and retiring devotees: Taoism, he declared, used to abhor politics and struggle, but "after the Liberation this was changed, and the Taoists went though indoctrinations and are taking part in social activities. They entered politics in a patriotic spirit. This has never happened in history before." [47] Similar feats were achieved within the Buddhist ranks, as we shall see in a later chapter.

Christianity suffered most from the new policies, because of its intimate association with foreign activity. Only in 1946, on the eve of Communist rule, did the Vatican reconstitute the old missionary organization of the Chinese Catholics into a regular hierarchy, and when Mao Tse-tung became Chairman of the People's Republic only sixty per cent of the Catholic priests and nuns in China were Chinese. It was easy for the Communist Party to portray the Catholic Church as essentially a foreign body, and much the same could be said of the Protestant groups (which claimed about 700,000 faithful in 1949, against the Catholics' 3.3 million). Article 88 of the new Constitution of 1954 guaranteed freedom of religion in the sense that atheists could not give sermons in churches, nor could theists preach outside the churches (and the government also insisted that ministers of religion should not preach "in areas where class relations are complex," in other words that they should keep quiet during periods of sharp struggle such as the land reform). But the various religions should, the Communists maintained, become self-governing (i.e. independent of foreign personnel and external authority), self-supporting (i.e. independent of foreign funds) * and self-propagating (i.e. they should not go out to proselytize). These were the three "autonomies" which the churches were expected to accept. From some of the Protestants there was an immediate response to this policy, and their spokesman, Wu Yueh-tsung (who had been one of the pioneers of the YMCA movement in Shanghai), spoke strongly at a political meeting in 1957, taking the government to task for being so lukewarm about the patriotic Christians. The government, he said, ought not to condemn religion as such, for there can be progressive priests, after all, "like Hewlett Johnson"; yet Christians were still discriminated against, even though they

---

* After the land reform, it was difficult for the churches to pay their way and the Government even extended subsidies to them and considered tax remission privileges. Good salaries were paid to the "patriotic" priests, for example 300 *yuan* monthly to one in Harbin. "Patriotic" in this context has been cynically defined by one commentator, as "the epithet for those whom the Party does not trust, yet wants to use." (See CNA 173, 22 March 1957, and 185, 21 June 1957, p. 5.)

had thrown off the Western churches and now stood on their own feet.[48]

The Catholics were less cooperative, although the government told them in 1951 that it expected "the Chinese Catholic Church to have its religious affairs run by Chinese." [49] A few months later, all Chinese Christian churches were ordered to sever their relations with America and with American-financed missions. Catholics came under strong attack, especially those in the Legion of Mary and the Society of Jesus. It was at this period that charges were freely made of nuns' having murdered babies in the mission orphanages; three Canadian nuns who were expelled from China in 1952 said that they had been stoned and spat on by the crowd after having been tried for infanticide.[50] A film was made and distributed describing Catholic "espionage" in Shanghai. The Papal Internuncio, Monsignor Riberi, was arrested for espionage and for instructing priests to oppose Communism, and in 1951 he was expelled. Monsignor Pollio, the former Archbishop of Kaifeng, said in Rome after his expulsion that he had been flogged before 5,000 people in 1950 for opposing the Chinese National Church.[51] All the Catholic churches were renamed, and new inscriptions put up with the phrase "Catholic Patriotic Union." [52] At last, in 1957, some Catholics were persuaded to form the Patriotic Association of Chinese Catholics.[53] Christianity did take deep root in some places; in 1955 the *People's Daily* revealed that two hundred literally underground Catholic churches had been discovered in the province of Hopei.[54] But the numbers are so small that they do not worry the government, which is quite happy to have apparently normal Christian services regularly conducted in the principal cities, to the surprise of many foreign visitors.

In 1960, possibly angered by the visit to Taiwan of the late Cardinal Tien, China's most distinguished Catholic, the Communists again clamped down on leading priests. The Catholic Bishop of Shanghai, Ignatius Kung Ping-mei, was sentenced to life imprisonment for "serious crimes of high treason," and Bishop James E. Walsh, an "American imperialist spy," was given twenty years' imprisonment.[55]

The average intellectual in China would probably agree that drastic social changes were long overdue, only regretting that they happen to make life so dull and frustrating for himself. To put it another way, one can perhaps say that the present generation of intellectuals is paying for its predecessors' neglect and inactivity. A society in which the élite could measure a 2,000-year gap between its own luxurious life and the depressed, despairing existence of the peasants whom it hardly ever saw, could not go on. The Communists began with much goodwill, if for no other reason than that the ousted Kuomintang had been cruel and oppressive in its policy towards the country's educated élite. Much of that goodwill has been expended, however, and it is difficult to say now that the Communists are really more popular with the intellectuals, particularly since the excesses of the Red Guards in 1966–8.* The future will depend very heavily on the next generation of intellectuals and on the way in which it responds to Communism. It becomes important to examine the Party's policy towards the family in general and the country's youth in particular.

5: THE FAMILY

New Obligations

ON 10 DECEMBER 1958, THE COMMUNIST PARTY'S CENTRAL Committee adopted a Resolution in which it was said:

> Mr Dulles of the United States . . . knows nothing about things in our country, but likes to pretend to be a China expert. . . . What breaks his heart especially is that we have supposedly destroyed the marvellous family system which has been handed down for thousands of years. True, the Chinese people have destroyed a feudal, patriarchal system. This patriarchal system, it must be noted, generally disappeared long ago in capitalist society. But we go a step further and estab-

* After the purge of rightists which succeeded the Hundred Flowers, there were periodic calls for more imaginative policies towards the intelligentsia. A senior official, Chang Chih-yi, wrote in *Youth of China*, No. 4 of 1959, that because of "the historical and practical conditions of China, culturally backward and scientifically underdeveloped and urgently needing a large number of intellectuals," a new lenient policy was to be followed. The intellectuals' expertise "is indispensable for socialist reconstruction" and constitutes a "social treasure." It is therefore "extremely wrong" to talk of suppressing bourgeois intellectuals, rather "we must conduct a long, recurrent, patient, delicate and persuasive education." Again, in January 1963 Liu Shao-chi and Chou En-lai entertained scientists and scholars to reaffirm their prestige. But the main interest of these sallies is in the field of science, and this is more fully discussed in Chapter Thirteen below.

lish a democratic, united family and this is generally rare in capitalist society. . . . As to nurseries, kindergartens, and workers' canteens in the factories, these also first appeared in capitalist society. . . . Such undertakings run by us . . . facilitate the . . . emancipation of the individual personality of man. They have truly and completely emancipated the mass of women and enabled the children to receive better education and care. . . .[1]

One of the earliest pieces of legislation made by the Communist Government was the Marriage Law of 13 April 1950, which abolished child marriage, polygamy and concubinage. This was not an academic matter. Mao Tse-tung was married by his parents "when I was fourteen to a girl of twenty, but I had never lived with her—and never subsequently did." [2] China's only living woman General, Li Chen, was given by her family as a child bride at the age of six.[3] These reforms were badly needed, and they were welcomed by all modern-minded Chinese. It is difficult for the average American to imagine the bondage of the oldstyle Chinese family, in which the grandparents decided who should marry whom, all income went to the head of the family, one had to obey one's seniors, marriage was lifelong and widows could not remarry. It resembled a small, authoritarian state.

More controversial were the Communists' new provisions for divorce. Any existing marriage which had been concluded "feudalistically" by the mere will of the four parents could now be dissolved on application. It was unkindly said by some that the real purpose in making divorce easier was to legalize the Communist Party cadres' new "city wives" acquired during their entry into the towns and cities in 1949, and the law was popularly referred to as the "Divorce Law." [4] The new freedom released many people from marriages they had never really wanted, though it was also taken by a few cadre workers as a signal for the institution of free love. Almost a million divorces were reported in the first two or three years of the new law, mainly of government officials and Party members working far from their original homes.[5] One unforeseen result was a wave of suicides, which the *People's Daily* admitted had to be attributed to the excessively vigorous implementation of the divorce law by local cadres.[6] The *cause célèbre* was that of the Fushun woman trade unionist, Yang Yun. A Party member, she had married another Communist at eighteen but had lost contact with him during the civil war, as happened with many couples at that time. In 1949 she found him again, but by then he had married another Party member and, obliged to choose between them, he found he was more attached to his second wife. The Court gave him a divorce from Yang Yun, who promptly ended her own life by taking poison. "I live for you," she wrote him, "I joined the revolution for your sake." But in the press correspondence which followed this affair, there were many critics of Yang Yun's behaviour. "When the fatherland is building up socialism," said one writer, "it is a great error to commit suicide because of a marriage case." Another commented: "The organization did everything to help her, but she did not believe in the organization. Her organization idea was weak." "The life of a Party member," a third rebuked, "belongs to the Party." [7] There were also murders, where a discarded spouse, or his or her relatives, took revenge on the one who had humiliated them by ending the marriage. The National Committee for the Thorough Implementation of the Marriage Law reported in 1953 that about 75,000 deaths or suicides could be attributed to marriage differences (over a period of a year.) [8]

The change in the customs of centuries was too sudden, too violently imposed. Within eighteen months of passing the law, the government admitted its widespread abuse [9] and ordered an investigation which eventually showed that only about fifteen per cent of the population really accepted the new system; sixty per cent were reluctant and twenty-five per cent had not been touched at all by the official propaganda.[10] The Party conceded that it had underestimated the strength of the old feudalistic outlook and social customs among the ordinary people, and the order went out that longstanding family customs could be changed only by patience: violence was to be avoided.[11] The Marriage Law Implementation Committee warned that its work would be "a long-term laborious task," and it restored the legality of matchmaking. The 1950 law had forbidden third parties to interfere in the conclusion of a marriage, but the village youth of China was not ready overnight to begin selecting its own marriage partners, and the traditional broker or go-between (who would sometimes receive as much as 600 *yuan*, or about $250, from the bridegroom's family) [12] had surreptitiously continued to ply his business. Now, the Committee conceded in 1955, marriage by introduction "can also be a form of self-determination."

The fuss about marriage and divorce having died down, attention turned to the relationship between parents and children. In the old Confucian tradition, to disobey one's parents was one of the worst sins. The revolt against this tight family discipline had begun before the Communist Party of China was born, and it was well in train when the Communist Government took power. The Communists' interest lay in accelerating the trend against paternal authority, for they knew that their future lay with the next generation. By encouraging children to resist their parents' pressure in the matter of their own marriage, the Party ensured its popularity with the younger generation, but it soon found itself obliged to prevent things going too far. The *Youth of China* magazine ran an editorial at the end of 1956 entitled "Maltreatment and Abandonment of Parents must not be Permitted," warning adolescents, however keen in their ideology, not to become too unfilial and behave harshly to "backward" parents.[13] The Party, after having encouraged teenagers to bring any unpatriotic or antisocial behaviour of their parents, from tax evasion to food hoarding, to the attention of the authorities, now sought something of a revival of Confucian ethics within the new, Communist family relationship. The *China Youth Daily* said in 1962:

> Marxism doesn't deny old moral concepts, it rejects merely the idealistic errors of the old ideas; it gives them new scientific content, creating a new Communist morality. Old virtues of the labouring people have a deep social foundation; they must be continued and further developed. Such a moral virtue is that of taking care of father and mother.[14]

So the Party of revolution became, after assuming power, the Party of conservatism, following the classic path of revolutionaries. Social justice demands a minimal care of the aged by their children, and the Party realized that in helping the young to shake off the too-rigid authority of their parents it ran the risk of leading them to become resistant to authority as such—including that of the Party itself and of the state. The same mistake was made by Mao on a massive scale when he unleashed the teenage discontents in the cultural revolution in 1966.

In 1958 came the People's Communes and the social experiments which provoked such unfavourable comment from Dulles and other foreign observers. Over-enthusiastic cadres in some districts arranged for men to work together in one village, women to work in another, with communal institutions for the care of the elderly and the children. These Orwellian experiments were disowned by the Party leaders in the Resolution quoted at the beginning of this chapter. This is what it had to say on communal living arrangements:

> The existing old-style houses must be reconstructed step by step; townships and village housing estates with parks and

woods must be built by stages and in groups; these will include residential quarters, community dining rooms, nurseries, kindergartens, the "homes of respect" for the aged, factories, threshing floors, livestock sheds, shops, post and telecommunications offices, warehouses, schools, hospitals, clubs, cinemas, sports grounds, baths and public lavatories. . . . We stand for the abolition of the irrational patriarchal system inherited from the past and for the development of family life in which there is democracy. . . . Therefore in building residential quarters, attention must be paid to building the houses so that the married couples, the young and aged of each family, can all live together. . . .

The communes have helped to hasten the breakdown of the old family ties * in indirect ways. For one thing, wages are paid, for the first time, to the individual worker instead of to the head of the family. This means that a son may have more money than his father, a sister more than her brother, and nothing could be better calculated to promote individual independence within the family, as any study of Western industrial society shows. For another thing, the institution of mess-halls, nurseries and kindergartens on a wide scale in both villages and towns has released housewives for agricultural or industrial work, and a corresponding enhancement of the prestige and independence of women in society has been observed. The promotion of family planning and birth control has also improved the position of women: this is discussed in Chapter Eleven below.

Before the Communists, women played little part in public life. Now Madame Soong Ching-ling, widow of Dr Sun Yat-sen and sister of Madame Chiang Kai-shek, is still, in her late seventies, much in the public eye as Vice-Chairman of the People's Republic. Another woman, Li Teh-chuan, was for many years Communist Minister of Public Health. Two women rank high in the Party Central Committee; Tsai Chang (wife of the economic planner Li Fu-chun) and Teng Ying-chao (wife of Prime Minister Chou En-lai). Both are Party veterans who were on the Long March and who have dedicated their lives to the emancipation of China's womanhood (they were instrumental in drafting the controversial Marriage Law of 1950). In 1966 Mao's wife (his third, if the one mentioned at the beginning of this chapter is excluded),

---

* In Taiwan, under the Nationalist Government, the family is also undergoing change but at a slower pace. The single-line three-generation family, where grandparents live with their eldest son and his children, is considered now the ideal. The old large family, in which many brothers stay with their parents even after marriage is disappearing.

Chiang Ching, emerged as a powerful political figure in her own right.

Women such as these personify the austere puritanism of the Party, disdaining both make-up and pretty clothes. One of the reported quarrels between Chiang Ching and Liu Shao-chi's wife (the two rival "first ladies" of China) concerned the latter's wearing showy jewelry during one of Liu's official tours abroad.[15] Many a visitor to China finds a disturbing lack of femininity in the modern Chinese woman. Cosmetics are frowned upon except when they are professionally used by actresses and compères. They are not forbidden, however, and can be seen on sale at department stores. The position can be inferred from an article in the *China Youth Daily* in the summer of 1964 criticizing the worship and pursuit of make-up: it is legal but lamentable.[16]

Dress is equally austere. Most Chinese men wear the high-collared suit (*chungshan*) which Sun Yat-sen made the uniform of the Kuomintang: the Communist innovation is to extend this also to women. During the Hundred Flowers period gay dresses were encouraged, but almost all women in China are still to be seen in the unflattering *chungshan* in one of the three standard colours (navy blue, grey or earth-brown). The only difficulty the authorities have over dress is with the Overseas Chinese students, children of families living in Southeast Asia where American fashion prevails, who introduce what the Communist Party considers undesirable styles—especially in Shanghai where the younger generation is receptive to such fashions. During 1964 there was an official campaign against "US-capitalist-style narrow trousers," "missile shoes" and other eccentricities.[17] A girl in Shanghai insisted on wearing tight slacks, arguing that they did not necessarily reflect bourgeois thoughts, but the *People's Daily* pointed out that such clothes could not fail to be associated in the Chinese people's mind with the immoral American films that used to be shown before 1949.[18] The problem has also arisen of unusual hair styles, as Cha Kui-min, a Peking barber, has pointed out in an article in a learned Peking journal at the end of 1963, under the heading: "Class Struggle Exists in Barbers' Shops, Too":

Is there class struggle in barbers' shops? We were not clear about this at the beginning. Everyone has his own taste in hair-dressing, and I used to do whatever the customers asked.

Recently, however, we have learned Chairman Mao's theories about class struggle and have come to a new realization of the problem. The struggle between two kinds of ideologies and between two roads in our society is reflected in every aspect of our social life. Viewing hairdressing from Chairman Mao's standpoint on class and class struggle, we have discovered that there exists a reflection of class struggle in barbers' shops.

Why do people come to have their hair dressed? In a word, it is for beauty. But different people have different opinions on beauty; each class of people differs from the others on this. What the proletariat consider true, good and beautiful the bourgeoisie considers false, bad and ugly. This also finds expression in people's choice of hair style. People with a bourgeois view of beauty always ask to have their hair dressed not in the style which the majority of people prefers but in peculiar and strange styles such as the "spiral," the "do-re-mi-fa-so," the "typhus," etc. . . . .

To these people we offered patient persuasion, telling them that peculiar hair styles are not in harmony with the time. Some people insisted on having their hair dressed in these strange ways, whereupon we told them we do not know how to do them.[19]

A few months later the Beatle haircut appeared. A woman complained that one could not tell whether her young nephew was male or female, and the barbers, after talking the matter over with the Party branch secretary, agreed not to execute such confusing styles. One young customer, however, indignant at his request's being refused, stalked out of the barber's shop. Unnerved, the barbers again took Party advice, only to be met with the rhetorical question: "Should we follow such extravagant Western habits?" The *China Youth Daily* set the official line by advising its readers not to insist on everyone's having a uniform hair-style, but at the same time to avoid "such a non-proletarian trend which considers only food, drink, and enjoyment." [20]

The poverty of the economy, the diffidence of the Chinese personality and the ardour of the revolutionary leadership combine to give Chinese life a puritanical austerity reminiscent of Cromwell's England. Publicly organized prostitution has ended [21] and punishments for sexual crimes have been stiffened. There have been cases of primary schoolteachers being executed for raping girls in their schools.[22] The sudden removal of the traditional barrier between the sexes and the breaking down of the reserve so long cultivated between young men and young women led to excesses. A Party magazine criticizes "scandalous rowdy dancing parties in the Party's cultural palaces" and chides the Youth Corps because it "cares only for political ideology, indoctrination and conscientious work, and takes no care of the private life of the young." [23] Parents are rebuked for neglecting the moral education of young people, and Lenin's remark is quoted: "Sex and family life are by no means a private business."

In 1963 the Kwangtung province branch of the Chinese Musicians' Association held a meeting of critics to consider the continuing popularity of Western light music and "yellow songs." * The critics, a report said, condemned the aria "La Donna è Mobile" from *Rigoletto* because it was "full of ideological poison and decadence, depravity, licentiousness, shamelessness and insults to women. . . . [The] sparkling and frivolous melody and the very 'gay and carefree' manner assumed by the singer with subtle seeming carelessness often produce a 'spicy' effect . . . [and] draw particularly strong response from some of the concertgoers who have bourgeois ideological inclinations. . . ." Even light musical numbers with relatively healthy lyrics were sometimes rendered decadent: "A tendency still exists to 'jazzify' them and so distort or exaggerate their content through distasteful styles of performance . . . in [which] the players often sway 'crazily' and move about the stage and even spin the double-bass as if it were a toy. The effect produced is disgusting." [24]

People's Music, the official musicians' magazine, was shocked to find in 1961 that a gramophone record of love songs had been produced in the Northeast: Chinese youth did not need such things, it said.[25] Shortly afterwards came the astonishing affair of the novel *Returning Home* by Liu Shu-teh, a love story in a modern setting of social struggle, published in Shanghai in 1962. At first it was well received, but in the spring of 1963 a conference of writers and artists was given an exposition of the new political line emphasizing continuing class struggle, and this novel fell victim to the new campaign.[26] "Love," said one critic, "is of secondary importance. . . . One should certainly not write about being intoxicated by love and absorbed in personal feelings and family quarrels; the effect of the novel would be the creation not of the new man but of the old." [27] "The story of the love of individuals is meaningless," concluded another critic; "it has no ideological content." [28] A reader said in the *Kuang Ming Daily,* the Peking newspaper: "To write that a young man, 'tempted by her beautiful appearance, wanted to give

* During a visit to Canton in 1964 I heard some nonconformist playing an old record of "There's an Awful Lot of Coffee in Brazil" in a back street. One of the hopes for the future, incidentally, is the frequency of visits by Cuban, African and other fun-loving foreign delegations who try—but are too often dissuaded by their embarrassed hosts—to show, as General Booth did for an earlier age of zealots, that "the devil has no monopoly of the best tunes" (or dances).

her his heart,' is to abandon all moral principle; such a violent outburst of emotion is indecent and wanting in composure." [29] But the magazine *Literature* noted in the summer of 1963 that in spite of the disapproval, "young students are fighting to get this book and discuss it among themselves." [30]

Love sometimes finds a way. A young postal worker, Chiao Ching, wrote in the *People's Daily* in 1964 that he preferred to go to movies and drama rather than to the organized activities of his collective dormitory, and that he particularly enjoyed taking his girl friend to films "portraying people in love." The leader of his collective group had argued with him that his tastes were "eccentric and peculiar," but, he explained disarmingly, "I found these recreational activities very purposeful . . . for through them I in many ways gained a better understanding of my girl friend." [31]

The family has not been destroyed in China, nor has morality. What has happened is that the Communists, in accelerating an existing tendency for the younger generation to assert its independence, have had to remind it that there should be a place in society also for the elders. The economic material base is too weak for any quick development of large-scale new housing units for the "small family," with concomitant institutions for the aged, the sick and the young, but this is the direction in which the Communists intend Chinese society to go. In this respect the government is a vigorously modernizing agent. The fact that it has such a strong and relatively simple ideology creates an almost Victorian atmosphere of prudishness and conformism, against which the new forces released by these social reforms sometimes collide and explode. The pity is that people have to behave so carefully and prudently, in their speech and in their relationships, to survive the pressures: the victim of this phase of the Chinese revolution is ordinary friendship. [32]

Steaming the Crooked Wood

"LET THE TOTS KNOW THE HAPPINESS OF SOCIALISM, THE poverty of workers' children in capitalist countries, the miseries of life in colonial and semi-colonial lands, the effects of imperialist invasion in colonial countries, and, most important of all, let them understand that American imperialism is the worst enemy of the peoples of the world." So declared the *People's Daily* in an editorial, referring to children under seven.[1] As Hsun Tzu, the third century BC Chinese philosopher, remarked: "Men are born with the love of gain, . . . crooked wood must be steamed and forced to conform to a straight edge." [2] The Chinese Communists, like the Jesuits, start the steaming early.

They inherited in 1949 a twelve-year system of primary and secondary education which existed more on paper than on the ground in many areas: probably fewer than twenty per cent of school-aged children were attending classes, and the rest remained illiterate. Their initial concern was to expand this network and to aim, first at universal primary schooling and then at universal secondary schooling. Even the first objective soon came up against the harsh realities of the Chinese economy, and four years after coming to power the government had to halt its programme because of insufficient funds. In 1956 the drive was resumed, and Chairman Mao announced two important new educational targets: the complete abolition of illiteracy through adult schools within twelve years, and compulsory universal education for all children within five or seven years.

There were also changes in the content of education. The old-fashioned parts of the traditional school curriculum, "old stuff from the nineteenth century," were abandoned and more stress was placed on mathematics (as a preparation for science) and foreign languages (as a preparation for the later acquisition of technical knowledge). Russian was the most popular first foreign language up to about 1960, since when the tide has turned in favour of English again. With the aim of rooting out the affectations of traditional learning, the government also introduced "productive labour" to the school curriculum, usually for about six hours a week, and although concern is periodically expressed about the effect of this on studies, it has continued because of the high priority accorded by the Communist Party to overcoming the natural contempt of the educated for physical work.

In 1957 it was realized that the national budget could not afford even to provide nine years of compulsory universal schooling by 1967. It was decided that the main burden should be put on the countryside itself, on the cooperatives and later the communes. So in 1958 tens of thousands of so-called *minpan*, or people's, schools were established, largely vocational in orientation and financially self-supporting through their own productive labour.[3] The spare-time agricultural secondary school was the most common type, and by 1960 there were about 30,000 of these (or roughly one to each commune) with an enrolment of three million students. As Lu Ting-yi said in an article in *People's Education* in 1960, regular secondary school education had "failed to penetrate" the rural areas: in 1959 there had been thirty-seven million children between the ages of thirteen and sixteen, only about one fifth of whom could be accommodated in the ordinary full-time secondary schools.[4] It was not only financial stringency that dictated this development. When Chou En-lai announced a renewed stress on spare-time education in 1964 he said that these schools "can train men of a new type, who are developed in an all-round way and are capable of doing physical labour as well as possessing culture and technique; the conditions will thus be created for gradually eliminating the difference between mental and manual workers."[5]

The *minpan* schools teach four main subjects: Chinese language, mathematics, politics and basic agricultural science. They were not always popular at first, some critics deriding them as "schools for beggars." The quality of the new teachers was variable, two thirds of them coming from city life with no previous teaching experience. "Every knowledgeable person can teach" was the official line, and local functionaries as well as experienced peasants were installed at the schoolmaster's desk.

The idea of spare-time study is even applied to higher education. Shanghai, for example, has a Spare-Time Industrial University offering five-year courses in engineering theory and practice for over 4,000 secondary school leavers with some intervening factory experience. They put in sixteen hours a week for productive labour, which pays for the expenses of the institution, and eight hours' study. The rest of the time they carry on their normal factory work outside.

The ordinary universities spent their first few years of Communist rule changing over to the unfamiliar and not very popular Russian style. They were reorganized into highly specialized institutions, each one designed, after the Soviet model, to turn out a given kind of professional person—one university for scientists, another for engineers, a third for administrators and so forth. But by about 1956 this initial enthusiasm for Russia had waned. It was opposed, or made not to work well, by many of the professors who had been educated in America or Western Europe and who considered the switch to the Russian model as either unnecessarily confusing or bound to lead to a downright reduction in standards. It was only in 1957, during the reign of the Hundred Flowers, that the full extent of resentment against Russian methods and Russian arrogance came to light. Two posters exhibited at Peking University during those exciting days of free speech give some of the flavour of the protest. One concerned literature:

On being told that many young people liked to read Romain Rolland's *Jean-Christophe,* the secretary of the Youth League exclaimed: "Don't poison yourself! Romain Rolland is a French writer, of a capitalist country, therefore his work contains poison!" We ask the School: why do you want to seal off Western literature from us? The time devoted to the teaching of Western literature does not even amount to half the time devoted to the teaching of Russian literature. Why do such great masters of world literature as Balzac, Byron and Shelley deserve only a two-hour lecture, whereas we had to study Pushkin alone for several weeks? Other excellent writers of world stature like Diderot, Hardy, Stendhal, Rolland, Dreiser, Twain, etc. . . . do not even deserve to have their names mentioned! Alas, these great writers were unfortunate: they were not born in a Slavic nation! We are tired of simple-minded Soviet books filled with chauvinism, propaganda and boasting. We want equal consideration of the whole world literature and not always to have some—ski,—ov,—aia,—na, presented as an idol or super-being.[6]

Another poster expressed some opinions in the Department of History:

Some dogmatists lack the most elementary decency: even products that have nothing to do with Marxism are imposed on us as if they carry the trade-mark "USSR." Some say the

Russo-Swedish war was a just war because it gave Russia an outlet on the Baltic Sea. It was not aggression because this land belonged to Russia in antiquity, besides it was necessary for the historical development of Russia. Nelson is presented as a warmonger and a parasite, whereas Suvorov of Russia is presented as a hero who liberated the peoples of Europe from Napoleon's tyranny! Let us not forget that the peoples of Europe greeted Napoleon with bread and salt whereas Suvorov reimposed on them the shackles of feudalism.[7]

Professor Liu Pu-tung explained, also during this Hundred Flowers period, how easy a profession teaching had become: in one university the "three-copy" system was practised, by which the teacher copied on the blackboard a Soviet text which he had previously copied into his own notebook and the students then copied from the blackboard into their notebooks. "In the event of a student not understanding a point, the teacher would confront him with the stick, with the remark: 'This teaching material originates in the Soviet Union.'"[8]

Much of all this is more a reflection on the level of Chinese university standards than on the Russian scholars, some of whom also probably lamented the way in which their work, after passing through the hands of the officials of both countries, was presented to Chinese students. In any event the pendulum gradually swung back: after 1958 the references to the Russian model were entirely omitted, and from then on the principal tug-of-war between the Party and the professors was over the importance to be attached to the class struggle. The Communist Party did not insist on its members being specially favoured in university entrance examinations, but it did require that a larger proportion of new students be drawn from peasant and proletarian backgrounds. The older universities were most reluctant to do this. Peita (Peking University) was told by one of its senior administrators in 1958 that "only . . . nineteen per cent of the students are worker and farmer students, and even these are gradually being eliminated from the school because the professors, the majority of whom come from exploiting classes, think that the workers are coarse, dull, not equipped to study and not able to learn a foreign language."[9] The Communists insist on a degree of manual work: most university students put in a month every year, in a factory or in the fields, and so do the teachers, all save the very old ones. Sometimes manual labour is regarded as a "punishment," as when the entire Philosophy Department at Peita spent a whole year in a village atoning for its ideological failings. This attitude of mind was carried to an extreme in 1966–7, when schools and universities were closed for a full year to do political work on behalf of the Maoists.

The rapid extension of higher educational facilities, and the almost military discipline * imposed on the students, also found the Party and the professors usually on different sides. In 1958 there was a Great Leap Forward in university extension, as in almost everything else, and the number of colleges and universities was brought up to more than a thousand. In the first fifteen years of the Communist Government something like 1,300,000 students graduated from colleges and universities, about one third of them engineers.[10] No one can doubt the need for such large numbers, but standards are difficult to maintain during such phases of rapid growth.

The Communist Party makes its influence felt on the younger generation not only through its control of the schools and universities themselves but also through the "junior" organizations, which were originally the Young Pioneers Corps (usually known as Red Scarves) among primary schoolchildren and the Communist Youth League for teenagers (from fourteen to twenty-five). About half of the primary schoolchildren were enrolled in the Young Pioneers, and their red scarves made a pretty sight when you saw a crocodile of them walking along the street. The *Peking Review* reported this example of their work in 1958:

> A man, while strolling along the street, suddenly spat. He was immediately approached by a little girl who politely asked him if he had spat. The man admitted that he had and was about to walk away when the girl stopped him and gave him a discourse on the evils of spitting. She smiled when she had finished, handed him a slip of paper, apologized for having taken up his time, and wished him good day. The man looked at the slip of paper. The girl was a member of a Young Pioneers' Health Inspection Team which was doing its part in the campaign against spitting.[11]

The Youth League, which numbered twenty million in 1956, aimed at educating young people in the Party's ideology and policies and preparing them for future membership and leadership in the Party. It was within this organization that children were encouraged to inform on their parents' activities, precipitating one of the most difficult problems which a con-

---

* European students in residence at Peita have described its daily life, with loudspeakers blaring out the song "The East is Glowing Red" at 6.30 a.m., regular compulsory physical exercises and so on. See for example René Goldman's "Peking University Today," in CQ 7, 1961, p. 103.

temporary Chinese child of middle class background has to face. One Youth League member from a formerly well-to-do bourgeois family was shocked when his parents' home was ransacked by a crowd, looking for hidden valuables, during the Five-Antis campaign of 1952–3. Subsequently a classmate of his denounced his own elder brother, who had brought him up after the death of their father, and the brother was executed. A fourteen-year-old girl in his school was pressed to denounce her father for some anti-popular activity, and he committed suicide. These events were deeply imprinted on this young man's mind: "Inside of me," he wrote afterwards, "I had a feeling of nausea, but of course I, like all the others said nothing." Years later he fled to Hongkong.[12]

In 1966 the Red Guard organization suddenly replaced the Youth League, which was accused of being under right-wing leadership and was dissolved. Revolutionary youth became Mao's chief ally in the fight against Party orthodoxy, and millions of them went to Peking to see their leader in a series of march-pasts. But in the end these young heroes had to come to terms with those in authority.

A good deal of dissatisfaction is caused by the intractable problem of matching school-leavers or graduates with jobs. The Party makes it very clear to students that, in the words of one college president, "you owe your training to the blood and sweat of the labouring people."[13] Everything possible is done to suppress any shirking of the less popular types of work, or any reluctance to go to whichever distant city or region the authorities select for a young man's or woman's first post. The fact that a boy may be separated for years from his parents, or a bride from her husband, is considered secondary to the urgent construction needs of the nation. It is another part of the government's policy to promote the cohesiveness and unity of the country by mixing people from different regions in the ranks of the administration. A graduate from Canton may be sent to teach in a northern school, and a northerner sent south, with this objective in mind.

It is also an important aim of the Party to breed a familiarity with manual work. The *China Youth Daily* reported approvingly the case of a Cantonese university student who was sent to the countryside and spent seven years collecting night-soil, noting that when he came to work in Peking it took some time for him to accustom himself to the northern habit of carrying the bucket on one's back, for he feared that the contents might spill over him.[14] Eighteen pupils at another school volunteered to be the "new shift" of sanitary workers after their graduation.[15] But these reports have the smell of being publicized precisely because they are not common enough for the Party's liking.*

There are two different factors involved in these situations affecting the entry of young people into adult working life. First, there is the inconvenience of being given work in a place where you do not want to go. Secondly, there is the disdain still surviving from the pre-1949 social outlook, for certain professions considered lowly, such as school-teaching, or any kind of manual labour. But sometimes these unfavourable factors are all compounded. Such is the case with construction work in the "virgin lands" of the western interior, in Sinkiang and Chinghai, regions where there are only nine people to the square mile (compared with about 450 to the square mile in central and eastern China). From the early 1950s on, the government organized groups of volunteers to go for varying periods into these desolate areas. In Shanghai a year or two ago an exhibition was put on, entitled, "Shanghai Youth in Sinkiang," embroidering the theme of "offering our youthful lives to the motherland," in "beautiful and opulent Sinkiang." A rally of 10,000 young people was lectured on the importance of "going West," and selected returnees from these mysterious regions went about telling their old friends how marvellous it was there. Stations were set up for the enrolment of "social youth" (as the Communists describe, with delicate euphemism, the unemployed they claim to have abolished), and the newspapers urged doting mothers to let their darlings go: "Don't be muddle-headed parents . . . let our children fly away to be great personages of the time, and let them plunge themselves into the splendid frontier of our motherland to receive the baptism of the Revolution. . . [16] Accounts of heroism on the part of such volunteers are frequently published.

Another great movement, which began to reach its climax only in 1964, is the mass descent of educated youth into the countryside. This is much more than the earlier drives to send young people to the communes for a month or so every year. "In recent years," the People's Daily said in 1964, "a great number of educated youth have responded to the call of the Party and of the country and gone down to the villages to take part in agricultural production: . . . in future the number . . . will grow. Their feet will be set in the villages, they will be rooted there and they will bring forth flowers and

---

* Even Mao Tse-tung himself quarrelled with his father over the question whether Mao should be obliged to carry manure about the farm when he was really wanting to study and read novels (see CQ 16, 1963, pp. 2–3).

bear fruits. . . . They will radically change the look of our villages, will establish new socialist villages and a great modern agriculture." [17] It was revealed that no fewer than forty million young people had already gone as the first "pioneers." [18] In Liaoning province these new migrants represented already more than half of the rural labour force in 1963.

This is the logical culmination of many trends in Chinese Communist thinking over the years. How to stop the appalling exodus of intelligent children from the villages, where their minds were the peasants' only sure key to the agro-technical revolution? * How to break the financial bottleneck which prevented the government from providing by conventional means the technical personnel to spark off the agro-technical revolution on a really nation-wide scale? How to provide employment for the growing number of city school-leavers for whom the disappointingly slow pace of industrialization could not provide regular factory jobs? How to bridge the widening gulf between the monstrously overgrown Shanghais and the deadeningly deprived rural backwaters? How to reconcile these two halves of China which, far more than Disraeli's "two nations," had almost lost touch with each other? How to break the stultifying and stratifying myth about the superiority of white-collar and white-cuff labour? All these questions are massively answered by the ultimate audacity of marshalling an entire generation of school-leavers and having them migrate to the villages for good (many of them, however, took advantage of the chaotic administrative conditions of the Cultural Revolution in 1966–8 to return home again).

But one comes back to the question of social origin. In one of the rare personal asides on this controversial subject, Foreign Minister Chen Yi, addressing Peking graduates in 1961, said:

> Speaking of myself, my own mind is very complex; there are Communist ideas, there are also the ideas of Confucius and Mencius, and there are bourgeois thoughts. After taking part in the revolution for forty years I could not say I am "thoroughly Red." I can only say that Communist ideas are dominant, but the ideas of Confucius, Mencius and of the bour-

---

* A 1960 survey in a county of Shansi province had shown that of the 9,975 boys and girls who had graduated from the primary schools between 1949 and 1960, only *nine* were still working in the fields; and of the 1,554 who had been through secondary school, only *one* was presently tilling the soil. All the others had migrated to the cities. (*Kuang Ming Daily*, Peking, 2 July 1962.)

geois class are not completely chased away. . . . One should not exclusively emphasize family origin. A young person does not choose for himself whether he comes from an exploiting family or from a family of workers and farmers. A young person coming from an exploiting class family may be a revolutionary. Among the leading comrades of the Party Central Committee there are many who come from families of higher social standing and there are not many who come from worker and peasant families. Nevertheless they became leaders in the Party.[19]

Coming from a man of bourgeois origin himself, these are comforting words for a middle class youth. This is also a practical policy for a government which still relies, and will continue for some time to rely, on the scientific and technological know-how of the bourgeois class. Nevertheless the Party leaders have formally decided that their successors must come from worker, poor peasant and lower-middle peasant family backgrounds.[20] The Red Guards of 1966 were exclusively from such social classes, and the Cultural Revolution gave them a further impetus towards capturing the commanding heights of social leadership. Unfortunately the much-heralded new generation of this scrupulous pedigree does not always prove as ideologically reliable as the present "trustee" generation of bourgeois-born but revolutionarily-moulded leaders.

The *China Youth Daily* came to the heart of the matter when it conceded that there are "intellectual youths from worker and peasant families who, after acquiring knowledge and culture, have not come closer to the labouring people. . . . They want to wear leather shoes and suits made of good materials. . . . Others, after returning to the countryside, find themselves no longer accustomed to the peasants' plain and frugal way of life and to their coarse and homely fare. They refuse to participate in labour, putting on the airs of intellectuals." [21] An Indian who was present at the Peita "Hyde Park" forums in the spring of 1957 said afterwards that worker and peasant students were more critical of the government than the middle class students (presumably because the latter were more sophisticated and sceptical in the first place).[22]

A young mother asked, in a letter published a few years ago in the magazine *Youth of China,* what was wrong with enjoying quiet leisure at home with one's family? If building Communism and building socialism meant that everyone should live a dull, hard life always working for others, "then what is the use of building them?" [23] The new generation, said the *Kuang Ming Daily,* "think that everything is simple, that the construction of society is going ahead by itself, that happiness will fall into their lap, that there is no need for bitter struggle." [24] The aged Communist leaders are in the dilemma that the natural leaders of the next generation to whom they must eventually give way are, by definition and by inner thought, unreliable, but that the artifically promoted ones whom they hoped would fill the gap are still too green and vulnerable, easy prey to the watchful forces of reaction. The straight wood is too soft, the crooked wood too difficult to steam true.

7: THE NATIONAL MINORITIES

Who Is Chinese?

THE CHINESE CALL THEIR COUNTRY *Chung Kuo* WHICH MEANS "Middle State," a term carrying no racial or national connotations whatever. The Chinese Communists have given us many examples of the difference between the Chinese and the Western concept of nationhood. In 1953, for instance, when the People's Republic held a national census of population, it included an estimated count of all Chinese people living in foreign countries, even those who had become settled after several generations of emigration and who had taken another citizenship. The feeling is that if a family in, say, Canton, is still keeping records of its Indonesian, Canadian and Malgache branches, then the state should support the inference that these latter are still people of China. This was given even more formal recognition in 1954 when the new Constitution of China provided that the National People's Congress be elected by, among others, "Chinese resident abroad."

The immensely strong attachments which the Chinese feel to be forged by blood and soil, by family and ancestral home, were interestingly contrasted with the priority which the West accords to the individual's personal choice during the Korean War, when disagreement over the disposition of the prisoners on both sides almost wrecked the cease-fire negotiations. The

Chinese side insisted to the end on the principle of automatic repatriation of prisoners, irrespective of their individual wishes, whereas the United Nations took the humanitarian view that a prisoner should not be forcibly sent home if he did not want to return. This was the only issue, throughout the Korean war, on which the Asian-Arab group in the UN voted against China.[1]

The Chinese, then, do not follow the neat patterns of European thought when it comes to nationality. It becomes necessary to clarify what the Chinese mean by "China," to define who the Chinese are, or who they *think* they are. The fifteen million or more Chinese who live abroad (principally in Southeast Asia) are obviously regarded, and to a large extent regard themselves, as Chinese, but their position is discussed in Chapter Sixteen below in the context of China's relations with Southeast Asia. Here the discussion will be confined to the national minorities who share the territory of the People's Republic of China with the so-called Han race, or Chinese proper.

Roughly ninety-four per cent of the population of China are Han people, and the remaining forty million are of many different nationalities—Tibetan, Mongol, Kazakh, Thai, Korean and others. Most of these national minorities live in the western fringes of China, in territory sparsely populated and undeveloped. They speak different languages, use different scripts (or none at all), practise different religions and are culturally quite distinct from the Han people of eastern and central China. There are four principal groups of them:

1 Tibet: There are about five million Tibetans, mostly living in Tibet but some in the neighbouring areas of Szechuan, Yunnan and Chinghai provinces as well as in Nepal, Bhutan, Sikkim and India. They can assemble an imposing case for independence, as we shall see; they are culturally distinct and have been for substantial periods self-governing. Like the Mongols, they follow Lamaistic Buddhism.

2 Mongolia: There are some two million Mongolians, now divided almost equally between the independent state of the Mongolian People's Republic (sometimes referred to by the out-dated term, Outer Mongolia) which is under dominantly Soviet influence, and the administrative unit of China known as the Inner Mongolian Autonomous Region—with a few more inside the USSR itself. For China this situation raises two questions: what attitude to take to the independent Mongolians and how to treat the Chinese Mongols?

3 Sinkiang: This name merely means, in Chinese, "new

frontier," and it covers what used to be known as Chinese Turkestan: its full title is Sinkiang Uighur Autonomous Region, the Uighurs being a Turkic people of Central Asia who follow Islam and are the major indigenous race of Sinkiang. But Sinkiang also contains Kazakhs and other races shared with the USSR, and has always been a barometer of Sino-Russian power relations.

4 The Southwest: In Yunnan, Kweichow and Kwangsi, the three Chinese provinces of the southwest, are races of the kind also found in northern Vietnam, Laos, northern Burma and northern Thailand: Chuang, Miao, Yi, Puyi, Thai and many others. They aggregate some twenty million, or half of the total of national minorities in China, and in the southwest itself they account for one fifth of the population. But unlike the Tibetans, Mongols and Uighurs, these are relatively primitive people lacking the prerequisites of independence, and sometimes lacking even a written language.[2]

These peoples were all, of course, considered barbarians by the ancient Chinese. They were brought under the political control of the Empire primarily for the negative purpose of safeguarding China proper from the periodic incursions which people beyond the Great Wall felt tempted to make into its fertile, rich lands.* Only incidentally did the idea of cultural mission intrude, and only with Mao Tse-tung did this assume such proportions as to provoke, in Tibet, one of the bloodiest national rebellions of modern times. China's relations with the minority peoples have never been entirely smooth and successful. A century ago more than 100,000 Chinese were massacred by local insurgents in Sinkiang. Ulanfu, the Mongol leader, declared in an official report to Peking, published in the *People's Daily* in 1952, that "as a result of the extremely savage and cruel oppression of national minorities by pan-Hanism historically, the national minorities (including the Mongols) tend to regard the big nationality with suspicion and to cherish narrow nationalism."[3]

In Chinese political and intellectual circles before 1949 there were two broad streams of thought about the future of the minority races. The national pride of the Chinese, and their sense of having been cheated out of modern great-

---

* Americans used to their modern image of a poor, powerless China, may reflect on the phrase used by Marco Polo, who knew his world better than most, to describe South China: "The richest country in the world." Canton was then three times bigger than Venice, and mediaeval Arab and other Latin visitors endorse Marco Polo's estimate. See Hudson, Chapter 5.

power status, suggested a policy of integration of the other races into the larger national unity of China. Sun Yat-sen, who took this view, planned to open up Mongolia, Tibet, and Sinkiang by railroads, in the American style, and to fill them with Chinese colonists who would develop these territories: Chiang Kai-shek argued that the minorities shared with the Hans a common racial origin. But by the 1920s and 1930s there was a new school of thought, which held that in the post-Versailles world each nationality deserved its own sovereignty. The Communists in their early days in the wilderness leaned to the latter view. The 1931 Constitution of the Kiangsi Soviet Republic (of which Mao Tse-tung was Chairman) recognized "the right of self-determination of the national minorities in China, their right to complete separation from China and to the formation of an independent state for each national minority," while Tibet, Sinkiang and even the provinces of Yunnan and Kweichow were mentioned at Chinese Communist meetings of this period as candidates for independent statehood in the future.[4] The right of secession was, after all, reserved for the non-Russian peoples in the Soviet Constitution of 1936 (though in the USSR the problem was not the same, the non-Russians accounting for a very much larger proportion of the total population).

But in 1936 Mao, questioned on the point by the American journalist Edgar Snow, put it differently. The Mongolians, Mohammedans and Tibetans, he said, "will form autonomous republics attached to the China federation." Of the Outer Mongolians he used a curious phraseology clearly reflecting the inner contradictions in the Chinese Communist attitude: they "will automatically become a part of the Chinese federation, at their own will."[5]

This became the official policy of the Communist Government after 1949. The Constitution of 1954 proclaimed China as a "unified multi-national state" in which the minority nationalities, though "inalienable parts of the People's Republic of China," were guaranteed equality of treatment and the right to preserve their own customs.[6] There was no mention of secession or of independence. Well over a hundred autonomous governments have now been set up by minority groups, under a government decree which at the same time appealed to all government and Party officials to promote "racial equality, friendship, solidarity and mutual aid" and to combat all tendencies towards "jingoistic nationalism." Most of these autonomous governments are at the modest county or district level, but five, including Tibet, Sinkiang and Inner Mongolia, have the title of Autonomous Region, which is the equivalent of provincial status.

But autonomy, whatever the literal provisions of the Constitution, turned out to have two important limitations. It must, the *People's Daily* remarked in 1956, exist within the unity of the great family of peoples, the People's China, under the guidance of the Communist Party and the Central Government. It must also "tend towards socialism." [7] A senior official wrote in 1957: "If autonomy came to mean that no Communist Party or Chinese Government agent helped, it would not be the right sort of autonomy," [8] and the *People's Daily* in the following year pinpointed the racial aspect of the Communists' dilemma: "Without the help of the Chinese race, socialism is nearly impossible among the national minorities." [9] It is the modern version of the old Chinese civilizing mission: the Peking leaders sincerely want the minorities both to rule themselves and to follow the Communist path, but if these objectives become irreconcilable, then the second must naturally take priority. What autonomy means is that the minorities, once they are firmly on the socialist road and have trained their own cadres, will be free from direct Han participation in their administration; also by implication, that they are allowed more time and more latitude than the Chinese people themselves in taking their first painful steps towards socialism. As Chen Yi said in Lhasa in 1956: "The transition of the nationalities of our country to socialism will be achieved separately and in different ways." [10]

A Central Nationalities Academy in Peking has been training administrators from the minority races since 1951, and there are similar institutions in other cities. But it takes years to build up a reliable nucleus of able and right-minded administrators in any nationality, and in the meanwhile the burden falls on the Han cadres. Ulanfu, Peking's original chosen leader for the Mongols (but a victim of the Cultural Revolution in 1967), had this to say about the Chinese cadres in Inner Mongolia in 1951:

> As most of the veteran cadres are Han Chinese . . . they tend to look down upon or distrust Mongol cadres. . . . They do not want to study the Mongolian language, they do not consider carefully the mentality and feeling of their Mongol comrades. . . . We [must] educate the Han Chinese, in particular Han Chinese cadres, to . . . respect the equal rights and opinion of national minorities and to eliminate the tendency towards the superior outlook of a big nationality. . . ."

Mao is well aware of the answer to this problem. "The key

to the solution of this question lies in overcoming Great-Han chauvinism," he said in his famous February 1957 speech. But how? The Central Committee puts out a creditable barrage of propaganda and counsel to its seventeen million Party members and cadre workers, but it takes more than words and arguments to change a man's innermost attitudes, and it is exceptionally difficult to ensure that a relatively uneducated and untravelled local cadre worker will treat other nationalities under his wing with courtesy and restraint, when he is also being told that at last the Chinese nation is standing up to its foes and enemies, and that he has a right to be more proud of being Chinese at this time than for many years past.* Thus the Red Guards in 1966–7 again brought to the surface the Communist's intolerance of Buddhist and Muslim customs. So the first twenty years of Communist rule have seen regular confrontations between local minority nationalism and Chinese cadre chauvinism, with Peking coming down now against one side, now against the other, in an attempt to keep both tendencies under control.

"War is declared," the *People's Daily* announced in 1958, "against all backward customs which stand in the way of progress and are an obstacle in the way of developing production. . . ." It was explained that only the evil customs were to go, so that no decent person need fear a consequent elimination of the various national peculiarities. But the newspaper spoilt the effect of this argument by adding that,

---

* The Chinese are naturally most reticent about their own racial prejudices, regarding these as products of a type of education and society which has now ceased, the surviving remnants of which can be quickly eradicated. We are not obliged to share their optimism, but we are given an occasional glimpse of prejudice. In 1955 a film was made, *Dawn on the Meng River*, showing the life and struggles of a Tibetan tribe in Yunnan province. Two Tibetan students at the Central College of minorities in Peking protested that the film misrepresented their people as primitive, poor and brutal (*Films of the Masses*, Peking, No. 2 of 1956, cited in CNA 133, 25 May 1956). But these critics may have been oversensitive. Again, when a collection of Tang Dynasty poems of the seventh and eighth centuries AD was republished in 1958, those written in border areas were omitted lest they throw a bad light on the minorities (see the review in *Literature*, No. 9 of 1958, cited in CNA 289, 23 October 1959). This does, however, show the tact of the new administration in curbing prejudice. Sometimes one reads correspondence about parents opposing a mixed marriage, but it is usually the minority side which objects, as in a Han-Hui case discussed in *Youth of China*, 16 October 1958 (quoted in FEER, 22 January 1959, p. 107). Sometimes a critic cites a reference in the Chinese press to the need for study of venereal diseases being confined to the minority areas as evidence of prejudice (see CNA 98, 2 September 1955, citing *People's Daily*, Peking, 21 April 1955); this would indeed seem to have more basis in fact than in prejudice.

in any event, it was a good thing to have "an ever-growing convergence of the nationalities." [12] One of the Party's minorities specialists warned in 1964 that "nationalist elements" had become "very rampant" in the past few years, "under the influence of imperialists, foreign reactionaries and modern revisionists, as well as reactionary elements inside China." Their slogan, he added, was "anti-Han, independence and no reforms." [13] The Minister of Culture, introducing a campaign of festivals for new propaganda plays and songs in the minority languages, explained that the feudalist class was training young minority people so that "one generation after the other will fight us." [14]

What is the ultimate aim? A discussion in the Department of History at Peking University in 1959 showed a divergence of viewpoint on this. The historian Chien Po-tsan said that the trend towards amalgamation of all the nationalities within China was a historical fact and should be accelerated by force, following the natural law that the stronger always absorbs the weaker. Others opposed the use of force. [15] A writer in 1962 suggested that it would be a Great-Han chauvinistic attitude to "ignore or want to extirpate national peculiarities and national differences," [16] but Liu Chun put the official line of the Party ideologists in 1964:

> The question of nationality is a question of classes; it is only with the coming of Communism and the gradual extinction of classes that, by the merging of nationalities, national peculiarities and differences will disappear. [17]

The Chinese have been most active in promoting the economic development of the neglected minority areas, some of which, notably Sinkiang and Tibet, are probably rich in mineral resources. They have also put much effort into the improvement of public health and education. Two cultural matters have attracted their special attention: language and religion. At the beginning of their rule, the Communists proposed to introduce a Latin alphabet for the Southwestern minorities (some of which had no script at all), but to follow the Soviet example of using the Cyrillic script for the Central Asian minorities which they shared with Russia. In 1958 this was changed, and Chou En-lai announced that "every nationality will have to use the Latin writing as the foundation" for language reform. [18] Latin letters, the *People's Daily* declared, would "facilitate the unification of the country and the amalgamation of nationalities." [19] This reverse was apparently prompted partly by the convenience of standardizing the alphabet (and Latin had already been preferred to Cyrillic for the honour of providing Mandarin, the national language, with its alphabet), and partly by a growing suspiciousness about Russian motives and policies in Central Asia. It is mainly Sinkiang which is affected, and Latin has not yet been imposed on Tibet or Inner Mongolia (where it suits the Chinese to continue the use of the old Mongol script, which was abolished in the neighbouring Mongolian People's Republic a quarter of a century ago in favour of the Cyrillic alphabet: now the "Outer Mongols" are made to feel envious of their brothers inside China at least for their ability to retain their own traditional script.) [20]

As convinced atheists, the Chinese Communists aim eventually to suppress all religions in China,* and they work continuously to discredit and weaken the Buddhism and Islam traditionally followed by the Central Asian minorities. They propagate popular songs such as this:

> Knock over the Gods!
> We do not Believe!
> We do not Pray!
> We labour, and the Mud will become Gold! [21]

Initially this propaganda was aimed at the local priests, the Lamas and Imams, many of whom were proverbially oppressive, cruel and corrupt; these vested religious interests were also hit hard by the land reform, suffering a loss of revenue. But their influence is not so easily destroyed.

As with Christianity, the Communists have sought to maintain the outward forms of Islam and Buddhism, but to render them innocuous in substance and incapable of hindering their programme of reforms. Islam probably claims ten million followers in China, including the Uighurs, the Kazakhs and the Hui. In 1952 a Chinese Islamic Religion Association was formed, under Communist Party guidance, and this body has set up a College of Islamic Religion which teaches the Koran and Arabic. But Muslims, the *People's Daily* insisted, must "love the country, accept the Government's policy on freedom of religion,† and take part in the movement to protect

---

* The Dalai Lama records that Mao once told him: "Religion is poison. It has two great defects. It undermines the race, and secondly it retards the progress of the country. Tibet and Mongolia have both been poisoned by it." (*My Land and My People: The Autobiography of H.H. The Dalai Lama,* London, Weidenfeld and Nicolson, 1962, p. 102.

† i.e. that the priests may expound their religion only in the mosques, while the Communist Party preaches atheism everywhere else; that the mosques must be self-administered and financially self-supporting without income from rents; that the priests must keep quiet during periods of land reform, etc., and must be patriotic.

world peace." [22] The situation of the average priest is perhaps conveyed by a news report of 1959 that four thousand Imams in Ninghsia had "taken off their long gowns and started working in the fields and local industry." [23] The Communist attitude to the pork question is that it is acceptable for Muslims to refuse pork on hygienic grounds but not out of unsupported superstition, and that if the taboo is based on hygiene then Muslims ought to try to understand the developments of modern science.

Buddhism presents a much bigger challenge to the Communists, especially among the Tibetans. A Chinese Buddhist Association was formed in 1953, and in 1956 a Chinese Buddhist Institute was formed at the Fa Yuan Monastery in Peking, giving two-year courses for monastery administrative workers and four-year courses for scholars and masters of *dharma:* the Tibetan and ancient Pali languages are taught. The government has restored such famous old buildings as the White Horse Temple at Loyang, considered the country's first Buddhist temple, and it has reconstructed the thirteen-storied Pagoda of the Buddha's Tooth which had been wrecked by European soldiers in the nineteenth century. [24] The government also subsidizes certain monasteries, particularly in the big cities, has revived the block-printing of ancient canons, compiled a Buddhist Encyclopaedia and introduced a monthly magazine called *Modern Buddhism.*

Most of the monks and nuns now spend much of their time being "remoulded" by manual labour. It is said that: "A Buddhist must throw himself into real life, and must strive to build up a richer and stronger country; that is the future of Buddhism"; and that: "The idea of parasitic life is being abandoned and replaced by the idea of labour." [25] Chao Pu-chu, Secretary-General of the Chinese Buddhist Association, wrote in 1955 that China's First Five-Year Plan "is the initial blue-print for the Western Paradise here on earth." [26]

The most startling change which the Communists seek to make in Chinese Buddhist thought is to discredit the pacifism and the refusal to take life which most Buddhists profess in some degree. In 1951, during the Korean war, the priests were urged "to join the army directly and learn the spirit in which Shakyamuni as the embodiment of compassion and our guide to Buddhahood killed robbers to save the people and suffered hardships on behalf of all living beings. To wipe out the American imperialist demons that are breaking world peace is, according to the Buddhist doctrine, not only blameless but actually gives rise to merit." [27]

During the Jordan–Lebanon crisis of 1958 a joint meeting

of Buddhists and Taoists in Peking issued a statement: "We good Buddhists and Taoists always love peace and abhor war; but we are never afraid of war. We must kill the war-provoking devils in defence of world peace, only then will we be following the Buddhist and Taoist doctrine of true compassion.[28] One reason for the Communists' interest in retaining an outwardly respectable Buddhist church is their international diplomacy. Japanese, Indian and Southeast Asian Buddhists can be readily impressed by the Chinese Government's policy. "China today," said Bhadanta Ananda Kausalyayana of India after his 1956 visit, "is a country which compared to many others is already Heaven." [29] The Nepalese Buddhist leader Amritananda remarked during a tour of China: "Before coming to China there were doubts in my mind: in the course of my present tour I have learned for myself . . . that there is genuine freedom of religious belief. . . . To provide a better life for the people conforms to the basic spirit of Buddhism." [30] The Peking Government cultivates foreign Buddhist opinion skilfully; it lent its tooth of the Buddha to Burma in 1955 and to Ceylon in 1961, both events causing a considerable stir in those countries. The Chinese delegation usually conducts running battles with the Americans, Taiwanese and other hostile nationalities at the triennial conferences of the World Buddhist Fellowship. The Chinese withdrew from the Bangkok conference in 1958 because of the admission of Taiwan; they almost split the Phnompenh conference in 1961; they did not attend the Sarnath conference in 1964.[31] In 1963 an eleven-nation Asian Buddhist Conference in Peking helped the Chinese Government's diplomacy by protesting atrocities against Buddhists in South Vietnam, although the stubbornness of the Nepalese, Japanese and Cambodian delegates (warned by their own governments to avoid politics) deprived Peking of an explicit reference to American intervention in Vietnam.[32] In general, other Asians are more impressed by Chinese reforms than upset by the regimentation of Chinese Buddhism,[33] although the discourtesies of the Cultural Revolution in 1966 helped to abate their enthusiasm.

Islam is also used by the government to assist its Middle Eastern diplomacy. Chinese Muslims began to make pilgrimages to Mecca in 1955. But it is not so easy to impress Arab scholars whose own governments are already doing more for Islam than any Asian government does to promote Buddhism. Politics are always at the forefront: the Darul Islam movement rebelling against Dr Sukarno's authority in Indonesia was denounced by Chinese Muslims as a "tool of colonialism."

No one has seriously questioned Chinese sovereignty in its Southwest minority areas, and there is no international controversy about Peking's rule over the Hui or the Manchus. The Russians, who are China's neighbours at this point, do not challenge Peking's rights in Sinkiang (though there are small differences over the precise delineation of the border), and the Uighurs, who still account for over half of the Sinkiang population in spite of large-scale Han immigration,[34] are not by nature rebellious: Peter Fleming called them "spineless" and "very easily ruled." * The only areas where Chinese sovereignty has been squarely challenged are Tibet and Mongolia.

Unlike the Uighurs, the Mongols constitute a distinct nation which did, after all, conquer China and even parts of Europe in its twelfth-thirteenth-century heyday. Having first sinicized their Mongol conquerors, then repelled them and finally, in the seventeenth century, reabsorbed them into the Chinese Empire, the Chinese regard the Mongols as their dependents. Mao, as we have seen, felt in the 1930s that they would return as a matter of course to the Chinese fold, though he did not, as the independent government of the Mongolian People's Republic now indignantly reminds us, consult them on the point. The Mongols managed to obtain Russian Communist support for their independence, and show no sign of wanting to exchange this for re-entry into the Chinese family—as a plebiscite proved in 1946.† Mao was obliged to accept this Mongolian *fait accompli* in 1949, and his Government behaved generously to the MPR in the following few years. It lent several tens of thousands of Chinese workers and technicians and gave some $85 million in aid to the Mongolian economy. This policy probably yielded a secret undertaking by Khrushchev in the mid-1950s to allow the MPR gradually to evolve out of the Soviet and back into the Chinese sphere of influence.[35]

* The tension between the Han and the indigenous Sinkiang races has been exploited by the USSR in recent years, even to the point of encouraging minor risings among the Chinese-ruled Kazakhs at Ili, adjoining the Soviet border. But this is only a minor aspect of the Sino-Soviet dispute. See P. H. M. Jones, "Sinkiang and the Split," in FEER, 23 July 1964, p 159.

† The result of this plebiscite was at first accepted by the Kuomintang Government, but since retiring to Taiwan, Chiang has reversed this, and the MPR is now shown on Taiwanese maps as Chinese.

But the Mongols had forgotten their earlier links with China after forty years of Russian influence, and when the Sino-Soviet partnership began to crack they remained firmly under the Soviet wing. The Mongolian Communist Party had openly condemned the "racial discrimination" shown by the Chinese Communists towards their national minorities,[36] and its representatives in Peking suffered during the Cultural Revolution. China is unlikely, however, to press its quarrel with the USSR through the medium of Mongolia. If the premise of Mongolian independence is accepted, a good argument can be made for the cession of Chinese-ruled Inner Mongolia to the MPR, and this would make northern China look very vulnerable. As the Russian Communists have said, "one can also prove that the borders of the Chinese People's Republic pass along the line of the Great Wall of China, which is only sixty miles away from Peking." [37] China's best strategy, if she wants the Mongols eventually to revolve around her sun, is to await a partial resolution of her dispute with the Soviet Union. Russia has little inherent interest in Mongolia aside from its relations with Peking, and would probably offer it again as a bargaining counter in return for some other Chinese concession.

In the barren sand-covered lands of Inner Mongolia, the Chinese have courted popularity. They have given honour to Buddhism (empty honour, as some would say, but in Asia the gestures of outward respect count for more than in Europe), they have allowed the traditional language and script to reign unchallenged, and in 1962 they supported the celebration of the 800th anniversary of Genghiz Khan.* In all these respects the Chinese attitude contrasted favourably, in Mongolian eyes, with the Soviet. But at least the Russians refrained from physically colonizing the MPR. In Inner Mongolia the Mongols are today vastly outnumbered by Han Chinese immigrants.

Indeed, in almost all the autonomous areas the Han are now, through deliberate recent settlement, in a majority—or are sufficiently numerous to weaken the position of the dominant local race. Of the sixty-three million inhabitants of autonomous areas of various kinds, some fifty-seven per cent were, at a recent official count, Chinese. This is bound up with the question of economic development. The Chinese population pressure, the economy's need for more oil (in

---

* This was organized by the MPR, but against Russian wishes, and the leaders involved were later dismissed. Russia accused the Chinese of refusing to join the world in condemning Genghiz' invasion of Europe as a "great historical tragedy."

which Sinkiang is rich) and minerals, and the political desirability of associating, in the minority nationalities' eyes, Chinese Communist rule with rapid material progress and modernization—all these combine to dictate a policy of colonization. In turn this raises the question of the ultimate future of the minorities as distinct national cultures.

There is no doubt whatever that the vast majority of Chinese regard it as China's destiny to rule Mongolia, Sinkiang and Tibet, and for a Westerner, who from Peking or Shanghai is seen as the arch-imperialist of all times, to suggest otherwise is interpreted as yet another attempt to delay the entry of China into her birthright as a great power in the world, equal to Europe or America. It is difficult for a Chinese to believe that a Westerner can have a genuine concern for the welfare of the ordinary Mongol or Uighur or Tibetan, and, if concern *is* expressed, it is taken to refer to the "old society" of feudal and benighted injustices which the Chinese are firmly dismantling.

I suppose the new generations of Mongols and Uighurs and the rest will bless the day that these essential reforms came and brought the twentieth century to their doorsteps. But by the same token that they will have become liberated from a mediaeval economic and social system, they will also have become so politically articulate and ambitious as to assert their own future path, even if this diverges from the Chinese. Peking will not be able to escape the odium of having been the agent of destroying the old any more than it can forfeit the merit of having been the agent by which the new was constructed. Just as Africa has mixed emotions about its nineteenth-century European embrace, Central Asia will both hate and thank the Chinese Communists for their dedicated work. And nowhere is this more true than in Tibet.

8: TIBET

Freedom or Progress?

THEIR HANDLING OF THE TIBETAN QUESTION PROBABLY LOST the Chinese Communists more international sympathy than any other aspect of their policy in the 1950s, and some of the

Peking leaders probably regard it as their single most embarrassing problem. The Tibetan question is also an extremely difficult one on which to judge. Very few people know anything about Tibet: probably fewer than two hundred Westerners have ever visited it, and of those only a score or two are still living.*

Until Chinese Communist rule Tibet was a primitive theocracy of about three million people, living in an area of half a million square miles—almost twice the size of Texas. Most of this inhospitable terrain lies over 15,000 feet, but its lower southern strip is cultivable and supports the majority of the population. The best land was owned by the Buddhist monasteries, and one third of the male population were monks. The Dalai Lama is traditionally god, king and priest all in one; he is believed to be a reincarnation of the Buddhist figure Avalokitasvara and when he dies a successor is found, by a complicated ritual, from among children born soon after his death. The present Dalai Lama is the fourteenth. He was born in a poor peasant's family, and is now thirty-five years old. The Tibetans are small in numbers, but they are also by tradition and temperament disunited, the various tribes being usually at odds with each other.†

No one doubts that Tibet possesses a unique culture and a recognizable distinct nationality. The controversial question is whether it was, in 1949, a sovereign independent state or not. The argument of the then Tibetan government (i.e. of the Dalai Lama, the leading monks and nobles) is well put in its letter of 7 November 1950 addressed to the United Nations:

> Tibetans have for long lived a cloistered life in their mountain fastnesses, remote and aloof from the rest of the world, except in so far as His Holiness the Dalai Lama, as the ac-

---

* As an example of the narrowness of the channels through which we obtain our information about Tibet, it may be recalled that in 1950, when the outside world was following the drama of the Chinese Communist entry into Tibet, the nearest point to which outsiders could go was Kalimpong, the Indian border town and centre of Tibetan *emigré* activity. Yet there were then only four non-Tibetans in Kalimpong able to speak the Tibetan language: a Russian scholar, an Austrian professor, the anthropologist Prince Peter of Greece and Denmark, and the former Plymouth Brother missionary George Patterson (George N. Patterson, *Tragic Destiny,* London, Faber, 1959, p. 64). The two latter were subsequently asked to leave by the Indian Government.

† George Patterson remarks, of the 1958 fighting between Chinese troops and Eastern Tibetan tribesmen, that: "For the first time in a millennium Tibet became a fully united country again" (*Tragic Destiny,* London, Faber, 1959, p. 180), a revealing comment on one of the factors preventing Tibet from establishing her independence in the eyes of the world.

knowledged head of the Buddhist Church, confers benediction and receives homage from followers in many countries. In the years preceding 1912 there were even indeed close and friendly relations of a personal nature between the Emperor of China and the Dalai Lama. The connexion was essentially born of belief in a common faith, and may correctly be described as the relationship between a spiritual guide and his lay followers. It had no political implications. As a people devoted to the tenets of Buddhism, Tibetans had long eschewed the art of warfare, practised peace and tolerance, and for the defence of their country relied on its geographical configuration and on non-involvement in the affairs of other nations. There were even times when Tibet sought, but seldom received, the protection of the Chinese Empire. The Chinese, however, in their natural urge for expansion, have wholly misconstrued the significance of the time of friendship and interdependence that existed between China and Tibet as between neighbours. To them, China was a suzerain and Tibet a vassal state.[1]

Like the Mongolians, the Tibetans had their days of glory when they caused their neighbours to tremble, but since the tenth century they have been on the defensive. On two occasions in the eighteenth century they invoked Chinese help against invaders from Sinkiang and Nepal, and each time the Chinese took the opportunity to strengthen their presence in Tibet. The Emperor appointed *Ambans,* or Residents, in Lhasa whom he regarded as overlords or governors, though the Tibetans deny that they had this status. The evidence about the exact nature of the relationship at this time is unsatisfactory and confusing.[2] The Tibetans were happy to make an occasional gesture of deference to Peking if it helped them pursue their *de facto* independence, while China was willing to allow a large degree of *de facto* independence in return for the untroubled acceptance of what China herself regarded (and expected third parties to regard) as the outward signs of subjection. Perhaps one should add that whenever any third power or foreign visitor sought to achieve anything in Lhasa it usually found the Chinese *Amban* ineffective and dealt directly with the Tibetans themselves. But the Chinese regarded Tibet as their conquest, and most international maps of the nineteenth century showed Tibet as within, or under the influence of, China.

Paradoxically, the nineteenth century was the period of China's greatest weakness and only in the first decade of the twentieth century, in a last spasm of activity before its downfall, did the Ching Empire attempt to reassert itself in Tibet. Alarmed at the growing interest of Russia in Tibet and by the

British expedition to Lhasa in 1903–4, Peking sent troops to Tibet in 1910, for the first time against the wishes of the Lhasa government. But the imperial throne tottered two years later and from 1913 to 1950 Lhasa was left to its own devices while rival republicans fought it out in China proper. The Tibetan government signed a treaty, the famous Simla Convention, with British India in 1914, and during the Second World War it caused much anger in Chinese, Indian and Western circles by stubbornly refusing to become involved with the war by allowing Chinese military supplies to pass in transit through Tibet. In 1949 Lhasa sent a trade mission to Britain, the USA, India and China, the delegates travelling on documents issued by the Tibetan Government, much to the annoyance of the Chinese.

Yet by 1950 Tibet had no formal relations with foreign countries, had no regular diplomatic representation abroad, and was not a member of the United Nations. "So far as I know," Nehru told his Parliament in 1958, "there is not one country in the world which recognized the independence of Tibet. We definitely have not." [3] The Tibetan government had agreed at Simla in 1914 to a description of itself as under Chinese suzerainty and of Tibet as part of Chinese territory, but this was part of a proposed overall tripartite agreement which also involved a diminution of the Chinese presence in Tibet (China was to recognize Tibetan autonomy, station no more than 500 troops there, and accept an agreed China–Tibet border—which had been the subject of controversy between them in the preceding decades). But the Simla pact was never accepted by Peking, and the Tibetans argue that they are therefore not bound by it.[4] The Delhi government sought to have the best of both worlds by dealing with Tibet as a separate state but also paying lip-service to Chinese "suzerainty." The British wanted none of the responsibility for Tibet, and preferred to see it in the hands of a weak China rather than of an expansionist Russia. British India and China, Tibet's only two neighbours, made it common ground that Tibet was in some degree under China. The word "suzerainty" appears to have been selected by the British because it sounded less precise and less complete than "sovereignty," but the distinction, if there is one, has baffled international lawyers and means nothing to the Chinese.

I think that one is bound to conclude, of the Tibetans, that "political independence was beyond their grasp," as one scholar puts it.[5] To the sympathetic outsider, Tibet in 1950 was a country deserving independence, but lacking the degree of cohesion and determination necessary to assert and achieve it. Certainly no third country was willing to intervene on its behalf. The ideal solution for Tibet, and this was the hope of Nehru as well as of many Chinese liberals and well-meaning observers in other countries, would have been the sympathetic tutelage and material assistance of a new, modern-minded China leading later to equal status within a Chinese federation (the Kazhak solution, to borrow an example from the Soviet side of Central Asia) or perhaps to actual independence on Mongolian lines.

What happened in fact is well known. The Chinese Communist government proclaimed from the start that the "liberation" of Tibet from foreign influence was one of its urgent remaining tasks. It told the Tibetans that they were part of the greater Chinese family, that they should cooperate in their own "peaceful liberation," that it would "fully respect their freedom of religion" and that they should send plenipotentiaries to Peking to save their country from "unnecessary losses." [6] Tibetan emissaries did indeed start out, but they dallied in India on the way and in October 1950 an impatient Peking ordered the People's Liberation Army to "liberate three million Tibetans from imperialist aggression and complete the unification of the whole of China." [7] The Tibetans now sought, many years too late, the help of India and the United Nations.

But the need for violence was averted: a group of Tibetans in Peking signed an agreement in May 1951 and this was subsequently endorsed by the Dalai Lama (who claimed afterwards, however, when in exile, that the agreement had been gained by trickery, including the use of a forged seal, and that the Tibetans had no alternative but to give in to the Chinese demands or face armed attack).[8]

The Chinese told the Tibetans that they were motivated not by a desire to interfere with Tibet but by fear of foreign intervention in China *via* Tibet.[9] In 1951 there was some basis for these fears. The visit to Tibet of Lowell Thomas, the American broadcaster, and his son in 1949 aroused Chinese suspicions; a top secret military briefing on Tibet for American troops was circulating in Kalimpong and was known to the Chinese representatives there; and in the summer of 1951 the Dalai Lama's brother, whom the Communists had at first hoped would be their man and perhaps eventually replace the Dalai Lama, "escaped" via India to the USA.[10] The Chinese undoubtedly saw Tibet as a weak link in their frontiers, vulnerable to British,* American and perhaps even Stalinist Russian probing.[11] Since the citizens of "imperialist" countries in Tibet during 1948, 1949 and 1950 could be counted on two hands, Chinese fears may seem exaggerated, but they should not therefore be dismissed as pure invention.

So the Tibetans accepted Chinese rule and the Chinese agreed that Tibet would enjoy autonomy and freedom of religion. We have already seen, however, that in the Chinese Communist dictionary "autonomy" does not involve a complete freedom of domestic action, and that freedom of religion means freedom of the Communist Party to spread atheism without rebuttal by the monks save in the monasteries themselves.† Anyone familiar with the differing backgrounds of the two parties could have predicted the outcome. Peking pressed for a broadening of the basis of the Tibetan government, wanting to reduce the power of the highly conservative monks and nobles. But whom could it put up instead? The Chinese sent hundreds of young Tibetans to their cadre training schools, but most of them were illiterates who could not even read or write Tibetan, let alone Chinese.[12]

Things were made worse by a growing hostility between the Chinese soldiers and the Tibetans. The former had come expecting, from what their political lecturers had told them, to be welcomed as liberators. Instead they were received after their extremely tough march sullenly, as enemy occupiers, and they soon fell into the trap into which their imperial predecessors had fallen before: their presence placed tremendous strain on the meagre food supplies (until December 1954 there was no road or railway linking Lhasa with China) ‡ and created a shortage, with consequent price rises. This increased their unpopularity. There were also some Chinese officers who thought in terms of settling accounts with the Tibetans for their lack of cooperation first during the Commu-

* Peking's analysis at that time was that the British still effectively ruled India, a point of view which derived plausibility, perhaps, from the fact that English officials continued for some time after 1947, in Lhasa and Gangtok, to represent India in its relations with Tibet.

† In one town, according to the August 1958 Manifesto to the UN of the rebel Tibetan Chul-ka-sum, "the Chinese have actually made our head lamas study Marxist dialectics. . . . The Communists preach day in and day out to our simple people and monks that religion is nothing short of an opium to distract the human mind from hard work" (quoted in Patterson, *Tragic Destiny*, pp. 215–6). The Manifesto also complained: "Our Tibetans are expected to treat these Chinese settlers as their aunts and uncles" (*ibid*, p. 214).

‡ The Chinese Communist Administrator, General Chang Ching-wu, took up his post in 1952 *via* Hongkong, Calcutta and Darjeeling!

nists' Long March in the 1950s,[13] and then during the war with Japan, when the Lhasa authorities had refused permission for supply convoys to pass. Add to all this the usual language difficulties and one can picture the progressive disenchantment.

Among the Tibetan communities in the regular Chinese provinces of Szechuan, Chinghai and Yunnan, the normal course of reform was followed: slavery was abolished, so was the old Tibetan institution of forced labour, and land was redistributed. These were not particularly socialist reforms, they were the basic modern changes on which even a non-Communist government might have insisted. But the Szechuan Tibetans opposed them in 1956, and their troubles caused a ripple of alarm to spread across the mountains. The Dalai Lama said:

> When recently from neighbouring provinces the news of reforms reached Tibet, it caused doubt and anxiety. . . . Tibet has no other way to travel but the way of Socialism. But Socialism and Tibet are still very distant from each other. A gradual reform has to be carried out, but . . . it will be carried out by the leaders and the people of Tibet and will not be imposed on them by force by other people. This instruction was given repeatedly to our visiting delegations by Chairman Mao.[14]

At the end of 1956 the Dalai Lama went to India to take part in the celebrations for the 2,500th anniversary of Buddha's death. Convinced that the Chinese were set on ignoring Tibetan autonomy, he determined not to go back to Lhasa. Only the persuasion of Nehru, combined with the promises of Chou En-lai, made him return.* Chou took the position that the Dalai Lama should be quite frank and make detailed complaints which he, the Prime Minister, could then take up in Peking. Unfortunately it is a long way from Peking to Lhasa, and the discrepancy between what Peking commands and what the Chinese in Lhasa carry out was consistently underestimated, both in Peking and New Delhi. The Dalai Lama himself wrote, after his final flight to exile in India: "I still find it hard to believe that these oppressions had the approval and support of Mao Tse-tung." [15]

---

* At one point these three statesmen were locked together in discussions in New Delhi on this matter, a scene which was the high point of embarrassment for China in what was altogether a profoundly distasteful situation. Nehru performed a signal service for China by prevailing on the Dalai Lama to go back. But in Chinese eyes this involved him in the general humiliation to which China was exposed by the whole affair, and the incident did not help Sino-Indian relations.

Little more than two years later the whole of Tibet flickered into rebellion. This time it was started by the proverbially troublesome Golok * and Khamba tribesmen of eastern Tibet, made angry by new taxes and grain requisitioning, by Chinese attempts to indoctrinate their children at schools, and by the general Chinese effort to bring them into a more modern state of mind. The Dalai Lama fled and the Chinese took over the direct control of the country. They battled with these tough, simple-minded tribal fighters and are still battling, although the odds against the Tibetan guerrillas are now tremendous.

Chou En-lai accused the Dalai Lama and his court of breaking the 1951 pact by maintaining relations with foreign imperialists, of refusing to put into effect "a democratic regional autonomy with the participation of the people," and of wanting to "force the Tibetan people to live perpetually in the abysmal darkness of a life of barbarism and cruelty worse than that of the Middle Ages in Europe." [16] Chinese propaganda always stresses the cruelties of Tibetan life. Hugh Richardson, the last British Head of Mission in Lhasa, regards these claims as exaggerated. "Communist charges of brutal oppression in Tibet will be discounted by anyone who knew the country before 1950," he writes.[17] "Cobbett and de Tocqueville on conditions in England and Ireland less than 150 years ago make far more distressful reading than anything [I] saw or heard in Tibet. . . ." † In his book *Tibet and its History* Richardson goes so far as to claim: "It must be concluded that the Tibetans accepted their long-established way of life and their social inequalities not merely with passivity but with active contentment." [18]

Perhaps an outsider's view of the Tibetan question will largely depend on his approach to social change. If slavery and forced labour are apparently accepted philosophically in a country so isolated that nothing better, or nothing different, is imagined, should we stand aside or should we intervene and artificially inject or inflame the spirit of revolt? Are primitive communities museum-pieces to be preserved in their distinctive entirety, or are they clients for progress? Nehru was an advocate of the slow approach. "When a type of soci-

---

* The Goloks had the habit of sending captured Chinese soldiers back to their camp with their noses cut off, to which the Chinese retaliated with similar atrocities (Patterson, *Tragic Destiny*, p. 156).

† This sounds like a generous, and a Lhasa-based view. Patterson who never reached Lhasa, describes cruelties, injustices and irrationalities in eastern Tibet that have a decidedly pre-Cobbett ring (see the early parts of his book, *God's Fool*, London, Faber, 1956).

ety," he said in the Tibet debate in the Indian Parliament in May 1959, "has existed for centuries, forcible uprooting is painful whether that society is good or bad. Such a change can only take place effectively and with the least harm if it is carried out by the people themselves. The moment it is done by imposition, it becomes a bad thing." [19] Such a gradualist, Fabian approach means waiting for one or two generations before genuine change can begin. The Chinese Communist leaders lacked the patience, or they underestimated the strength of the traditional Tibetan social fabric.

Sympathizers with the Tibetan cause say that the Dalai Lama himself is a reformer and would have done far better than the Communists if allowed. In the years before the Rising he did advocate a rationalization of the antiquated and unjust taxation system, as well as a programme of moderate land redistribution with compensation. One must nevertheless doubt his power to overcome the conservatives in his own court. As even Richardson, an eloquent spokesman for the Tibetan case, admits, "the Dalai Lama, although the summit and master of the system, was also its creature. No Dalai Lama, however autocratic, could possibly ignore determined pressure from the general body of monks." [20]

Since 1959 the Chinese have pressed further with reforms, beginning with land redistribution. "Temples and monasteries," said their own chosen (but since disgraced) Tibetan leader, the Panchen Lama, in mid-1959, "will inevitably be involved in the reform, since they and some of the high-ranking lamas in them possess manorial estates and are serf owners. It will not be beneficial to religion if the serfs of the aristocratic feudal government are emancipated while the serfs of the lamaseries remain in bondage. Genuine and philanthropic religion must not retain any stigma of serfdom." [21] Such are the grounds on which, almost apologetically, the promise not to interfere with religion is broken. A supporter of the Tibetan case has to commit himself to this system of Buddhist monks' owning slaves,* for if no helping hand were lent it might be centuries before the slaves themselves rebelled. This was part of a campaign with five aims: to abolish slavery, abolish forced labour, abolish rebellions, reduce rents and reduce interest on loans. Within a year, the first steps to collectivization began with Mutual Aid Teams for simple cooperation among producers. But the reforms seem still to meet resistance, and remain only partially implemented. [22]

---

* Just as a nineteenth-century opponent of British imperialism in India would have had to countenance the continuation of *suttee,* or the sacrifice of widows on their husbands' funeral pyres.

China has sent a large number of Han immigrants to Tibet, some say more than the total number of Tibetans, as part of the effort to develop the Tibetan economy. Some critics assume that one of the motives of this is to overwhelm the Tibetans racially, and Patterson talks of forced mating and "mass hanization." [23] Probably there are numbers of Chinese immigrant men who, far from their normal home life, have taken (or tried to take) local wives or mistresses, but it is another thing to prove that this has been officially encouraged on a massive scale with an ulterior motive. There have also been reports of Tibetans being deported to other parts of China, and of Tibetans being sterilized. Even the sober Dalai Lama has accused the Chinese of "wanton and reckless murder of my people," and has complained to the UN that by sterilization China aims at the "total extermination of the Tibetan race." [24] The International Commision of Jurists, following the investigations among refugees by a very able anti-Communist Indian lawyer passionately dedicated to the idea of Tibetan independence, has concluded that there is a *prima facie* case of genocide against China. [25] If these charges are only partially true, then the Chinese must be unequivocally condemned. But it must be pointed out that the evidence is necessarily second-hand and from partisan sources, and at least one eminent Western legal critic finds it "far from convincing." [26] China does not help its case by refusing to accept an impartial committee to investigate these grave charges, but this could as well be explained by the general suspiciousness of the Chinese, dictated by their ancient and recent history, as by fear of an unfavourable verdict.

What will happen now? The Chinese have failed to secure a strong following in Tibet,[27] and have only just been able to complete the elections which began in 1962 and produce a representative Tibetan congress which can be counted on to rubber-stamp their policy. Even the Panchen Lama has now been disgraced because he could not keep up the pretence of agreeing with Chinese policies. There are occasional efforts to persuade the refugees in India and elsewhere, from the Dalai Lama downward, to come back and make a fresh start. Much publicity is given to such cases as that of Phuntsog Wangdue, who on returning to Tibet in 1964 was given grain, a milch cow, eight sheep, a set of tools and one and a half acres of land "already green with young barley." It is suggested that the mistakes which the Chinese made had been inspired by wrong, Russian-style policies and would not be repeated, and that the cadres at fault would be sent home to

China.[28] Naturally this has little effect. But it is a pointer to the future.

The world has become very concerned with the freebooting tribesmen and the corrupt nobles who have been the chief victims of Chinese rule. But the future lies with the younger generation of Tibetans which was sickened by the venality, cruelty and lethargy of the old government,[29] and which genuinely welcomes the material progress which the Chinese have introduced (though not necessarily their methods). For the first time Tibetans have seen a metalled road, motor vehicles, electricity, modern aircraft, machinery of various kinds and modern aids to agricultural production. Patterson, no friend of the Chinese, says of the early 1950s in Tibet:

> The new generation were determined to push ahead with the buildings when they could, irrespective of whether the providers of them were Chinese or Communist, on the assumption that the Chinese would have to leave eventually and by that time the schools, hospitals and dispensaries would be so strongly established that they could not be removed.[30]

For this is a country so blindly, stubbornly primitive that its so-called leaders would close a school or a dispensary, if they were free to, on account of its competing with the traditional monopoly of the monks.[31] The Chinese have saved the Tibetan herds from the gradual degeneration of inbreeding in that thin mountain air, and they have forced the authorities to accept mining (which was formerly thought to lead to the sterility of the soil). Tibet is probably rich in minerals, in gold, copper, boron, iron and possibly uranium, and an enlightened government could transform the economy over a period of years.[32] This is sensed by the intelligent younger generation of Tibetans, and the pull of economic modernity, once it sets in, will provide a powerful lever of social and political change.

No end of the present political impasse is in sight. The best hope is that the next generation of leaders on both sides will be better informed about each other and better equipped to cooperate. The next generation of Chinese leaders may be less obsessed about Western penetration through the Himalayas and may feel able to apologize to Tibet for the misdeeds of the past. It is worth recalling that not all the Chinese agree with their government's policy in Tibet. In 1958 some 5,000 Chinese soldiers and cadre workers in Tibet were arrested because of their sympathies with the Tibetans [33] and the Dalai Lama cites the case of one Chinese officer who fought in the ranks of the guerrillas and subsequently became a refugee in India.[34] The concluding words of the Dalai Lama's autobi-

ography express the hope of future reconciliation: "Our enemies are not Communism, or China; our only enemies are
some of the Chinese Communists. The atrocities in Tibet
have been committed by Chinese of the lowest sort, a small
proportion of their soldiers and Communist officials who
were corrupted by the knowledge of having the power of life
and death." [35] In a sense the Tibetan tragedy is one of conflicting inexperience: the Chinese hoped to be good trustees
and overlords but underestimated their difficulties, while the
Tibetans could hardly have chosen worse than first to rebuff
the outside world and then to have pitted themselves in hope-
less physical combat against the largest and toughest army in
the world.

Why do the Chinese feel so strongly that Tibet is a part of
China? Chiang Kai-shek and Mao Tse-tung, like Sun Yat-sen
before them, both share this passionate belief. In Mao's case
there is a clearly defined mission for the Chinese in Tibet, to
spread Communism, but one has to look further than Communism to explain the tenacity of Chinese feeling on this
matter.

One has to remember the extraordinarily vivid sense of
loss which the Chinese feel about their nineteenth-century humiliations at European hands, and how these have become
symbolized by British and Russian activity in Tibet during
the past hundred years. To "retrieve" Tibet was, in the minds
of thousands of educated Chinese who have never been remotely near that land and have no conception of what it and
its people are like, a fixed target of national honour. It is only
a later generation, able to take for granted the restoration of
national honour, which may be persuaded to see things in a
more rational light.

9: COMMUNISM

Ten Thousand Years of Struggle?

THE CHINESE COMMUNIST PARTY IS NOW A LEVIATHAN OF
more than seventeen million members. The great majority of
them are post-1949 recruits, but their mood and discipline
are dictated by the few thousand survivors of the Party's

early days, on the Long March and in the fight against Japan. This is a Party which demands complete control over its members' personal life: no member, for example, would dare to marry without first obtaining the blessing of his local Party Committee, and there have been instances of suicide provoked by a Party member's falling in love with an ideologically unsuitable partner.[1] When it was a small, compact, dedicated group of guerrilla fighters, the Party astonished Chinese and foreigner alike by its discipline and rectitude. It was rare to hear of Communists looting, raping or embezzling, common to hear of their showing a courtesy and consideration in dealing with ordinary people which previous contenders for power in China had notably lacked. It was more difficult to maintain such standards after 1949, when the Party could not prevent the entry of opportunists and careerists into its ranks and when the petty temptations of power became much more numerous.

The corporate morality of the Party deteriorated noticeably during the grim years of food shortage in 1960-2. The *People's Daily* in 1962 was reduced to the somewhat lame comment: "There are . . . people who ask: Is it not stupid to be so honest? . . . We say, very well, let the honest be stupid, but such stupidity is lovable. . . ." [2] Refugees have come to Hongkong claiming to have been engaged until quite recently in smuggling opium into China from Hongkong and selling it there, with the connivance of Party cadres, and one has said that a People's Liberation Army officer will pay 1,000 *yuan* (about $400 at the official exchange rate) for an ordinary, smuggled, Swiss watch.[3] Such offences are probably not common; but petty abuses of power, particularly to favour one's own family or friends, are frequently reported.

Above all, the Party is bureaucratic. Lord Lindsay of Birker, who by an accident of history became the radio adviser at the Communist headquarters in Yenan in 1944, tells a story that is typical. The standard time of the Yenan government was that of the sundial in its courtyard, because this was "close to the masses." Lord Lindsay pointed out that from the point of view of keeping to radio schedules across the whole of China this was inconvenient, and he urged the use of West China Standard Time. Not until he wrote a personal letter to Chairman Mao (who sent him a courteous letter of thanks in reply) was the change made, because no one of lesser rank dared to complain against an official order.[4] These are some of the Party's faults, and they have become magnified by the task of administering a country as large as the whole of Europe. So abysmal is the record of previous governments that one can nevertheless say that the Communist Party is the most honest and efficient body ever to rule in China.

It is led by a dozen or so men who have worked closely together for almost four decades. Between 1935, when Mao established his personal supremacy in the Party, and 1966, when a profound power struggle broke out within the Politburo, there were only two public cracks in this extraordinary display of unity. In 1955 Kao Kang, who had carved out what his critics called an "independent kingdom" in the Northeast and who dealt with Moscow directly rather than through Peking, was dismissed from his post and committed suicide. Four years later Peng Teh-huai, Minister of Defence and hero of the Korean War, was disgraced for carrying his criticisms of the Great Leap Forward and of the Chinese part in the Sino-Soviet split to the point of discussing them privately with the Soviet leadership: he wrote a letter of confession asking to be rehabilitated by agricultural work, and was appointed an executive in a State Farm.[5] Otherwise the Chinese leaders kept their internal quarrels to themselves, until Mao in 1966 publicly attacked his chief Politburo colleagues and more or less denounced the Communist Party itself as a counter-revolutionary force.

In the Party itself the commanding figures, after Mao, had been Liu Shao-chi, the Chairman of the Republic, and Teng Hsiao-ping, the Party's Secretary-General who usually acted as Prime Minister in Chou En-lai's absence abroad. Liu is an austere, unimaginative man who shuns the limelight: like Mao, he came from a reasonably well-off Hunanese peasant family, and he actually went to the same school as Mao in Changsha.[6] At sixty-nine, he was second in the Party hierarchy. Teng is a short man with a bad limp about whom little is known. He is reputed arrogant and irascible. These two represent the more conventional Party *apparatchiks* against whom Mao declared war in 1966.

Another group of leaders, with smaller followings in the Party ranks, centres loosely on Chou En-lai, the Prime Minister, who sided with Mao against Liu in 1966. These have been called the technocrats, or the government bureaucrats, because they seem more interested in practical problems of nation-building than in the niceties of doctrine. While Liu's speeches sound like the sermons of a revivalist preacher, Chou's resemble a managing director's report to his Board. Unlike Mao or Liu, Chou had some early experience of Western Europe, having studied in Paris and worked briefly at the Renault car factory and in a German coalmine.

Born into a family of imperial officials, Chou is the most urbane and charming of the Chinese leaders. Unfortunately his aristocratic parentage and his grace earn him suspicion in certain quarters of the Party, and it used to be said that he would never be acceptable as its supreme leader. But in 1966, when he opted for Mao rather than Liu, he seemed to emerge as an acceptable conciliator in the Party's inner struggle for power. Chen Yi, the jovial, colourful Foreign Minister, is Chou's closest associate, while the few senior Party men who specialize in economic affairs, notably Li Fu-chun, are usually regarded as supporters of Chou.

The next important group is the Army leadership, in which Lin Piao, the tubercular sixty-year-old Defence Minister whom Mao picked in 1966 as his preferred successor in place of Liu, and Lo Jui-ching, Lin's chief opponent and a former Army Chief-of-Staff, are the dominant personalities. "Political power grows out of the barrel of the gun," Mao Tse-tung once said: "Our principle is that the Party commands the gun, and the gun shall never be allowed to command the party." But there are contradictions between the professional and the ideological elements among the senior officers.[7] Firstly, the People's Liberation Army is conceived as a social and not merely as a military force. It is expected to take part in economic construction, flood relief and even in political campaigns (when its contribution is usually "writing letters to mobilize . . . relative and friends and to encourage them" to do whatever is currently being called for).[8] During the Great Leap the PLA supplied about fifty million man-days a year in village work. The officer who is keen on technical specialization naturally resents his men "wasting" their talents in the fields. He also resents the devaluation of his professional status by the "Everyone a Soldier" campaign which began in 1958. In that year 200 million volunteers enrolled in the People's Militia units which are part of the People's Commune organization.

There is also dissension about rank. Originally the PLA was the most democratic of all armies, with little distinction between ranks, but in 1955 Russian-style distinctions were somewhat apologetically introduced between officers and other ranks, and salaries were instituted (nearly $3 a month for privates, nearly $250 for generals) to replace the old free supply system. Mao even conferred the new rank of "Marshal" on ten senior generals and awarded decorations for the first time. The *People's Daily* felt it necessary to explain that this was all quite different from the class distinctions of capitalist armies.[9] But the purity of the Party line was reaffirmed in 1965 when rank was abolished. At times of ideological excitement, as in 1958, officers spend one month in the year in the ranks (much as engineers go to work at the bench).

The final cause of strain between the professional officers and the Party is the question of equipment. Since the break with Russia the technical and logistic position of the armed forces has deteriorated. In the summer of 1961, when things were at their worst, a military official admitted in a secret report:* "The air force ought to fly more but cannot fly more. The navy ought to go to sea but cannot go to sea. The army ought to move its transport vehicles but cannot move them much: there is a contradiction between the need for training and the obstacles imposed by available material. This is the real situation." Things have got better since then, but the forces are still badly short of fuel, spare parts and equipment. Some professional officers probably feel, as Marshal Peng Teh-huai apparently did, that it would have been better to have gone along with the Soviet ideological line and retained the benefits of Soviet military aid until the Chinese army could really stand on its own feet.

The Army is potentially an important force in China's domestic power structure. It has 2¾ million men, and some economic independence (in 1960, for example, it owned 700 farms with 280,000 acres, and furnaces producing 42,000 tons of pig iron annually).[10] In 1966 it became Mao's chosen instrument for reforming the Communist Party structure, and in the following year it was the only organization standing between China and total anarchy: the new Party Constitution of 1969 confirmed its status above the Communist Party.

The top forty men of the Peking hierarchy are all over sixty years old. Mao is seventy-five, and Liu and Chou seventy. When Mao disappears from the scene, a period of rapid turnover in leadership is likely, because so many senior leaders are already in their sixties. The younger people, now in their fifties, who will succeed to supreme power in the 1970s are mostly from families of reasonable means, fairly well educated but with no more first-hand experience of the outside world (beyond the Soviet Union, which most of the leaders have at one time visited) than the present inner circle.[11]

Indeed, there are pessimists among Western diplomats who argue that China will be led in future by men even more parochial in their outlook and less in tune with the world than

---

* Captured by rebels, smuggled out of Tibet and subsequently made public by the US Government: most observers believe it genuine.

the present leaders. In economic affairs, for instance, the government has until now been able to command the services of men who learned about international business by participating in it in pre-1949 Shanghai or Tientsin. These ranks are now thinning as the years pass, and their successors in the Trade and Industry Ministries will be men who will have spent their whole adult lives under a Communist government and are suspicious of the outside world. On the other hand the generation about to reach the higher rungs of power is likely to set more store on efficiency, technique and national prosperity, possibly above ideology, and the "technocrats" will presumably exercise a greater influence on the leadership in the future.

Still, towering above everyone else, the unquenchable figure of Mao dominates China. Born in a peasant family which, by hard work, succeeded in owning its own land and using hired labour to cultivate it (so that it would nowadays qualify as the enemy in the rural class struggle), Mao left the fertile ricefields, bamboo groves and pine-clad hills of Shaoshan village (where his father's farmhouse is now a national museum) at fifteen. He was a student of eighteen who had just defied tradition by cutting off his queue when the Ching Dynasty finally tumbled: he was then reading John Stuart Mill, Adam Smith, Darwin and T. H. Huxley (in translation: he has never mastered a foreign language). He placed great faith in physical training, toughening himself by long walks in spartan conditions. At twenty-eight he was one of the twelve men who founded the Chinese Communist Party, and since then he has never looked back, leading the Chinese Communists through the pitfalls of Stalin's bad advice, Kuomintang treachery and Japanese attack.

His sister and his two brothers were all killed in the Communist cause, and his eldest son fell in the Korean War. He is indifferent to personal appearance, and is often seen with socks falling around his ankles, shoes unpolished and collar or cuffs frayed. He delights to use the coarse words and epithets of his peasant youth even before foreign visitors. Though largely self-educated by avid reading, he is an established Marxist philosopher and also a poet whose verses "would have secured him a place in contemporary Chinese literature independent of his pre-eminent position in the political sphere," in the judgment of Dr Jerome Ch'en, his non-Communist Chinese biographer. As a military strategist he was unequalled in China, and his texts on guerrilla warfare are still studied in African and Latin American cities.

Mao is personally austere and impervious to the trivialities of power, and yet he is worshipped more than Stalin was in Russia. This is a curious paradox. The Chinese Communists have always been on guard against personality cults, from which China had suffered in the past, and in 1949 Mao forbade the public celebration of any leader's birthday or the naming of streets and towns after living men. The contrast with Stalin was striking, and when Khrushchev began the de-Stalinization campaign in Russia the Chinese said smugly that they had always taken measures to prevent such idol-worship —adding, however, that "love and support for leaders . . . has nothing in common with the worship of any individual." [12] Mao could be loved, and indeed *is* loved by many Chinese, but gradually the line has been crossed from love to worship, perhaps in consequence of his declining personal hold on the minor activities of the Party, perhaps as a means of maximizing national unity and morals during the difficult years after 1960 when economic disaster and the loss of Russian support reduced the Party's popularity.

Nowadays Mao's portrait or bust is seen everywhere, in every schoolroom, at every celebration, in every public office. The Secretary of the Young Communist League described him in 1964 as "the sun, lighthouse, food, arms and compass of the Chinese people," [13] and in 1959 he was referred to as a living Buddha.[14] In a much-quoted editorial, the *People's Daily* in 1964 declared: "The moon without the sun gives no light; young rice plants with no rain water will wither; without the study of the thoughts of Mao Tse-tung, even with your eyes open you will miss the direction." [15]

The means by which the Party controls both its members and the public are unique: the Communists utilize not only the emotion of loyalty but also those of hatred and shame. They incite hatred against those whom they wish to destroy, and capitalize on the shame in which the Chinese social tradition plunges any individual who breaks the prevailing ethos. The "struggle meetings" of the land reform period, when the petty feudal tyrants of the villages were publicly condemned and often executed, were typical occasions for the arousal of mass hatred. Chou En-lai, asked by an old liberal friend to explain, replied: "Hatred is a powerful social lever." [16] It enables a tradition-ridden society to make a sudden break with the past and provides the basis of a new set of loyalties. This is what the novelist Lao She refers to when he describes an accusation meeting in 1951:

The only feelings that are of value, that are to be prized, are hatred of your enemy, love for your country. . . . One of the accusers was attacking his own father! In any other times but these, how could such a thing happen? I was ready to shed tears. In the old days, Chinese people specialized in "son covers up for father, father covers up for son." So everyone covered up, and truth and justice were hidden away beyond hope of discovery. Today, the father-son relationship can no longer bury the truth beneath it.[17]

The "struggle meetings" are the public face of this manipulation of emotions. Thought reform (which the Party calls ideological remoulding and its critics brainwashing) is the personal side of it.[18] His social tradition does not equip a Chinese as effectively as a European for martyrdom to an idea: it renders him much more vulnerable to the personal pressures of grandfather, father, grandmother, mother, brother and sister, son and daughter, schoolfriend and classmate, professional colleague and confidant. The stronger-minded can thus be attacked through the weaker-minded in his personal circle. This is what the Communists do. We have seen how soldiers write letters to persuade their relatives to follow the latest Party directives, how children urge their parents to obey the law or observe the new morality. During the marriage reform the Party Central Committee even considered, but rejected, a suggestion that every single family in China be rigorously and personally investigated.[19] In theory the transformation of minds from non-socialist to socialist ways of thought is approached with the scientific meticulousness of the horse breeder or the horticulturalist. In practice, since the Party has to work mostly through men of only average intelligence and imagination, the guinea pigs often have to suffer all the inconveniences of brainwashing without the benefits of its success. The trouble is that the surgery of bad thoughts is every bit as tricky as the surgery of bad tissues. Chinese surgeons are very proud of their operations to restore severed fingers and hands, yet the surgery of the mind is often left to amateurs. In the short-term, however, the Chinese play on shame is successful. This is how a foreign resident,* working in a paper mill, describes it (the Party has to persuade a factory meeting to accept reduced food rations during the 1961 shortage):

A Party activist would stand up and declare that he required only a pound and a half of bread a day. Then everyone pres-

---

* Albert Belhomme, the American soldier captured in the Korean War who chose to stay in China. He married a Chinese girl and settled down as a factory worker for several years but finally left in disillusion (Stanley Karnow, "The GI Who Chose Communism," in *Saturday Evening Post,* 16 November 1963, p. 106).

ent would be asked to state his needs. There'd be some discussion, and finally an official would set a ration figure. You couldn't oppose it without losing face. Besides, there was always a Comrade who could claim that he watched you in the canteen, and you ate too much anyway. So you went along with the ration. Then, a few months later, at another meeting, the "plan" would be reviewed. Officials would show some more crusts of bread and complain of waste, and you'd agree to reduce your ration. Everything in China is "voluntary."

The succession of campaigns, drives and purges that the Party has carried out gives abundant illustration of the difficulties. The trouble is that the Party bullies and sycophants seek victims more earnestly than offences. The critics of the Party say that, because Chairman Mao once remarked that about five per cent of the personnel in most organizations were "bad elements," each branch of enterprise or office regarded this as a target.[20] This naturally meant false accusations,* usually directed against the few independent-minded individuals in the organizations concerned.

In 1955 another series of witch-hunts, the so-called *sufan* campaign, began. It lasted just over two years, and the Minister of Public Security announced at the end of it that the political history of 1,800,000 people had been investigated by 150,000 full-time cadre workers. A total of 535,000 people had been penalized as a result, either by loss of their job, or by sentences to corrective labour † or death.[21]

But as Confucius had said: "If a ruler . . . does not rectify his own conduct, how can he rectify others?" In April 1957 a rectification campaign was launched for the improvement of the Party's style of work. The public was invited to criticize the Party, under the Hundred Flowers slogan, with

* The case of a thirty-four-year-old graduate who was tortured in the 1952 anti-corruption drive and made to confess false crimes and embezzlement, which in turn implicated other innocents, and who later fled to Hongkong, may be read in CNA 454, 1 February 1963. The Minister of Public Security called on cadres in 1956 to cease the practice of torturing in order to extract confessions.

† "Regulations on Corrective Labour" were published by the government in 1954. This is a punishment for enemies of the people, the labour being "forced, unpaid and subject to strict control." There are agricultural labour reform camps (which the West calls forced labour camps) and industrial establishments for the same purpose. The *People's Daily* on 7 September 1954 ridiculed UN criticism of these camps. See Keesing, p. 12786. Chou En-lai announced in 1957 that of all apprehended counter-revolutionaries, seventeen per cent had been executed, forty-two per cent were doing corrective labour, thirty-two per cent were still under surveillance and nine per cent had been released after serving mild sentences.

the consequences that we have seen in Chapter Four above. When it came to the point, individual Party members were not ready to admit serious mistakes: as a Wuhan Professor complained during the Hundred Flowers, "when they speak of submitting views and making criticisms, they are . . . referring to other people; they regard themselves as completely correct, progressive and in need of no more education, reform or criticism. These people create the impression that they are 'born saints' in the true sense of the term. This is like a Christian believer saying 'I represent God.' " [22]

Since 1962 there has been a more or less continuous campaign of class struggle and socialist education throughout China. Its basis was most clearly expressed by Premier Chou En-lai in his report to the National People's Congress at the end of 1964:

> It is entirely wrong to underestimate the danger of the restoration of capitalism in a socialist country. . . . The landlord class, the bourgeoisie and other exploiting classes which have been overthrown will remain strong and powerful in all socialist countries . . . and new bourgeois elements, new bourgeois intellectuals and other new exploiters will be ceaselessly generated in society, in Party and government organs. . . . [23]

China today is urged to imitate the life of Lei Feng, the half-real, half-legendary, poor peasant's son who suffered at his landlord's hands, worked on a collective farm and at the Anshan steelworks, joined the Army and spent all his spare time helping other people. His diary was published in 1963. "I cannot express my gratitude," the entry on the Party's fortieth anniversary reads, ". . . I, an orphan who reared pigs, could become a soldier, a Party member, a representative of the people. . . ." In 1962 he had written: "A man is like a cog in a machine . . . A cog may be small but its value cannot be overestimated. For ever I want to be a cog, well kept and clean, that will not rust." [24]

The prospect of struggle stretches out into the distant future. The First Secretary of the Young Communist League warned in 1964 that the period of transition to Communism would last for "five to ten—or even more—generations," i.e. some 300 years.[25] Even then, there is no guarantee of Communism; it could become side-tracked, as has already happened in Yugoslavia and is now happening in Russia.

The threat of revisionism, or the development of a Khrushchev-style brand of Communism in which social controls are relaxed before ideological purity has been inculcated and in which goulash takes precedence over the Marxist gospels, is regarded seriously in Peking. "Revisionism," warned the *China Youth Daily* in 1964, "can implant the idea that class struggle is not humanitarian, together with a horror of war and the feeling that one should love every human being no matter what class he belongs to." [26] The Peking press often refers to the prediction of Dulles ('of putrid memory') that Communism would undergo "peaceful transformation" in its third generation. [27] The Director of the Party's Organization Department wrote in 1965 that the Party's class enemies were "placing their hopes on our third and fourth generations": they had decided, "viewing the development of revisionism in the Soviet Union, . . . that the day would soon come for them to regain power. . . . They made the following fortune-tellers' predictions about China: poverty leads to changes, changes lead to riches and riches lead to revisionism. They saw that whoever wins the hearts of the youth will gain state power." [28]

So the search for revolutionary heirs was begun. The question was, the Chinese public was told:

> . . . whether or not there will be people who can carry on the Marxist-Leninist revolutionary cause started by the older generation of proletarian revolutionaries, whether or not the leadership of our Party and state will remain in the hands of proletarian revolutionaries, whether or not our descendants will continue to march along the correct road laid down by Marxism-Leninism, or, in other words, whether or not we can successfully prevent the emergence of Khrushchevite revisionism in China.* In short, it is an extremely important question, a matter of life or death for our Party and our country . . . a question of fundamental importance to the proletarian revolutionary cause for a hundred, a thousand, nay, ten thousand years. . . . To cultivate and train successors is a major, thousand-year project in the cause of Revolution. [29]

---

* A few months later, reporting to the National People's Congress on the work of the government, Chou En-lai spoke in grimmer, almost pessimistic terms: "The restoration of capitalism is not inevitable. In China we have a firm and fighting Marxist-Leninist Party, a proletarian power which is increasingly consolidating itself, a powerful and revolutionary People's Liberation Army, an enormous number of cadres, a people of high political consciousness and a glorious revolutionary tradition. Of especial importance is the fact that our Party and state can count on a leading nucleus guided by the thought of Mao Tse-tung. All of this makes the restoration of capitalism very difficult in our country" (*Peking Review*, 1 January 1965). The confidence sounds strained.

The 1966-8 Cultural Revolution reflected this dilemma. Mao was disturbed by the concessions to petty capitalism and to Party bureaucratism on which his colleagues in the Party leadership had insisted in the aftermath of the three bitter years of 1960-2. His misgivings about the ideological integrity and personal loyalty of some of his colleagues came to a head in 1965, as his control over policy became increasingly subverted by those in charge of the Party machine who were set on avoiding any repetition of such blunders as the Hundred Flowers movement and the Great Leap Forward. Mao was made to feel ignored, his prestige in the Party having suffered from the failure of those campaigns.

He therefore decided that the Party itself had become an obstacle to change, being too establishment-minded and insufficiently responsive to public opinion. In this final iconoclasm of his extraordinary career, he turned for allies to two elements in Chinese society with which he felt more in tune than with Party officialdom—the Army and the students. Lin Piao was chosen to forge the Army into a spearhead of Party reform, and between them, Lin and Mao organized a new body of militant youth—the Red Guards—to serve as their shock troops.

Towards the end of 1965 Mao made his first strike—at the crucial propaganda organs of the Party. Criticism of certain journalists, playwrights and other writers led to dismissals and purges which secured for Mao the allegiance of the radio stations and the newspapers throughout the Cultural Revolution. Gradually the radical Maoist group, backed by the mobilized fervour of the Red Guard, raised the level of its challenge until Peng Chen (the powerful Mayor of Peking), Tao Chu (the Kwangtung Party boss), Teng Hsiao-ping (the Party Secretary-General) and Liu Shao-chi himself were all named as "revisionist" opponents of Mao Tse-tung.

But Mao's group was not strong enough to clinch a victory over the well-entrenched Party organization. Although Mao was personally loved and admired, his radical policies were not acceptable to the average Party official. As the Cultural Revolution (which combined the intra-Party power struggle with an unprecedentedly thorough campaign for Party criticism and ideological remoulding) rocked the entire country through most of 1966 and 1967, it became apparent that Maoism in the strict sense was virtually a one-man affair. The hard core of Mao's faction proved to be his own wife, Chiang Ching, and his personal secretary of long standing,

Chen Po-ta. Of the Politburo members of real stature only Chou En-lai and Lin Piao sided with Mao against Liu Shao-chi and the Party machine. Neither had any cause to like Liu, but at the same time neither proved to be uncritical echoers of Mao's policies.

Chou seemed to be in the curious but understandable position of preferring Mao to Liu as a person, while at the same time valuing Liu's more pragmatic policies above those of Mao. At any rate his role during the Cultural Revolution seemed to be to encourage the nation to follow Mao's leadership, while seeking to temper and moderate the actual effects of that leadership. Whenever the Maoists and the Red Guards sought to wreck the economy or alienate China's foreign neighbours in the interests of stirring up revolutionary fervour at home, it was Chou who tried—often successfully—to restrain them. Lin Piao failed to take the leading role in the Maoist faction which his nomination as Mao's successor suggested for him. Whether out of ill health, out of a sense of shame at his failure to deliver the entire General Staff to Mao as converts, or out of his own differences of opinion with Mao, Lin seemed to fade into the background during the Cultural Revolution. The Army certainly enhanced its prestige and its power vis-à-vis the Party, and it was the regional or provincial Army commanders who in the end brought the anarchy of the Red Guards under control, but the Army finally emerged as powerful in its own right rather than as enfeoffed to Mao. Indeed, most of the senior Army officers seemed to be neutral in the internal squabbling of the Party, concerned only with the interests of law and order, national unity and the development programme.

When Mao Tse-tung joined the university students in composing and displaying big posters calling for the "bombardment of the Party headquarters," and justifying rebellion against Party authority, he must have known that some degree of confusion would result. In his own calculation, the short-term losses in terms of law and order, development and national unity were far less important than the long-term gains to be derived from freeing the Chinese people from their traditional subservience to authority and lack of independence of mind.

In the end, neither side was able to win the day, and a somewhat ragged compromise emerged. A certain amount of new blood was introduced into the Party leadership at all levels, but the policy differences remained unresolved. Mao stands for an all-out commitment to the goal of perfecting human nature; Liu stands for a more realistic settling for half, in which, for example, a private sector would be permitted in an economy which is in all important respects controlled by the Communist government. The most likely outcome of Mao's last campaign would seem to be a continued recognition of Mao as the father-figure of Chinese Communism, but a gradual reversion in practice to the "revisionist" path after his death. The new Party Constitution put out in 1969 and the expected Ninth Party Congress of that year suggested a degree of normalization after the Cultural Revolution, though with a weakened central government, a stronger army and provinces and a continuing inner struggle for the succession to Mao and over policies to be pursued.

Those Chinese who went along with Communism because they believed that a short course of drastic reforms was worthwhile, however painful, must now be bitterly disappointed. The Communists have reconstructed rural society on a sound basis, eliminated the injustices of exploitation by landlords and moneylenders and put China at last well on the road to universal primary education. They have modernized the laws relating to the family and promoted more tolerant attitudes within the family. They have united the country, and brought the "lost territories" of Tibet and Sinkiang firmly back into Chinese hands. They have provided China with its most honest and efficient administration of modern times. Such benefits are not to be expected without paying a price, and for the non-Communists of China I suppose that the price has been paid in the form of four major sacrifices: first, the loss of personal freedom; second, the vanishing of trust from family and personal life; third, the isolation of China's artistic and intellectual life from the rest of the world, even, now, from the Soviet Union; and fourth, the failure to provide a substitute, in terms of security, for the peasant's loss of ownership of land. I would guess that many rural non-Communists and some urban ones regard the price, so far, as worth paying; but if the pressure is to be maintained for several generations, then the original valuations might be revised.

"Young people," wrote the *Reuters* Correspondent in Peking in 1957, "are beginning to judge the situation on its merits instead of by mere comparison with the past." [30] Young Chinese want things now to be better than they were in 1955 or 1960, and are increasingly unimpressed by the knowledge—which they take for granted—that things are better than they were in 1948. The Communists, to succeed in their ambitious aims, must not merely keep the minds of China's youth ideologically pure, but also ensure a perceptible and continual improvement in the standard of living and in economic growth.

TWO: *ECONOMY*

10: AGRICULTURE

Feeding the People

"THE ONLY COMMUNISM POSSIBLE IN CHINA TODAY IS THE Communism of poverty, a lot of people eating rice out of an almost empty bowl." The words of Borodin,[1] Sun Yat-sen's Russian adviser, forty years ago are still true. Communist rule has indeed achieved a higher food production, but not by a very great margin, and large quantities of foodgrains have still to be imported.

The two-day train ride from Canton to Peking offers a moving picture of Chinese agriculture: starting from the semi-tropical ricefields which are tended as lovingly as green gardens and are about as small; crossing the two rivers, the Yangtze (which cuts the country into two halves) and the Yellow (China's "River of Sorrows"); and ending in the vast bleak northern wheat and cotton plains covered, if it is spring, with the fine yellow dust which piercing winds carry over the hills from the Gobi desert. China is larger in area than the USA, but most of the land is too high for farming, and the agriculture on which China still depends for over half of her wealth is concentrated in 250 million acres in the eastern third of the country.

By enforcing a peace and order which the Chinese countryside had not known for decades, by resuming normal public works and by encouraging farmers to extend their acreages and their double-cropping, the Communist government quickly restored the rural economy to its pre-war position. The foodgrain harvest, which used to come to about

140 million tons in the days before the Japanese invasion, but which the Communists estimated at only 108 million tons in 1949 (a year of political chaos and bad weather), exceeded 150 million tons in 1952.[2] Mao was then ready for his first full-scale assault on the problem. During the First Five-Year Plan (1953–7) the state allotted almost 8 billion *yuan* ($3 1/5 billion), or ten percent of its total investment, to agriculture. The result was a claimed twenty-five per cent increase in production, representing an annual growth rate of 4.3 per cent (Professor Choh-ming Li, the American economist, believes that this is exaggerated and that the actual increase was nearer three per cent a year).[3] In the most vital sector of all, foodgrains, the officially claimed increase was only twenty per cent (representing less than four per cent a year).

The Second Five-Year Plan (1958–62) envisaged a gradual quickening of this tempo, and so did the Twelve-Year Agricultural Development Plan (1956–67) which was launched in the middle of the First Five-Year Plan period. But both of these blueprints were thrown out of the window in 1958 when the Chinese announced a Great Leap Forward in their economic development. Impatient with the equivocal results of the more orthodox Russian economic techniques which they had been using till then, the Peking leaders decided to make an all-out mobilization of every available resource. During the 1957–8 winter a record amount of fertilizer and manure was laid on the fields. Rice and other grains were sown over a much larger area than before, and the authorities promoted the new techniques by which they hoped a breakthrough could be made in the production drive—deep ploughing, early sowing, close planting and so on. The whole country was in a frenzy: a million city-dwellers were transferred to work in the fields, investment in agriculture was boosted by forty per cent in one year, and the cooperatives were rapidly merged into the final collectivism of the People's Communes. Everywhere eager Party workers, not all of them versed in agronomy, chivvied the peasants into adopting the new techniques. It was the year in which the Party knew best, and the peasant's hoary old instincts about the soil and its behaviour were at a discount.*

* Afterwards, when the harm caused by the indiscriminate use of new techniques had been realized, peasant lore was reinstated. A *People's Daily* article (12 November and 2 December 1960) said: "We still cannot control nature completely. . . . Traditions which have come down to us from our ancestors all contain some truth. There were places where the nature of the soil was disregarded, systems and methods of cultivation which did not suit the nature and condition of the

It all culminated in the announcement, made in awed tones, that the harvest had been doubled, to reach the incredibly high total of 375 million tons. But doubts soon set in: foreign comment was uniformly sceptical, and it gradually became clear that the newly-established commune authorities had, in the excitement and in the pressure to meet targets, exaggerated what was admittedly a bumper crop (blessed for once with excellent weather). The 1958 harvest, an astonished world was eventually told, had been only 250 million tons, not 375 million.

The Central Committee of the Party, meeting at Lushan, was obliged to halve the target for 1959. Deluded by its own propaganda, it had seen no reason why a doubling in one year could not be followed by a further forty per cent increase the next year, and had set a target of 525 million tons (which China will be lucky to achieve by the end of the century) for 1959: this was reduced to 275 million. But the weather, as if to punish the Central Committee for its presumption, proceeded to inflict on China not just one disastrous harvest but three successive ones, in 1959, 1960 and 1961.*

In the summer of 1959 heavy rains spread from south to north, destroying the crops, and not until 1962 did Chinese farmers shake free from a complex of flood and drought that set the production figures decisively back. The best indication of official disappointment is the fact that 1958 was the last year for which figures for the various crops were published. For 1959 the Government announced a total foodgrain harvest of 270 million tons, less than its target, but it withheld the usual breakdown (into rice, wheat, potatoes, etc.) and has published no figures at all for subsequent years. Unofficial estimates by foreign observers (who regarded even the revised 1958 figure, of 250 million tons, as exaggerated) put the harvests of the "three bitter years" 1959–61 all below 175 million tons. At the end of 1960 China began to import Western foodgrains. From 1962 onwards conditions improved, and the harvest is now back to its 1957 level: the 1968 harvest was probably in the order of 190 million tons.[4]

---

place were adopted. . . . It is extremely dangerous not to consider the traditions of former generations. . . . The masses must be daringly trusted."

* Some critics feel that Peking blamed too much on the weather and too little on its own policy errors. The natural calamities were not, however, invented (though they may have been slightly exaggerated), and Peking did admit that its human mistakes played a part in the débâcle. 1959–61 was certainly among the worst three-year periods of the century for natural calamities.

The collapse of the Great Leap Forward changed the Communists' minds about agriculture, which they now regard as their highest economic priority. In the First Plan industry attracted most of the attention and investment, but the experience of 1958–9 convinced Peking that agriculture is the foundation of its economy, providing, as the Minister of Agriculture pointed out in 1960, half of the state revenues and seventy per cent of its exports.[5] In chastened mood, the Party leaders who had blandly accepted in 1959 the myth that the foodgrain harvest could be doubled in one year, now asked whether it could be doubled in one decade.

There are only two ways of getting a larger crop: to extend the area you are cultivating or to raise the yields you are getting from each acre. At first the Communists set high store on the first alternative, arguing that the proportion of the total area actually cultivated could surely be doubled from one fifth to two fifths. Indeed, the increase in grain harvests during the Communists' first fifteen years was three quarters due to extended acreages,[6] only one quarter the result of raised yields per acre. But the official attitude towards expanding acreages is equivocal. The idealists in the Party dream of a Chinese landscape no longer bruised by the plough or disfigured by the tractor but reverting to its pristine beauty. "In the years to come," the Central Committee declared at the height of its self-delusion in 1958,

> . . . local conditions permitting, we should try to reduce the area sown to food crops each year, say to about one third of what it is at present; part of the land thus saved to lie fallow by rotation or to be used for pasturage and the growing of green manure, for afforestation nurseries, extensive cultivation of flowers, shrubs and trees, to turn our whole land, with its plains, hills and water, into a garden.[7]

But this utopia is not much discussed nowadays, and the main objection to a determined campaign to open up virgin lands to the plough is the expense.

"Reclamation requires from the State a large amount of capital for communications, water regulation, immigration of people and many other complicated operations which are not easy," a *People's Daily* editorial explained in 1958,[8] and it was officially estimated that reclamation cost the equivalent of $115 per acre [9] (so that doubling the arable land would cost almost $28 billion or more than China's entire annual budget). Hasty reclamation can in any case do harm, and there have been official complaints of the consequent erosion of topsoil (in pastoral Inner Mongolia, for example, and in hilly Chekiang and Kweichow provinces) [10] and of soil ex-

haustion (because of local cadres' reluctance to wait the sta-
tutory year before sowing on reclaimed soil).[11] Double-cropping on soil already under the plough has been extended, but
the amount of new land opened up has been relatively small.
The physical area cultivated is now about 265 million acres,
and the maximum practicable extension is by a mere twenty-
five per cent to 330 million. Obviously the future prosperity
of the Chinese people must rest on rising yields rather than
expanding acreage.

The first factor in raising yields is water control. The average ton of grain needs over 400 tons of water supplied at the
right time, but some soils absorb water a thousand times
faster than others. In the northern plains the tardiness or failure of seasonal rains is the worst crop-killer, but the flooding
of the big rivers when heavy summer and autumn rains wash
into them is equally damaging in the south. Three times the
Communist government has had more than one tenth of its
farmland flooded in consecutive years, in 1953–4, in 1956–7
and, worst of all, in 1959–61.

Mao inherited a water control system creaking from the
destruction and neglect of two chaotic decades. The fact that
the ditches, the crucial link between the reservoir and the
field, involved requisitioning land, compensating the owner
and allocating costs between individual proprietors or cooperatives, was one of the problems which led to the establishment of the communes. In 1957 Mao launched a mass irrigation drive, the success of which prompted the Great Leap
Forward in the following year. A hundred million peasants
were put to digging canals, and in a few short months the
ratio of cultivated land which was irrigated soared from
thirty-one per cent to a fantastic fifty-six per cent.[12] The people, when organized, could triumph over nature—though not,
as it was learnt in 1958 and 1959, on all fronts at once, and
not unless the technical directions were correct. After the
failure of the Leap it was discovered that many canals had
been dug so quickly, without proper supervision or materials,
and without a well-prepared national or regional plan to follow, that half of the water escaped from them; the water
table had been caused to rise in many places and the condition known as "cloudy soil" or alkali soil, on which crops
would not grow, had spread (by 1963) to six per cent of the
cultivated land. If water is led into a field, but there is no
adequate drainage for it, then the water table (normally six
or seven feet underground) rises and brings salts to the surface. In Hopei province, where the water lacks outlet and the
plain had been on the verge of salinity for decades, the care-

ful balance which the farmers had constructed, using little dams and dykes, was shattered by the canal-digging drive of 1959.[13] Even today, with 300 scientists at work in the well-equipped Soil Science Research Institute at Nanking,[14] the problem of the water table of the North China Plain and of spreading alkali soil remains unsolved.

Similarly the early hopes about taming the Yellow and Yangtze Rivers quickly have faded. The Russians helped with the dams and reservoirs which are to control the Yellow River, but the technical difficulties are enormous and the work is impeded by the reclamation of land in the upper reaches of the river, causing soil erosion and an increase in the silting of the reservoirs. The Sanmen Gorge dam is complete, though there has been delay in fitting the turbines for electricity generation (the Chinese make most of the dams pay their way by generating power). Even after the dam was built, however, the Yellow River still flooded to almost unprecedented heights in 1958, reaching 22,300 cubic metres per second on 17 July,* and China's planners must have been disappointed at the relatively small effect of the Sanmen dam.[15]

In South China water control and mechanization of agriculture are almost one and the same thing: the wet paddy-fields around Canton need electric pumps for irrigation and drainage just as much as the wheat plains around Peking cry for tractors. You can still see from the train Cantonese peasants in their pointed wicker hats pulling canvas pails of water up from the main irrigation canals and pouring it into the smaller channels serving their own particular fields—by hand. But the gradual spread of mechanized pumping releases labour for other essential purposes, especially the upkeep of the canals and the preparation of manure.

Mechanization is the second major factor in raising yields. Its most obvious manifestation is the tractor, status symbol of every rural Communist imagination. Under the spell of their

---

* The chaos caused by bad floods is heart-rending. One of the worst experiences of the present government was the Yangtze flood in the summer of 1954, causing ten million people to flee their homes in three provinces. On 18 August the Yangtze swelled to a height of ninety feet, and many villages had deliberately to be flooded in order to save the large cities. Soldiers at Wuchang formed a human wall to contain the breaches in the dykes, on which more than a hundred helpers died (including an eighteen-year-old girl who threw herself on the mud to prevent a breach in the dyke). Probably forty million people were ultimately affected by this disaster, and seven million were without shelter during the following winter. "Under the present government no human lives are lost in such disasters," the press says proudly. But the state still cannot prevent the misery they cause.

Russian advisers, the Chinese at first eagerly welcomed the large tractors with which their new ally began to supply them. But the Chinese landscape is one of small, irregular plots with no lack of hands to plough them by ox or buffalo.* This is especially so in the southern ricefields where the use of tractors "showed no increase in yield," as one newspaper commentator in Peking rather crossly remarked two or three years ago, "because in quality, mechanical ploughing was found to be no better than cattle ploughing." [16] True, a tractor took only one-twentieth the time, but what would the peasant do with his saved time? He tended to regard the tractor as a way of avoiding heavy work rather than as a release for more urgent tasks.

In the north, and particularly in the less thickly populated northeast, tractors are more helpful, and are indeed essential if rain delays ploughing and forces it to be done in a rush. Heilungkiang, which borders Russian Siberia, enjoys only a short frost-free period suitable for cultivation and consequently is the most mechanized of all provinces. But in China as a whole only one acre in twenty is machine-ploughed, and at the end of 1967 there were only about 50,000 tractors in use (one to every 5,000 acres, one to every 12,500 peasants, one to every People's Commune).[17] In five spring weeks of travel about China I did not see a single tractor being used. Ideally a million tractors are needed, but the Chinese admit that it will take at least two decades to get them. A 15-horsepower tractor costs 15,000 *yuan* ($6,000), and one Peking economist reckons that it would take the communes twenty years to buy the machinery they need out of their own accumulated funds, without state help.[18]

In any case the Communists have revised their earlier ideas about developing large-scale mechanized farming units on the Russian or American pattern: "We have no oil," the *People's Daily* explained in 1957, "too few animals, steel is expensive, the cost of machinery is prohibitive. Mechanization will come, but gradually. . . ." [19] The stress now is on machines specially adapted for Chinese conditions, unlike the Soviet-designed models for which the two principal tractor plants, at Loyang and Chang chun, were designed. Loyang specializes in the 54-horsepower *East is Red* caterpillar tractor, but the communes prefer the 35- and 28-horsepower tractors made in

---

* In times or places of animal shortage the men themselves pull the plough. The *People's Daily* reported that in one district in the spring of 1957 "there were 58,000 people pulling ploughs. In northern Anhui it is a very common sight" (24 October 1957). This is perhaps the best indicator of the traditional poverty of the Chinese farmer.

Shanghai and elsewhere—and a 7-horsepower "walking" tractor now designed for hilly areas and small plots. Even in the
northeast the Russian and European vehicles are too heavy,
with shares going too deep into the soft Manchurian earth,
and now a Shantung factory has brought out a half-weight
tractor more suitable for use there.[20]

The third factor in yields is the contribution of chemistry.
The southern Chinese soil is deficient in phosphorus, while
nitrogenous fertilizing is generally needed for raising yields
throughout the country. At first the Communists assumed
that the traditional sources would suffice: green manure, animal manure and human night-soil. "I think of the stomach of
every man and of every animal," said the Party's agricultural
expert in 1957, "as a small fertilizer factory." [21] From about
1957, however, the Party gave more attention to artificial
fertilizer. But domestic manufacture presented challenges:
China had no reliable indigenous source of phosphates
and no experience in this kind of industry; it took six
years to construct a large chemical fertilizer plant and they
were costly.[22] The Kirin plant which was commissioned in
1957 cost the equivalent of $85 million, and the Wuching
plant of 1963 (the first to be built exclusively by Chinese
technicians from their own designs, independent of Russian
help) cost $25 million.[23] There are now a number of large
plants producing about five million tons of the principal fer-
tilizers a year, and these are now joined by a British and a
Dutch plant just constructed in Szechuan province. This is
now one of the fastest-growing industries in China, and yet
domestic production represents still less than one tenth of the
countryside's real needs, the Chinese farm acre receiving only
about one tenth of the chemical fertilizer which is applied to
a Japanese or American acre. Large quantities are still imported (between two and three million tons a year in the past
two years), but, at over $25 a ton, these represent a heavy
burden on China's foreign exchange and will probably be reduced as more domestic plants come into commission.

The provision of fertilizer is only half the story: the peasant has to be persuaded to use it, and to use it properly. The
newspapers reveal cases where the fertilizer burns the seed,
or is left out in the open air and loses its value; cases where it
is not selectively used in the places which really need it, and
where not enough trouble is taken in watering the fields properly, ascertaining the soil properties and choosing the right
proportions of fertilizer. There are complaints of uneven
quality and of excessive cost, and sometimes, even when the

fertilizer works, the peasants are frightened by the unnatural increase in the plants' growth.[24]

Pesticides and insecticides are also an important contribution of the chemical industry to the farmers. In the mid-1950s Peking launched an extraordinary nation-wide campaign to eliminate four pests—rats, flies, mosquitoes and sparrows. The whole of society was organized to take part in this unique campaign, people spending days in the treetops and on roofs beating drums, shouting and screaming until all the sparrows collapsed on the ground with exhaustion. In 1958 alone almost 1.9 billion rats and almost 2 billion sparrows were killed, the authorities announced, and Clement Attlee had found in 1954 that there were "no flies in China" (one or two have been noticed by visitors since then). Leeches were eliminated in 1958, as a sort of by-product of the campaign, and Chairman Mao was moved to write a poem called "Farewell to the God of Plagues."

But the sparrows were a mistake, it seemed. In 1956 the sparrow was "a glutton whose daily grain intake amounts to about thirty per cent of its weight," but after the campaign there appeared millions of destructive caterpillars, and it was discovered that "sparrows are the born enemy of insects": they were reprieved and their place in the campaign given to bed-bugs instead, a typical example of the ill-prepared attacks on nature's balance which marred so many of the Chinese Communists' early agricultural policies.[25]

The real breakthrough in Chinese agriculture will come in another thirty years or so when a more educated generation of farmers takes over. The state farms, modelled on the Soviet pattern, have not done well in China: they have consistently lost money and are called by the peasants "pig and cow mansions," too high faluting to inspire imitation.[26] But simple demonstration farms, more practical and less fancy, and agro-technical stations have been set up on a wide scale in the past five years or so to take the lead in extension work, promoting innovations and establishing test plots.[27]

Meanwhile the government, reconciled to the meagreness of its resources, has now agreed to concentrate them on the high-yielding areas, especially around the big cities, "to extend the area of farmland on which crops are protected and output is stable and high. . . ."[28] Yields can be raised very substantially: the Hua Dong commune in Kwangtung province, for instance, claims to have trebled its rice yield in fourteen years (from eighteen cwt per acre in 1949 to fifty-eight cwt in 1963).[29] But this commune uses about four times the national average per-acre supply of chemical fertilizer, and the average rice yield throughout China is still only twenty-two cwt per acre, or half as good again as when the Communists came to power.*

It is one thing to see that the grain is grown: another to see it fairly distributed. Most grain is retained at its point of harvest, for consumption during the year by the peasants. But the state acquires about fifty million tons each year, partly as payment of tax and partly by purchase, for distribution to food-deficit provinces, the cities, the export corporations and so forth. In spite of collectivization there is often reluctance to give up surplus grain to the state: feelings are said to be still sour, for example, in the great interior rice-bowl of Szechuan province, whose farmers fed five other provinces during the coastal floods of 1959 and 1960, but received little food relief from them or from the central government when drought struck Szechuan itself in 1961.

Those were years of unusual disaster: in normal times the government's chief concern is to feed the seventy-five million city-dwellers who, to receive sixteen ounces of grain a day, require about twelve million tons a year. It was the inability of the large towns and cities to obtain food from their immediate countryside in 1960 that led the government to import cereal from Australia, Canada and later from Mexico, France and Argentina. At first this was an emergency measure, but in 1968 Peking was still importing five million tons at a cost of some $400 million in hard-earned foreign exchange. This was partly to build up really safe reserves (perhaps against a world grain shortage as well as a Chinese crop failure), and partly a deliberate commercial policy of importing relatively cheap wheat (at about $70 per ton) in order to release more attractive farm products for export (rice, for example, of which China can export about a million tons in a good year, fetches some $115 a ton, and soyabean is another high-value export crop of which China could sell more).†

But the grim fact must be faced by the Communist leaders

---

* This discussion has been primarily about foodgrains, but broadly similar remarks could be made of other crops. Cotton has been one of the major disappointments for the Communists, who are still having to import raw cotton from Africa and Pakistan. "At present," said the *People's Daily* on 26 August 1963, "most cottonfields are not fertile enough, the cotton seeds have generally deteriorated, the prevalence of insects is serious and the strength for resisting drought, waterlogging and other natural calamities is still weak in the cotton-growing areas."

† The gaining popularity of bread at the expense of rice, which has been a notable consequence of modernization in Japan, Taiwan and Hongkong in the past two decades, is also being observed in China and this may be another factor in the policy of importing wheat.

that the 1968 foodgrain harvest was only about level with that of 1957. Ten precious years have, as it were, been lost in the drive to increase production. The average annual increase in the grain harvest has been only three and a half per cent since 1949, and if the comparison be stretched back to the pre-war years, then the annual increase has been less than one per cent. Now that the full cost, both financial and political, of the agricultural drive has been appreciated, these are sobering statistics. They take on an even greater urgency when it is realized that the Chinese population has been growing at more than two per cent a year over the past fifteen years, so that the extra food grown barely feeds the new mouths that cry for it.

11: POPULATION

How Many Millions?

THE INHABITANTS OF CHINA, WHICH IS THE MOST POPULOUS country in the world and accounts for one quarter of humanity, now number over 750 million and are increasing each year by about 18 million. To a nation which finds difficulty in producing enough food for its people, is added every year the equivalent of the population of Canada or New York State. This "Malthusian counter-revolution" blunts the successes of China's industrial revolution by providing more mouths to feed, more hands to employ, each year. In a typical year of reasonable weather the Chinese national product might expand, through good planning, costly investment and hard work, by five per cent; but half of this achievement would be offset by a two and a half per cent increase in population, leaving a net gain per head of only two and a half per cent. If China's economic planners are burdened by this built-in handicap to growth, which compels them, in the Red Queen's phrase from *Alice through the Looking Glass,* to run hard merely to keep their place, China's neighbours (Russia, no less than Burma or Thailand) are fearful of its political consequences. Could the demographic explosion within China lead her to seek *lebensraum* beyond her borders?

The Census which the Communist government held in 1953 was the first scientific attempt to count the population, which till then had been assumed to number less than 500 million. There was surprise [1] when it revealed a total of 583 million.* There should have been another Census in 1963, ten years later, but conditions were still too chaotic following the disasters of 1959–61 and the count was apparently postponed for twelve months. Some kind of simple enumeration was made in 1964, but in conditions of secrecy, and the results are unlikely to be published.[2] There is no precise means, therefore, of calculating the increase in the population over the intervening eleven years.

Some official estimates were published, however, of the rate of population growth between 1950 and 1957, based on sample surveys of certain towns and provinces. They show an annual increase of about two per cent, tending to rise slightly towards the end of the period. Chou En-lai told Edgar Snow, the American journalist, in 1964 that "with the improvement in the standard of life in the course of the last two years, our rate of increase in population has gone up again to two and a half per cent." [3] No more precise estimates have been given, but it seems fair to conclude that the Chinese population has been growing by at least two per cent a year since 1950, and that in the more recent years the rate has been nearer to two and a half per cent.†

Some observers consider that during the 1959–61 calamities the birth rate must temporarily have dropped and the death rate risen,[4] but it cannot be established that there was a net reduction in the population during those years. A conservative calculation would put the end-1969 population at 760 million, a more generous one at about 800 million. Chinese politicians refer in speeches and articles to "the 700 million Chinese people," but this is probably a layman's under-estimate pending a new official figure.

An annual increase of two and a half per cent may sound small enough, especially to politicians who envisage annual production increases of ten per cent or more. But if this rate were maintained for a whole generation, it would cause the population to double, and if it were sustained until the end of

* The grand total was 602 million, but this included seven and a half million in Taiwan, and almost twelve million Overseas Chinese.

† These rates correspond with the experience of other Asian countries during the same period. Asia's population rose by twenty per cent during the 1950s, while India's expanded at an average of 1.9 per cent annually in that decade—rising to an expected 2.3 per cent in the 1960s.

the century there would then be 1.8 billion Chinese. Medical
progress is the major reason for the high rate of population
growth. The extension of public works, hygiene and medical
relief throughout the countryside, following the restoration of
peace and order after decades of strife, resulted in a dramatic
fall in the death rate of an estimated seventeen per thousand
in 1953. By the same token, peace and medical advance
brought the birth rate up to thirty-seven per thousand, leaving a net natural growth of twenty per thousand (or two per
cent).[5] Clearly the Communist government expects to continue and even expand its medical and public works programmes, and these will probably bring the death rate even
further down and thus increase the rate of population
growth.

Eventually this development should be offset by a decline
in the birth rate, if the pattern of Europe is followed. The
Chinese birth and death rates are roughly comparable with
those of Western Europe during the early stages of the industrial revolution there. The effect on nineteenth-century Europe of improved sanitation, public health and transportation
was an immediate slump in the death rate, only later followed, after a century's interval, by a similar fall in the birth
rate. The medical revolution, which allowed more babies to
survive the rigours of early infancy, had an immediate effect,
whereas the social revolution, which reduced the economic
importance of the family, raised the status of women and popularized the practice of birth control, took many decades to
complete. In the time-lag between these two processes the
population growth temporarily swelled from its normal half
per cent a year to between one and two per cent, but once
the birth rate "caught up" again, so to speak, with the death
rate, the population growth resumed its normal modest
tempo.

In Russia, America, Europe and Japan, where this process
has already taken place, it lasted for about a hundred years.
In China, as in India and Southeast Asia, the birth rate is already higher than it was in nineteenth-century Europe because of the tradition of early marriage, while the death rate
is being reduced even more sharply because of the use of
low-cost medical techniques previously developed in the industrialized West. The temporary "gap" between the death
and birth rates which modernization provokes is thus larger
than the one Europe had to close, but on the other hand a
modern Asian state has at its disposal techniques of social
control and propaganda far more effective than those of previous days. The riddle cannot be answered until it works it-

self out. All one can say is that if the Chinese population is to be held down to a modest billion or so, then the Communists have only another decade in which to achieve a fall in the birth rate. It would seem far more probable, however, that another generation will be needed to accomplish this change in social attitudes, and that the eventual Chinese population cannot, therefore, be stabilized at less than 1¾ billion or so.[6] By that time, since the rest of Asia, Africa and Latin America is also growing at similar speed, the world will hold some 6 to 7 billion people, and China's share will have increased from its present twenty-three per cent to something nearer thirty per cent. In relative terms this should not seem alarming, though as part of a world-wide problem it is most serious.

The ingrained racial pride of the Chinese, reinforced by the Marxist antipathy towards Malthusianism, led the Communist leaders at first to make light of the population problem. The Census result prompted the Cabinet, however, to commission an inquiry into birth control by the Ministry of Public Health, and this was completed in 1954. It set out the facts and urged a programme of encouraging family planning. After some debate, in which it was pointed out that even the Soviet Union manufactured contraceptives and allowed abortions in certain circumstances, and that family planning would certainly not result in an actual fall in the total population, the government in early 1955 approved a modest programme to make techniques of birth control available to the public, without actually persuading them. The attitude of some Politburo members was clear from the remark of Chen Po-ta, in 1956, that China would double its food production in the coming twelve years and could therefore "find room for another 600 million people at least."[7] Mao himself referred to the topic in his famous speech of 27 February 1957: "In all regions with dense population, birth control will be propagandized and promoted so as to further planned parenthood, lighten the excessive burden of families and provide for better education and better chances of employment."

This speech was quickly followed by the first full-scale birth control campaign every to be waged in China. The *People's Daily* argued: "If we assume . . . that the yearly population increase is thirteen million, and if agricultural production is not raised further, there is the danger that the living standard not only cannot be raised but that it will fall."[8]

The campaign included propaganda for delayed marriages, the legalization of abortion and the dissemination of knowledge about the "safe" period and contraception. Visitors were surprised by the thoroughness of the campaign, the vividness of its posters and the directness of the village lectures. Exhibitions were held of drawings and diagrams with complete and intimate details (one spectator described them as almost animated), and lecturers gave commentaries without any squeamishness or prudery. "An exhibition like that wouldn't last for a day in our country," an Indian girl student commented.[9]

But not all the lectures were praised. A *Hopei Daily* report complained that "the same material is propagated to both young and old, men and women, without regard to whether the people concerned could accept it, and people were forcibly brought together to hear the propaganda. There were also some cases in which the propagandists failed to maintain a solemn attitude. . . ."[10] At the end of one lecture in Peking, the chairman said reprovingly, that "this does not apply to us; we are all married."[11] A Shanghai newspaper explained the difficulty thus: "Birth control is connected with sex, and for thousands of years no respectable man has spoken in public about sex. . . . Such feudal notions . . . still exert influence."[12] Birth control was the only issue on which Frederick Nossall, the Canadian correspondent resident in China in 1959–60, heard a state employee criticize the government: "We all considered," this man said, "that the State had no right to interfere in people's private lives. Raising a family is your personal affair, and has nothing to do with national progress."[13]

If this was the resistance to birth control in the supposedly sophisticated cities, one can imagine the reaction in the villages, where the universal advice to a young rustic had for millennia been: "Get an heir as soon as you can." The old sayings about "More children more happiness" and "Rear children to protect your old age" had far more weight than the new message of the Party spokesmen, many of whom were doubtless only half-hearted family planners themselves.

These difficulties were taken by the doctrinaire anti-Malthusians in the Party as vindication of their viewpoint, and in 1958 the birth control campaign was suddenly called off after only a year of trial. It was in any case quite in conflict with the premises and spirit of the Great Leap Forward, which allowed of no limit on the potential growth of production and which was based on the maximum mobilization of manpower. The Party organ, *Red Flag*, laid down that "the more people we have, the better, faster, greater, and more economical will be the results of our socialist construction."[14] The

line was once more taken that, in a socialist society undergoing rapid technological change, "the problem of population
does not exist." The Food Minister explained that, while the
population had been growing at two per cent a year during
the first eight years of Communist rule (1949–57), food production had been expanding at seven per cent a year, so there
was no need to worry (he could not have predicted the setback in food production during 1959–63). In 1961 an earlier
dictum of Mao in the same vein was republished:

> It is a very good thing that China has a big population. Even
> if China's population multiplies many times, she is fully ca-
> pable of finding a solution; the solution is production. . . .
> Of all things in the world, people are the most precious.
> Under the leadership of the Communist Party, as long as
> there are people, every kind of miracle can be performed.[15]

But the miracle of the Great Leap Forward collapsed, and
gradually, in the early 1960s, the more rational and scientific
view prevailed. Birth control measures were again promoted,
though with less fanfare.

Official pronouncements still depreciate the problem, but at
least they recognize it *as* a problem. One writer explained in
1963 that while population increase was desirable, "it may
also be a handicap, as at present; when the economy is rather
underdeveloped one has to face the question of arranging
clothing, food, lodging and work for the whole population." [16] But the birth control campaign nowadays is a
muted affair. Propaganda is made for contraception, but the
supply of ointment, pastes, sheaths and diaphragms was only
enough for two per cent of the reproducing population in
1958 [17] and has probably not dramatically improved since
then. An old herbalist, Dr Yeh Hsi-chun, persuaded the Ministry of Public Health in 1956 to add to the approved methods of birth control the swallowing of live tadpoles, but
other doctors condemned this practice as harmful and it is
not now recommended.[18] Little is said about abortion, but a
Japanese nurse said after working in a Chinese hospital recently that its surgeons induced abortions on three days a
week. No doubt the Japanese experience has been instructive
here: Chinese experts are now studying Japanese population
control methods, which rely heavily on abortion. Sterilization
is also being suggested, as in India: in the spring of 1963, for
example, the monthly *Women of China* described and recommended sterilization operations for both men and women,
stressing that they are safe and do not necessarily interfere
with a couple's sex life. There is also constant propaganda for

delayed marriage and late child-bearing. The minimum legal age for marriage is now eighteen for women, twenty for men, but in practice men are urged not to marry before twenty-eight, women before twenty-two. Parents bearing more than three chidren are now, in some parts of China, subjected to an effective discrimination: they do not receive maternity supplies or extra rations.

The stock Chinese comment on foreign apprehensions about this population explosion is to point out that China's density of population is still modest compared with other countries. At 180 inhabitants per square mile, China has fewer people for her area than, say, Britain or France, India or Japan. It would be more realistic, perhaps, to exclude the deserts and non-cultivable land which account for the greater part of China's total area. Even then, China is far less densely populated than Britain or Japan, though more densely populated than Russia or India.[19]

The fear of population pressure on China's border is exaggerated. For one thing there is room in the Chinese interior (in Sinkiang, Chinghai, Inner Mongolia and the Northeast) for large numbers of immigrants from the cities and the more thickly populated coastal areas. Only a tiny fraction of the population has so far migrated, but these areas provide a safety valve for any population pressures that may build up.[20] Another factor of importance is that the land immediately across China's foreign borders is not greatly attractive to Chinese emigrants: Siberia is too cold and bleak (which is why the Chinese were not unhappy at giving it up to Czarist Russia a century ago), while the Southern borderlands are too mountainous—and the flat land beyond, in Burma, India, Siam and so forth, is already almost as densely populated as China. It would be entirely out of character for the Chinese goverment itself to seek alternative homes for its people outside its borders, and indeed emigration was forbidden in China's imperial days. If Southeast Asian rice, oil and rubber are needed, China could obtain them more easily by economic diplomacy than by demographic aggression.[21]

Much more serious is the impact of the population explosion on employment. Already, in the first two Five-Year Plans, population growth exceeded the planned increase in employment. The doctrinaire Marxists in Peking deny that unemployment is possible in a socialist economy, but the prospect of large-scale under-employment, particularly in the cities and among the soaring ranks of school-leavers, must cause anxiety among Party leaders. One solution is the deliberate reversal of the drift to the cities which was so marked a feature of the pre-1949 China (as it is of India even today) and indeed of the China of the 1950s. Now young people are virtually forced to work in the countryside, where skills are easily absorbed. But the provision of satisfying jobs to the new teenagers of China's cities depends on the development of industry.

12: INDUSTRY

Is Self-Reliance Enough?

ON THE DAY THAT THE FIRST FIVE-YEAR PLAN BEGAN, THE *People's Daily* declared in an editorial, "Industrialization provides a guarantee that our people shall no longer be exposed by imperialism to treachery and humiliations, and shall no longer live in poverty." [1] The order in which these two objectives are listed is instructive. Industry, in the Chinese Communist mind, is a status symbol of national power more than a generator of higher living standards. Luckily the two aims are served by the same means, and China since 1949 has for the first time had a government determined systematically to construct a modern industry which will as soon as possible make the country self-sufficient in manufactured goods.

There was precious little to start from in 1949. The Japanese-built mines and metal-working industries in Manchuria had been devastated by war, dismantled by the Russians in 1945 and then ransacked by the Kuomintang before they came into Communist hands. The light industrial centre of Shanghai was deserted by its leading entrepreneurs and their skilled foremen on the eve of the Communist take-over. These, with Tientsin, were the only major sites of industry.

The First Plan (1953–7) envisaged a doubling of factory production and the foundation of a solid heavy industrial base, with the investment of almost 48 billion *yuan* (say \$19 billion) in basic construction. This was a steel-oriented Plan along Soviet Russian lines, and roughly seventy per cent of the investment was in heavy industry. The Anshan steelworks in the Northeast was refurbished and expanded, and new steel complexes were begun at Wuhan, in central China, and at Paotow, in Inner Mongolia. A vital bridge was constructed over the Yangtze River at Wuhan, work was begun on the Sanmen Gorge hydroelectric project, and a new oil industry was started in Sinkiang.

All this could not have been undertaken without Soviet assistance. Stalin provided 156 key industrial projects for China's First Plan, not as a gift but on normal commercial terms including an element of long-term credit. The relationship had its difficulties from the start. Chinese workers lacked the skills necessary for the new plant, and Chinese administrators had no experience of the detailed and precise organization that was called for. Accidents were frequent, the arrangement of raw material supplies to the new factories was often neglected, and Chinese engineers, many of them Western-trained, sometimes quarrelled with their Soviet advisers. Two hundred Chinese directors were summoned to the Ministry of Heavy Industry in 1954 and accused of "having neglected the faithful execution of the Russian experts' instruction." [2]

Professor Choh-ming Li of the University of California concluded, after a close analysis of the implementation of the First Plan, that:

> The development of heavy industry has already run into the bottlenecks of the supply of power and basic industrial materials. Coal and metal mining, crude oil and electric power have failed to grow rapidly enough to meet the demand of all other industries, while the production of iron, steel and construction materials is unable to keep up with the rising demands of the metal-working and machine-making industries. . . . The situation reveals a lack of integration and co-ordination in planning. . . . [3]

Towards the end of the First Plan the Chinese leaders reappraised their industrialization programme. They found it too costly, too slow and too dependent on foreign help.* The Second Five-Year Plan, which had been drawn up as a logical successor to the First and followed faithfully in its footsteps, was laid aside and in 1958 Chinese industry was shaken by the Great Leap Forward. For industry the Leap meant three distinct changes. Firstly, large-scale industry was decentralized, and most state-owned factories were taken from the central government's wing and put under local provincial or city authorities; this made them more efficient, but

---

* In 1956 the first signs of the Sino-Soviet split appeared, and it became clear to Peking that a substantial increase in Soviet aid was out of the question.

also less coordinated and less amenable to the discipline of the national planners. Secondly, technical innovations were demanded from workers and engineers: "Give full play," said Mao, "to the ingenuity of all workers by emancipating their minds from any sort of superstition"—such as the superstition that a certain industrial process must always be done in such-and-such a way, because that is how it is done in Pittsburgh or Kharkov, although there may be cheaper ways of doing it in China where different materials are available and labour is plentiful.

But the third and most dramatic change was the promotion of small-scale, labour-intensive industry using indigenous production techniques and materials. The *People's Daily* explained in the spring of 1957 that there had been "too much emphasis on large, modern, mechanized, high-standard construction with no regard to conditions in our country, which is vast, has an immense population and is economically backward." [4] At Anshan "there are machines and production equipment with automatic control not needed today; these could have been acquired at a later date." [5] The construction industry was being mechanized under Russian guidance, but by 1957 the machine utilization rate had reached only fifty per cent and Chinese officials belatedly realized the absurdity of imitating the USSR. "Machines should not be used, or should be used as little as possible," it was now laid down.[6] Perhaps the height of waste was the almost entirely automated Russian papermill at Kiamusse in Manchuria.[7] The large modern steelmills would remain the backbone of Chinese heavy industry, but the stress would henceforth be on smaller, less up-to-date plants because otherwise, "a great part of our limited resources will be concentrated upon a few industrial bases which for a long period will be economically sterile." [8]

This was the reasoning behind the village steel drive of 1958. Old villagers were asked to remember ancient mine shafts and coalpits in their district, and these were reopened and worked by the peasants. Thousands of pygmy hearths and primitive furnaces were built, and supplied with ore and coal from these local sources. At the height of the campaign, there were sixty million peasants working at these back-yard furnaces and producing rough pig iron. A nation-wide conference on village steel revealed that "a number of highly skilled cadres did not believe that steel could be refined from village iron," but technical innovations were proposed which were claimed to overcome all the difficulties of raising the necessary high temperatures in the small converters available, reducing the sulphur content of the steel, and economizing on costly silicon, manganese and aluminium.[9] This was, in the words of a National People's Congressman's speech:

> . . . a movement of the whole people to produce iron and steel. In every corner of the country, old and young took part happily in the work of smelting iron and steel and breaking through old superstitions that the smelting of iron and steel belongs only to the aloof few working in the iron and steel industry, and cannot be mastered by others.[10]

But an engineer who had been elected to represent the Anshan steel-works at a political conference in Peking, said of the village furnaces:

> The low quality of equipment and installation, the inadequacy of transport, the frequency of accidents add to the difficulties of production; the poor raw material, the lack of skill of the workers, and a labour organization which is not up to the need, create added confusion. . . .[11]

A total production of eleven million tons of steel had been originally claimed for 1958, but after a few months it was admitted that three million of these had been village steel unsuitable for industrial use.[12] Most of the hundreds of thousands of small furnaces were abandoned.

The idea of self-help was not confined to steel. One city received especial praise for its Leap in electricity. "The whole population creates electricity. . . . Clerks and workers in enterprises, cadres in government offices, teachers and students in schools and the population in the streets, have all been encouraged to create electricity themselves." Thousands of "very small and very native" generators, producing up to 200 or 300 kilowatt and operating by the use of string, were set up, and delegations came to learn from other parts of China.[13]

The atmosphere of the Great Leap was one of frenzy. A foreign resident working as an electrician in a papermill described how its equipment was speeded up beyond all precedent in the struggle to register dramatic production increases. The mill was fed with roots, reeds and straw, in addition to the usual raw materials, in the effort to produce more. The machines' bearings burnt out, and the woollen belts became tangled and torn. An experienced technician who dared to complain of the way the equipment was being treated was reduced to common manual labour. Then, in the autumn of 1958:

> We were told that China could get rich quick if everyone concentrated on iron and steel. So we dropped everything

else and built brick chimneys in the factory yard. Radiators, pots and pans and every bit of available scrap went into the ovens, and peasants from the countryside poured in to help. The whole place was raving mad. Furnaces were glowing everywhere, and at night the city glowed red. The streetlights had gone off to save electricity, and the bulbs in houses were a kind of dim yellow. People, machines, everything was being strained to the limit and cracking up. Workers who had to tend furnaces at night and go to the factory by day were having all sorts of accidents, smashing their hands or breaking their arms. But the drums and gongs went on beating, and at first people were really carried away. They felt proud that they could make iron. Besides, there were meals of dumplings and holiday dishes, and I guess the Chinese will do almost anything for good food. The trouble was, nothing human or mechanical could stand that terrible pace.[14]

Politics have been in command at the factories throughout most of the Communist rule in China. The director of a factory is responsible to his local Party committee, and since, on average, one in seven of his workers belongs to the Party, his authority is not always firm. The conflict between the economists and the politicians within the Party is never resolved: they may sleep on the same bed, but dream different dreams. The politician says: "The majority among engineers and technicians have a deep superstition. The old colonial times have left a mark upon them. They superstitiously believe in books and in European and American scientific achievements. . . . [Now they must] discover the creative force of the workers." [15] He regards the participation of workers in administration as a step towards the abolition of the hated distinction between manual and mental work, the counterpart of the engineer's participating in manual work. "The Chinese labouring class is an advanced class," a Party official in the Northeast boasted, "with high consciousness and infinite wisdom." [16] It was in this spirit that Anshan workers were told by their Party committee to change techniques at will, without reference to the engineers, in order to increase production.[17] But every now and again the economist in the Party's *persona* will emerge, and in the summer of 1961 the *People's Daily* said:

If special organs for checking are abolished and their staff sent down to the workshops, if the workers engage in production and at the same time they themselves, and not a special staff, check, then in fact technical supervision has ceased. If the material supply department and the finance department are amalgamated, then the same hand which receives also spends, and the supervision of finances has ceased. What is the result of all this? The quality of the production suffers, exact costing becomes impossible: economic management has ceased.[18]

The Leap was already failing in mid-air out of exhaustion and confusion, when the crop failure of 1959, followed by even worse disasters in 1960 and 1961, brought it crashing to the ground. Many factories came to a complete standstill in 1961, their workers weak with disease and hunger, their raw materials cut off. The Leap was officially declared over in 1961, and for the next five years Chinese industry groped its way back, without any national plan, to the point from which it had so proudly taken off in 1958. Its recovery was further set back by the sudden mass withdrawal of the 1,390 Soviet experts who had been working in China, mostly as advisers in industrial establishments, in the summer of 1960. Khrushchev also cancelled certain technical and commercial contracts and withheld sophisticated equipment which the Chinese had ordered from Russian factories. This blow was a severe one, and Chinese industry has only just recovered from it.

At Anshan, for instance, eleven Soviet engineers had been installing two groups of Russian machines which were to have formed the basis of a new section for cold-rolling steel sheets (badly needed for motor vehicle bodies). The first set was being tried out, and a part of the second set had been delivered, when the Russians packed their bags, taking the technical documentation with them; the remaining equipment never arrived. Since it differed from the first set, it could not simply be copied. "Our workers and technicians were angry and determined," Po I-po, then Chairman of the State Economic Commission, explained three years later, "and decided we must make these machines ourselves. They sent out a call for ideas from all Chinese workers who knew steel-rolling, especially in the Northeast. We had to invent from scratch. Within a year we had it operating. They may not be like the machines the Soviets would have sent, but they roll steel sheets with ninety per cent of them up to standard, while the USSR contract promised us only eighty per cent. . . ."[19] When I visited Anshan four years after the Russian withdrawal, the Superintendent of the newest blast furnace there told me unequivocally that they had still not overcome the difficulties caused by this event. The Russians would not have been there (at Chinese expense, after all) if they had not had something to give, in terms of knowledge and experience, which the Chinese themselves lacked, and the claim that the Chinese quickly made do without this technical advice, while it satisfies Chinese pride, lacks the ring of truth. On the other hand the Soviet walk-out has certainly stimulated Chinese inventiveness and resourcefulness.

China is very anxious to impress on the outside world the feeling that she is making great industrial strides even without Soviet aid. There are complete sets of Chinese-built equipment in "several hundred key construction projects in over twenty branches of industry," and at Wuching, near Shanghai, I saw one of these: a large chemical fertilizer plant which was apparently working well although there had been earlier reports of teething troubles. In the past four years or so "the first big rotary cement kiln designed, built and installed entirely by Chinese personnel" was commissioned; the first 220,000-volt capacitative voltage mutual inductor was built; and a 12,000-ton home-made hydraulic forging press, one of only twenty or so in the whole world, was put into regular operation.[20] "Now we have progressed," declared Po I-po in 1963, "from copying to independent designing." [21] But it stands to reason that the Chinese industrialization programme will miss the short cuts and the sophisticated experience which only the technicians of an advanced industrialized country can offer her.

Now the Third Five-Year Plan has begun (in 1966, a little late), and the painful readjustment made necessary by the excessive demands of the Leap, the chaos of 1959–61 and the quarrel with Khrushchev has been effected. The Chinese have strengthened their extractive mining industry and are now making about twelve million tons of steel a year: they still need to import certain special alloy steels, but are exporting simple steel products. They claim to be in serial production of diesel locomotives* and are turning out small quantities† of nine basic models of road vehicle (concentrating on goods vehicles rather than automobiles). They have built a 16,000-ton cargo ship, the *Leap Forward,* but ironically this sank on its maiden voyage in 1962, and since then only smaller vessels have been made.‡ The only aircraft being made in China is the piston-driven, eight-passenger *An-*

* China is badly served for railroads: the Communists inherited a mere 12,500 miles of track and have since added only another 10,000 miles (including double-tracking). China still has far less railway than India, and neither the key Peking–Canton line nor the Peking–Tientsin line is yet fully double-tracked.

† About 35,000 vehicles in all in 1968, probably.

‡ With an annual export-import trade involving at least 100 billion ton-miles of sea carriage and costing at least $225 million in freight (see Li, Chapter 7), China is bound to build up a large merchant fleet. In 1963 she had 150 ocean-going ships aggregating about 700,000 deadweight tons, mostly purchased from abroad, either second-hand or new.

tonov AN–2 produced at Shenyang under Soviet licence.*
Electricity production stands at about 50 billion kilowatt-
hours a year.

Light industry has at last been given the attention it deserves, after the neglect of the Russian-oriented First Plan.
The textile industry has expanded faster than the cottonfields
can supply it, and since 1957 synthetic fibres have been made
to supplement cotton. China has now exported complete cotton textile spinning and weaving equipment to such countries
as Burma, Indonesia and Cambodia. The plastics industry
made a start in 1961, and was accounting two years later for
almost one tenth of the consumer market.[22] The principal
aim of light industry is to provide goods for rural consumption which will stimulate agricultural production, to eliminate
the need for imports of consumer goods, and to provide export sales in Southeast Asia, Europe and other foreign markets.

China's most serious lack was, until a year or so ago, oil.
The joint development, with the Soviet Union, of the Yumen
oilfield in Sinkiang was never a smooth business and the
break with Russia put paid to it for a long period. China
even began to buy small quantities of oil products from the
West in 1960, and is still importing a portion of her needs
from Russia and Rumania. Her domestic production of crude
oil is about ten million tons, and her refining capacity almost
matches that amount. This is enough to carry on a limited
transportation effort, but every visitor comments on the paucity of road traffic by comparison with other countries, and it
is likely that China still imports certain special oil products
such as high-octane aviation fuel. It is known that the relative
inactivity of her badly-equipped air force is partly attribut-
able to fuel shortages. Recently a large new oilfield was discovered in the Northeast, but few details have been published
about it. In the end China will probably find within her vast
borders all the oil and other minerals she needs (nickel and

Recently Peking has ordered several new freighters in the
12,500–16,500 ton class from Western shipyards. But China-made ships
are now calling at African, Asian and European ports.

* The Chinese civil airline has six new Vickers *Viscount 810s*, about
fifteen *Ilyushin 18-Vs* (equivalent to the Vickers *Vanguard*) and fifty
or more low-speed *Ilyushin 14s* (the Russian *Dakota*). Chou En-
lai charters jets from Western airlines for his diplomatic travels. But
the Chinese aim to extend their own international air services (at present limited to Pyongyang, Hanoi, Rangoon and Irkutsk) to Colombo,
Djakarta, Cairo, Accra, Paris and Havana. To do so they will need to
buy modern jet aeroplanes, probably from Britain or France.

copper are the main metals she lacks), especially in the virtually unexplored areas of mountainous Sinkiang and Tibet. Peking now attaches high priority to geological prospecting. But it takes many years to bring mines into production even when the deposits are found, and the transportation problem is immense.[23]

A start has been made, and there are industries in which China offers an example to other developing countries. The nuclear explosions are also a product of a well-prepared industrial effort. A question-mark, however, hangs over China's technology. Spurning Russian or any other foreign aid (and always tempted to put her own engineers and technicians into political straitjackets from which they cannot play their full role in increasing the quality and quantity of production), can the Chinese Communist leaders be sure of safely "going it alone" in this constantly changing world of industrial technology?

13: SCIENCE AND TECHNOLOGY

A Question of Trust

AS DR JOSEPH NEEDHAM HAS SHOWN IN HIS MONUMENTAL volumes on *Science and Civilisation in China*, the Chinese maintained, in the millennium that preceded the European Renaissance, "a level of scientific knowledge unapproached in the West."[1] Iron was cast, the mechanical clock was built, and gunpowder, paper and printing were invented in China long before these techniques became known in Europe, although China played no part in the Western Renaissance. In modern times Chinese scientists have won the Nobel Prize, and are filling posts of importance throughout the Western scientific world. Of the several thousands of Chinese who were in 1949 studying natural or social sciences abroad, only a small fraction has returned to work for the Communist government, but this number includes a high proportion of outstanding scholars. Their worth was dramatically illustrated on 16 October 1964 when China exploded her first nuclear device in the Sinkiang desert, four years after the Russians had packed their bags and left her without external technological assistance.

The first Chinese atomic reactor, the experimental one in Peking, was supplied by the Soviet Union in 1958, and the Russians apparently helped also to build the gaseous diffusion plant at Lanchow from which the Chinese obtained the high-grade uranium 235 for their nuclear explosions. Almost a thousand Chinese nuclear scientists were trained at the joint atomic institute of the Communist powers, partly financed by Peking, at Dubna, in the USSR. But Chien San-chang, Director of China's Institute of Atomic Energy, had collaborated with Joliot-Curie in France, as had his wife, and the Chinese programme for the development of nuclear weapons is believed to be headed by Wang Kan-chang, a nuclear physicist specializing in fission processes who studied both in Germany and the USA. Chinese missile development is in the hands of Chien Hsueh-shen, a former Professor of Jet Propulsion at the California Institute of Technology. All three of these senior scientists have an imposing array of helpers with experience in universities and firms in America, Britain, France and Germany.[2]

This team has been able to put up two reactors near Paotow, in Inner Mongolia, for the production of plutonium; to complete the gaseous diffusion plant near Lanchow and manufacture uranium 235; and then to begin a series of test explosions in Sinkiang which made China the fifth member of the nuclear club and culminated in the successful development of a hydrogen-bomb. By the expenditure of rather more than $1 billion* and the diversion of a very large amount of electricity, and of the services of almost 2,000 highly-skilled specialists from other sectors of national construction, Peking has thus proved to the world that China is a power to be taken seriously and that, when it is important enough, her science and technology are not far behind the West's.

By 1960 the government was allocating between one and two per cent of its annual budget, or some $450 million, to science, and the proportion has probably risen since then. Almost all scientific visitors are impressed by the wealth of up-to-date foreign publications which the government makes

---

* The cost of acquiring a nuclear arsenal which would count either as a serious deterrent or as a force to be reckoned with in any nuclear war would, however, be inordinately heavy for China. See Chapter 15 below.

available to Chinese scientists and by the equipment which they have.*

China has good scientists, and is giving them a reasonable budget, and yet doubts about the Communists' science programme are raised by the predominance of political considerations in its implementation. Sometimes the political aims are justified. One has much sympathy, for instance, with the Communist Party's plan, inspired by the emotions of cultural nationalism, to marry Chinese traditional medicine with modern Western medicine and breed an entirely new integrated medicine of maximum usefulness and validity for the Chinese environment. The old Chinese practice of acupuncture, which involves the sticking of long silver needles into certain parts of the body (and by which many people have been cured of rheumatism, post-poliomyelitis paralysis and other ailments) has now been given a theoretical basis of startling novelty [3] and is no longer so uniformly despised by Western doctors. This policy makes sense in a country which could boast of only 60,000 hospital beds in 1949 (one to every 9,000 inhabitants), and which has 500,000 traditional-style doctors against a mere 40,000 Western-style doctors. It is true that the rival schools of the old Chinese tradition resisted its codification, and that many Western-trained doctors refused to see any value in it. The Dean of the Pharmaceutical Department of the Peking Medical College complained during the Hundred Flowers period that the Ministry of Public Health had "dragged back pharmaceutics to the eighteenth century." [4] The authorities did not help by setting absurdly over-ambitious targets for the herbalists and acupuncturists (who were told in 1958 that, as part of the Great Leap Forward, it had been decided that they should find a cure for cancer in five years). But the Japanese, upon whom there is no political pressure in the matter, have also reinstated some of the old Chinese medicine and intend to subject it all to modern verification and analysis.

The same nationalism which enables the Chinese Communists to make a sensible salvaging of their own tradition, however, also leads them to extremes of irrationality. When they declared, in 1955, that "The rotten capitalist system is an obstacle to scientific development; it definitely is not capable of

---

* Including, the *People's Daily* (7 January 1964) claims, electronic computers constructed since 1958 by Chinese research scientists and in use for weather forecasting as well as for agricultural and transportation calculations. But many Chinese laboratories lack air-conditioning or a steady flow of electric current, and consequently one hears reports also of difficulty in maintaining delicate instruments.

increasing production by using new techniques," [5] it was permissible to attribute such untruths to the Moscow line of that day. In 1956 the Russians came to terms with reality by officially recognizing the achievements of capitalist technology. But in 1958 the Peking magazine *Red Flag* was still declaring that bourgeois science and what was written in books was "a pile of garbage," to be replaced by a genuine Marxist, proletarian science. [6]

A phenomenon which puzzles many Western businessmen may be explained in this context of nationalist feeling. In 1964, when China bought six Vickers *Viscount* aeroplanes, the British manufacturers sent to Peking an expert on the Rolls-Royce jet engines used in the aircraft. He stayed there for a year as part of the purchase contract, and he was on call to the Chinese at any time to instruct, explain, demonstrate or merely discuss; yet he spent most of his time playing billiards in the saloon of the Hsinchiao Hotel. The Chinese called him only on the rare occasions when they could not deal with a fault in the engines. It would have been more rational to exploit his presence by constant talks on the technical ins and outs of this very sophisticated engine, but Chinese hate the role of pupil to any foreigner, and would rather patch something up than expose their own shortcomings, ignorance or inferiority.

It was this factor which made it so difficult for the Russian scientists who came to help with China's Twelve-Year Plan for Science which aimed at training over 10,000 advanced scientists and completing more than 580 major research projects by 1967. At the first significant joint conference of Soviet and Chinese scientists in Peking in 1955, the Chinese Communists recognized that their country was still very backward in science. "In order that we may catch up," Chen Pota concluded, "Soviet Russian scientists must be our masters." [7] But the Hundred Flowers in 1957 yielded this comment from the Assistant Manager of an electrical appliance factory in Shanghai:

Learning from the Soviet Union is a royal road; but some cadre workers do not understand and think that it means copying. I say if we copy, it will paralyse Chinese engineers. . . . I have been engaged in electric engineering for twenty years. Some of the Soviet experiences simply do not impress me. Of course, I suffered a good deal in the Five-antis movement because of these opinions. . . . [8]

When Khrushchev ordered all the 1,390 Soviet specialists home in the summer of 1960, Chinese science took a hard blow. Where it is important enough, as it is on the nuclear programme, Chinese scientists have proved they can succeed. But the nuclear programme is unique in being exempted from most of the normal harassments of political interference,* and it is these which raise doubts about the other fields. The main complaint is the systematic depreciation of scientific expertise. A vivid example is the 1958 play *Everywhere Floats the Red Flag,* in which an injured steelworker is rushed to hospital in the middle of the Great Leap: "I am not afraid of death," he explains, "my wife and children are provided for by the organization; what I am worrying about is the furnace, . . . steel. . . . We are surpassing England . . . surpassing America. . . . I cannot die, my furnace. . . ." The hospital doctor is Western-trained and has a "superstitious faith in scientific research." The Western medicine books said "amputate," so he proposed to amputate. But the local Party officials supported the steelworker in refusing amputation which would render him unable to work at the furnace again, and, in the end, despite the doctor's doubts, the leg was saved. A critic said after seeing the play, "This proves that what foreign science cannot do, the Party in new China can do." [9]

While bookish lore was downgraded (the Party even challenged Euclidian geometry), the first results of the campaign to encourage peasants to contribute to science were warmly applauded. The peasant Chen Yung-kang's theory of "three-yellow and three-black" as a criterion for applying fertilizer on ricefields was only popularized after expert checking, and he was skilfully used as a go-between linking the peasants with the agronomists.[10] But there were other cases where the Party preferred peasant hunches to laboratory testing. Even nuclear science was included in the 1958 campaign: "The pursuit of atomic science," the *People's Daily* assured its readers, "is not the privilege of a select few and it does not require long training; it can be carried out in wide circles and in a short time." [11] A Hunanese official said that, "Those of lower cultural standard are better than people with high education; . . . the expert scientists blindly worship foreigners and themselves and do not dare to do things which have not been done abroad." [12] The pendulum has swung back in recent years, but the basic attitude remains one of disdain and contempt, especially for pure science and research, which is regarded as a low priority compared with the immediate

---

* Even the nuclear establishments suffered from this during the Cultural Revolution of 1966–8.

needs of production. During the Leap, a Chinese professor trained in America wrote:

> There was a way of thinking according to which teaching of fundamental mathematics, physics and chemistry was empty and meaningless, because such teaching only explains natural laws which are unreal because they have no connection with production. Therefore it was proposed that fundamental scientific lessons should be curtailed or scrapped, and that the mathematical, physical or chemical notions required in specialized trades should be taught in the trade schools.[13]

An American scholar estimates that in 1961 there were only 1,200 scientists with advanced degrees or their equivalent actively engaged in original research in China,[14] and Mikhail Klochko, the Soviet chemist who spent a year in China before defecting to Canada, concluded that, by ignoring the need for a pure research base, China condemned herself to "imitate foreign prototypes and borrow alien ideas." [15]

The Chinese Communist love of secrecy also hinders science. Even such topics as land desalinization are rated as top-secret, so that scientific work on them cannot easily be shared, and there are cases like that of a girl in Kunming investigating a scientific problem which, unknown to her, had long since been solved in Peking. But above all, the time-consuming imposition of manual labour and political discussion on scientists, most of whom are, of course, of bourgeois origin, robs the country of a proportion of their talent. The mere fact that after the excesses of the Leap the universities should adopt (in 1961) the slogan: "The main task of higher education is study," and that the Party First Secretary at Yunnan University should add his own assurance that, "We shall do our best to put the emphasis on teaching and not on productive labour," [16] illustrate the lengths to which brain power is depreciated. Klochko concludes that Chinese science underwent 'complete stagnation' in 1958–60 when the "line of the masses" ruled.

It is not all nonsense: there is a genuine effort to bring scientists into closer contact with the reality of their country's needs and condition. But balance and perspective were lost in the Leap period. Recently it was necessary for the *People's Daily* to reaffirm that:

> All technical personnel who are willing to work for socialism should be treated on the basis of equality in our country . . . Leading posts of a technical nature should generally be filled by technical personnel, and technical problems must be decided primarily by technicians. . . . As far as technical problems are concerned, nobody is permitted to adopt an ar-

bitrary attitude, nor should divergent technical opinions be regarded as political opinions. . . . Technical personnel should, in the spirit of being responsible to the state and the people, dare to adhere to truth and persist in their opinions if they are correct.[17]

This is advice which speaks volumes for the degree of local Party interference which is taken as a matter of course in technological and scientific matters. Mao apparently had no qualms about China's losing a whole year of scientific education in 1966–7 in the interests of class struggle, and the Academy of Sciences had a tough time in the Cultural Revolution.[18]

Klochko believes that if the Chinese scientists are allowed to work properly, they will quickly outstrip their Russian counterparts. A group of British scientists who visited China in 1962 came back with mixed opinions, but many of them felt that China would go ahead of Britain in certain fields of research and technology within about ten years.[19] Chinese science is uneven, and many of the 250,000 scientists and engineers who have now been trained in post-1949 China lack the independence of mind and the habit of genuine free enquiry which the next generation will need. The potential is there, but, until a genuinely scientific-minded generation gains weight in the Communist Party, it will remain only partly realized. For this reason the prospects for economic growth on China's chosen basis of technological self-reliance are reduced.

14: GROWTH

Politics in Command

THE ECONOMIC CHALLENGE WHICH WAS PRESENTED TO THE Chinese Communist leaders when they took power in 1949 was daunting. The annual product of the average Chinese citizen was $50,* about the lowest in the world. China was

* For purposes of comparison with Western countries, this figure ought to be at least doubled, to take account of price differences. See Alexander Eckstein, *The National Income of Communist China*, Glencoe, Illinois, 1961.

much less developed, in terms of industry, railways and so forth, than either Russia or India had been on the eve of their First Five-Year Plans, and was devastated by twelve years of almost continuous warfare. There was no controversy over the need to build up the economy and develop a strong heavy industrial base. So weak had the Chinese entrepreneur class shown itself, that there was not even serious controversy about the need for basic industries to develop in state ownership: both Sun Yat-sen and Chiang Kai-shek were opponents of private enterprise in heavy industry. In all these aims the Communists carried educated opinion with them in China.

Obviously foreign help was necessary to accelerate economic growth: Chiang had been assisted by the American treasury * and the Communists were expected to obtain aid from Moscow. Pride led some Chinese comrades to oppose the acceptance of Russian help, and the fact that the Russians charged interest on their loans caused some resentment. A Governor of a Chinese province argued later that, "Russia's loans are an onerous charge: after ten years we are still paying interest. America's war loans were more generous and easy. . . ." [1] Russia did, however, provide the Chinese with about $2¼ billion of credits which they could not have obtained from any other source and which, together with Soviet technological expertise, were invaluable in realizing the Chinese First Five-Year Plan.

The USSR had in 1949 a quarter of a century of experience in industrialization, and it was natural that the Chinese should at first follow the same path. The First Plan (1953–7) achieved an annual six to seven per cent growth in the economy: [2] double the Indian performance during the same period, though hardly spectacular by comparison with the advanced European and American economies. Even this involved a degree of capital accumulation, of enforced saving on a nation-wide scale, that provoked anxiety. In the first year of the First Plan, which unluckily saw a bad harvest, the *People's Daily* felt obliged to answer the question: "If we embark now on large-scale industrial construction, will not this impose an intolerable burden on the farmers?" A fort-

---

* The USA committed over $2 billion to Chiang's government between 1945 and 1949, and has dispensed another $4 billion (one third economic aid, two thirds military aid) to Taiwan since then. See Neil H. Jacoby, *U.S. Aid To Taiwan*, New York, Praeger, 1966. Russian aid to the Chinese Communists during the same period amounted to about $2¼ billion, including both economic and military assistance. America has been more than twice as generous.

night later the newspaper returned to the defence of the Party's industrialization policy: "Perhaps there are people who think this way: the development of heavy industry is necessary, but could its speed not be slower? Why can we not have a break, a breathing space . . . ?" [3]

The year 1957, the last of the First Plan, was a sad one for Mao Tse-tung and his colleagues. It saw the end of their dreams of building a great modern empire full of fine buildings and river-harnessing projects, with a bottomless Russian purse open to them and wealth sprouting from China's yellow earth. The people could hardly be asked to tighten their belts still further in the interests of industrialization, and the leaders regretfully realized that modernization would be a far slower and more difficult process than they had expected.

The Russian advisers were counselling caution, urging China to be less ambitious and to settle for a slow, gradual, conventional growth into economic maturity. Mao's reaction was to discard these careful, pedestrian blueprints and budgets and invent a more heroic approach to the economic problem. He proposed to decentralize industry and release it from the suffocating embrace of the Peking bureaucrats; to "walk on two legs" by developing *both* the modern, large-scale, Westernized factories which the First Plan had produced *and* the small-scale, labour-intensive, native techniques and enterprises which the First Plan had neglected; to give more attention to light industry and agriculture, since heavy industry without these was a white elephant, lacking both raw materials and markets; and, most important of all, to mobilize the enthusiasm of the millions of peasants for whom the First Plan had meant practically nothing beyond stiff grain requisitioning. These strands of thought, tested by the mass irrigation drive in 1957, were woven into the Great Leap Forward of 1958.

"If we do not live tensely," explained the *People's Daily*, "how can we free ourselves from the burden of poverty and backwardness left to us by history?" [4] The Leap was defined as "a tense struggle between man and time," but it was also a battle against nature: "Demand grain from nature," a slogan went, "and declare war against the great earth."

There were plenty of sceptics. The Party First Secretary of Chekiang province wrote that, "In agricultural production, a number of comrades were of the opinion that a sudden Leap is possible; but others criticized what they called the Provincial Committee's excessive optimism, impatience and impetuosity, pointing out that in the past years agricultural production in Chekiang increased by a yearly average of only two or three per cent." [5]

The whole nation became delirious, intoxicated by the drama of its unusual exertions and by the lyrical slogans of its leaders. The *People's Daily* did justice to the situation when the ninth anniversary of the Communist government came on 1 October 1958:

> In agriculture the red flag is flying, . . . merging into the red flames coming from the steel plants: the sky has turned red. . . . The Greek mythology of ancient times was only a tale, a dream, an ideal. Today, in the era of Mao Tse-tung, heaven is here on earth. . . . Once the Party calls, tens of millions of the masses jump into motion. Chairman Mao is a great prophet. Through scientific Marxist-Leninism he can see the future. . . . Each prophecy of Chairman Mao has become a reality.

The steel production target was raised three times during 1958, and the Finance Minister explained apologetically in the summer of that year that, "At present the central authorities are compiling targets for the Second Five-Year Plan" (1958–62) "but have not been able to catch up with the swift changes in practical conditions that require upward revision of the targets almost every day." [6]

National fatigue became apparent as the Leap went into its second year, and Ko Ching-shih (Mayor of Shanghai) and Chen Yun (the economic specialist in the Politburo) were among those who took the opportunity to counsel a saner and more balanced policy which would restore the central responsibility for national planning. [7] The preliminary production results for 1958, released in early 1959, were prodigious. Combined agricultural and industrial production had soared by sixty-five per cent over the previous year, it was claimed; both the grain harvest and steel production had more than doubled during the year (to reach 375 million tons and eleven million tons respectively). But gradually the truth came out, and in August the Party Central Committee confirmed that the statistics had been exaggerated, though it still claimed a forty-eight per cent production increase and it still persisted in the Leap. Targets for 1959 were reduced, but the mass campaigns were continued. A Shanghai newspaper noted towards the end of 1959 that certain "rightist opportunists" were criticizing the Leap, saying that the economic gains of the 1949–57 period had been lost in the first six months of 1958 and "the wealth of the state . . . squandered with no effective results." [8]

When 1960 came, the statisticians claimed another thirty-one per cent production increase for 1959, which meant that production had doubled in the two Leap years 1958 and 1959 and that the almost forgotten Second Five-Year Plan had been overfulfilled before its term was even half-way. But the 1960 floods and drought ("the most severe natural calamities in a century") and Khrushchev's withdrawal of aid finally shattered Mao's dream. The curtain was officially drawn on the Leap Forward in January 1961, when the Central Committee, putting the best face on things, announced:

> Inasmuch as tremendous development has been achieved over the past three years, and as the output of major products has greatly exceeded the levels originally scheduled for 1961 and 1962, the last two years of the Second Five-Year Plan, the scope of capital construction in 1961 should be readjusted and a policy of consolidating, filling out and raising standards should be adopted on the basis of the victories already won.

This period of readjustment was to last for five years, and frugality was the watchword: no economy was too small, it was said, even of "a chicken feather or an onion skin." Party economists tried to put the Leap in a more respectable light by advancing a new theory of "spiral" economic development,* but its real condemnation was spoken by Po I-po, then the principal economic official in the government, in February 1961:

> It is wrong to think merely of production and not of the life of the people, to neglect harmony between work and rest, to disregard safety in production, to look merely at present-day production and not to look at the next step, to eat up the reserves in the storehouses, to use equipment and manpower to excess, and thus be unable to maintain a steady rhythm of production. These things are bad management.[9]

Po maintained the façade of Party unity, however, and vigorously defended the Leap as such. When Anna Louise

---

* "The experience of our country's economic construction proves that the development of a socialist economy is not a policy of advancing in a straight line but is an undulatory, forward and spiral upward motion," Liu Ku-kang wrote in the *Ta Kung Pao*, Peking, on 2 June 1961. This is quite different, he added, from the economic cycle in capitalist countries, where the production growth rate "only crawls forward very slowly and sometimes goes backward." In the same newspaper a year later Ho Pei-yu wrote that, "Socialist production and circulation of commodities are carried out according to plan and are determined according to planned proportions. . . . Such a thing as economic crisis does not exist" (6 August 1962). But Chairman Liu Shao-chi admitted privately to Party workers that the Leap was "like an eclipse of the sun" —an honourable mistake (Sven Lindqvist, *China in Crisis*, London, Faber and Faber, 1965, p. 30).

Strong asked him if the 1958 steel drive had been a mistake, he replied:

> It was not a mistake, it was indispensable. When you as a writer write 10,000 words and then cut it down to 5,000 this is no mistake. It enriches the result. That steel drive gave us a nation-wide steel industry faster than any other way.[10]

Suslov, the Russian Party leader, unkindly called the Leap an attempt to industrialize by "cavalry charges," and its extremism is indefensible. It did, however, make an important impact on the psychology of the Chinese peasant and of the village cadre worker, and it has resulted in a useful proliferation of primitive local industries which take the strain off the expensive large plant that requires foreign help. It is wrong to write the Leap off as a total waste, but it is equally wrong to assume that the Party has learnt the proper lessons from it. As economic recovery has proceeded in the first half of the 1960s there have been occasional murmurings from the Party ranks for another Leap Forward, and only time will tell whether this presages another outbreak of economic amateurism. Liu Shao-chi remarked on the Party's fortieth anniversary in mid-1961 that:

> Those who joined the Party before Liberation have gone through sanguinary revolutionary struggles and are now the backbone of our Party, but while familiar with revolution they have not yet had adequate experience in socialist construction. . . . There are many things about socialist construction we have yet to learn.[11] *

The most important feature of the Chinese economy after the Leap Forward is its new basis in self-reliance. Khrushchev's economic sanctions against China in 1960 provoked an intense rage in the Chinese Party. A Shanghai editorial, published as the Russian specialists were boarding their trains home, said:

> The USA and reactionaries of certain other countries † do

---

* A Peking Professor of Economics wrote in 1957 that, "The comrades in charge of the direction of the economy have no knowledge of economics. They proceed by trial and error" (*People's Daily*, 29 August); and two participants at an economic planning conference during the Hundred Flowers period called Li Fu-chun, the chief government planner, "an amateur" in economics (*People's Daily*, 9 June 1957). An example of the Party's economic innocence is the answer given by *Learning*, the Peking periodical, in January 1956, to a reader who asked whether, if a part of the national economy surpassed its target, the coordination of production would be affected. The answer was: No, it would spur other sectors to produce more (cited in CNA 119, 10 February 1956).

† i.e. the "Khrushchev clique" in the Soviet Union.

not let us progress, do not let us become powerful. . . . We are filled with anger. . . . But let them wait eight or ten years or a little longer, and then they will see what China is. . . . The enemy dares to cheat us, because although we have become stronger, yet we are still "poor and blank." [But this will be changed] by revival through our own strength.[12]

The sensitivities of the Chinese on the question of foreign aid are well illustrated by a *Red Flag* article in 1963, which stated:

> Everybody knows that our country's socialist capital accumulation, just as Stalin has said, cannot be carried out through methods imperialism uses in robbing colonies, cannot be carried out through methods capitalism uses to carry out foreign aggression and extort reparations, nor can it be realized by methods of relying on enslaving foreign loans. Imperialism will not make us any loans. The running dogs of imperialism and foreign reactionaries will also not make us any loans. We have no intention of accepting any kind of unequal conditions to obtain loans from imperialists, foreign reactionaries, or anyone else! [13]

How, then, is China to finance her development? By 1960 the government was raising budget revenues in the order of 70 billion *yuan*, or almost $30 billion a year.* Roughly one third of this derives from taxation, two thirds from the profits of state enterprises. In the early 1950s Peking had two additional sources of finance, Russian aid and the fines and confiscations of the economic reforms (the land reform is unofficially estimated to have yielded about $8½ billion to the state, and the Three-antis and Five-antis campaigns in 1951–2 another $2¼ billion, but these are only guesses).[14] Today Russian aid is suspended and the entire domestic economy socialized. The flow of remittances from the Overseas Chinese to their families at home, amounting perhaps to $100 million a year,[15] provides the government with useful foreign exchange but is not a net addition to its total resources.

China's domestic development funds must therefore come from her own savings, which cannot be raised much higher without risking severe discontent among the peasants and Party cadres. Her foreign exchange must come from her export surplus. Now that China has repaid all her debts to Russia, her

* In 1963 the Chinese budget had dropped, apparently, to around 43 billion *yuan* (according to M. Francois Durand, in his *Le Financement du Budget en Chine Populaire*, Hongkong, Sirey, 1965, p. 401: in China itself the Budget has been a state secret for many years), but it has probably now recovered to its 1960 level.

exports, which normally reach $2¼ billion a year, all represent purchasing power for imports. But the prospects of increasing them are not rosy. The demand for the traditional "native" products of China—hog's bristles, duck's feathers, soyabeans, tea, tung oil, furs, hides, rough wool, silk—is hardly expanding in the major world markets, and some of these commodities face tough competition from synthetic substitutes (nylon for the hog's bristle which used to go into toothbrushes, for instance). In any case it is not at all certain that China could substantially increase production of these items. As with India and, a few decades earlier, Japan, the most likely expansion in export earnings will be in new manufactured articles.

In 1958 China was making good headway in other Asian markets with light consumer goods; cotton and synthetic textiles, sewing machines, simple metal goods, householdware, torches and the like. Since then the economics of her cotton textile exports have been confused by her need to import raw cotton from Africa and Pakistan, but the export drive has been resumed. Many markets are politically hostile to China, however (the rich American market is closed to her, and many Southeast Asian and Western European markets restrict Chinese imports). It is difficult to envisage China's being able to increase her export earnings by any dramatic amount in the near future, though they will undoubtedly rise gradually year by year.

China's imports currently run to about $2 billion of which almost one quarter goes on Western foodgrains and another large amount on raw rubber, timber, raw cotton, oil products and chemical fertilizer. Only a relatively small proportion is allocated to the capital goods imports which must be the backbone of the economic development programme. China's export surplus is thus about $250 million a year, most of which probably goes on shipping, insurance, diplomatic expenditure and other invisible items, and the balance on China's own foreign aid programme to the Afro-Asian Latin American neutrals.* This is a tight budget, not allowing the Chinese much flexibility.

During the Leap, China was going to catch up with British industrial production in ten years, and intended to overtake America in fifteen to twenty years. Now the Chinese leaders

* There is some opposition to this within the Party, as Chou En-lai revealed in his report to the National People's Congress at the end of 1964: "Quite a few people actively advocated . . . in the international field . . . reduction of assistance and support to the revolutionary struggle of other peoples" (*Peking Review*, 1 January 1965).

talk in terms of reaching the *present* level of Western European development in fifty or a hundred years. In the First Plan an annual growth of six per cent was probably achieved (from a low base), but the past ten years have interrupted that growth curve and the Chinese advertise their poor performance by the very fact of not issuing any production statistics since 1960. It is unlikely that China is now growing faster than by four or five per cent a year, though she may be capable of accelerating once she has recovered from the Cultural Revolution of 1966–8. Whether that capacity will be realized depends on political considerations.

Peking has made it clear that it knew the economic consequences of pursuing its ideological quarrel with Moscow: "We knew that our criticism of the errors of the leaders of the Communist Party of the Soviet Union would be followed by their revengeful acts and that inevitably this would bring with serious damage to the socialist construction of China. [But we must] hold firmly to the truth," * said the People's *Daily* in 1963.[16] The Communist leaders may also realize the economic cost of their political objectives in the Chinese countryside. Much of the recovery in 1962–5 was due to the incentives of the private plot and the rural fair, and the independence of the small production team. The astonishing capacity of the small Chinese entrepreneur to retain his commercial instincts is, in the words of a Peking journal in 1958, "terrifying." This reference was to Madame Yang Shou-ying, who began as a small trader in Chungking with 300 *yuan* ($120) and by speculation accumulated a tremendous capital, operating, almost on a guerrilla basis, on a wide scale throughout northwest China and the big cities—all under Communist rule.[17] The Chinglienko teahouse in Shanghai was in 1958, after nine years of Communism and with complete state control of the economy, still maintaining its pre-Liberation reputation as a trading mart: a local newspaper reported the case of a purchaser from Inner Mongolia who wanted a generator for his enterprise and who failed to get

---

* There is strong evidence that some Peking leaders would have preferred a compromise on ideology in order to save the economic development programme. Tao Chu, the influential Kwangtung province First Secretary, told a local meeting on the eve of the economic break in 1960 that, "The condition essential to the smooth progress of socialist construction" was to "make our utterances and our actions beneficial to international solidarity" (*Nanfang Daily*, Canton, 13 May 1960, quoted in CQ 8, 1961, p. 2). Later in the Cultural Revolution, one of the accusations against Liu Shao-chi and his supporters, including Tao, was that they were willing to sacrifice their ideological integrity in order to regain Soviet aid.

one through the official commercial channels in Peking, Tientsin, Wuhan or Shanghai, but who succeeded at last through a visit to this teahouse.[18]

This perhaps explains the *Red Flag* editorial of 1 January 1967, proclaiming the extension of the Cultural Revolution into the economy:

> Some muddle-headed people counterpose the revolution to production and think that once the great cultural revolution starts it will impede production. . . . These comrades have not thought through the question of what is the purpose of farming, of weaving, of steel-making? Is it for building socialism, or is it for building capitalism?

Because the Communist Party leadership contains more ideologues and guerrilla fighters than technocrats, it may continue to dissipate national energies on a fruitless quest for a social utopia, and thereby lengthen what already promises, because of China's poverty, to be a long hard road to prosperity and modernity. This was borne out in the Cultural Revolution of 1966–8. It is admirable to keep intellectuals in touch with their compatriots by regular manual work, but it makes no sense for one of the few men skilled in the processing of coke to spend twelve months in the fields. It is excellent that peasants should learn the rudiments of steel-making, but ridiculous that a modern chemical factory should stop work for three months in order to make improvised steel in its backyard.

China can feed her people at the low level to which they are accustomed, but she needs costly fertilizer to make the meals more nourishing and a serious birth control campaign to accelerate her economic growth. She is industrializing, but it is questionable whether her own technological resources are adequate to the needs of really fast growth. She has the advantage of a sound rural organization (lacking, for example, in India) and a considerable experience in the techniques of mass mobilization. If her decision-making could pass from the guerrilla generals to a new efficiency-minded élite, and if she could bring herself to a reconciliation with Russia, then her economic outlook would indeed be hopeful. As it is, she has not even felt able to announce the targets of the Third Five-Year Plan which was officially launched in January 1966.

THREE: *DIPLOMACY*

15: TAIWAN AND THE WEST

Island Irritant

THE CHINESE COMMUNISTS CAME TO POWER AT THE HEIGHT of the Cold War, and their ideology made it certain that their relations with the West would be difficult. This basic hostility has been hopelessly compounded, however, by Mao's inability to complete his conquest of China and expel Generalissimo Chiang Kai-shek from the island to which the Kuomintang Army and Government retired in 1949. Taiwan was originally inhabited by primitive tribes who now form a negligible minority of 200,000 in a population of some twelve million: the vast majority of today's Taiwanese are Chinese whose ancestors crossed to the "Beautiful Island" (Formosa, as the Portuguese called it) from the maritime provinces of China at various times during the past five centuries. This process of colonization qualified Taiwan as a province of China in Chinese eyes, but in 1895 imperial Peking was obliged to cede the island to Japan. During World War Two the allied leaders, Roosevelt, Churchill and Stalin, agreed that Taiwan would be returned to China after their victory, and in 1945 they accordingly authorized the then government of China, the Kuomintang, to receive the surrender of Japanese forces in the island after its half-century of Japanese colonial rule. The great powers thus tacitly acknowledged Taiwan's status as a part of China. The Kuomintang, however, soon alienated Taiwanese opinion by the outrageous behaviour of its soldiers and officials, and more than ten thousand Taiwanese lost their lives in the tragic clash between Kuomintang troops and local citizens in February 1947.

Since 1949 Taiwan has been the province from which Chiang has maintained the illusion of being still the President of China, and, because the Communists lack a naval fleet or air force of any consequence, he has been able to survive there undisturbed, his annual pledges to lead the Kuomintang armies back to the mainland appearing less plausible as the decades pass. If it had been left to the Chinese themselves to resolve, no doubt the superior numbers of the Communists would long ago have decided the matter, but Chiang had powerful allies across the Pacific Ocean.

When Mao proclaimed the People's Republic in 1949, Chiang was heavily discredited in American eyes. His weak leadership, together with the corruption and effeteness of his officials, were held largely responsible for the Communists' success. When Chiang asked for American military aid in defending Taiwan from Communist attack, President Truman refused, and for a few months in 1950 there was a chance that the two rivals for power in China would be allowed to play out the last act of their thirty-year drama without foreign intervention. But the Korean War spoilt that chance. Truman viewed the outbreak of fighting in Korea in the summer of 1950 as an attempt by international Communism to extend its sphere of influence by the use of force, and he saw no reason to assume that it might not be followed by a Communist invasion of Taiwan as part of a general Communist offensive in the West Pacific. He therefore ordered the US Seventh Fleet to maintain the peace in the Formosa Straits and prevent either side from attacking the other.

The Chinese Communists, who had probably not co-sponsored the Korean War,* saw this as an American decision "by armed force to obstruct our liberation of Taiwan," in the words of Chou En-lai. Washington thus became involved both in supporting the separate status of Taiwan, and in resuming American intervention in the Chinese civil war, not as a calculated policy, but as a hurried by-product of defensive preparations for a threatened new Pacific War.

President Eisenhower revoked Truman's order in 1953; his recall of the Seventh Fleet left it open to Chiang to stage a return to the mainland without American opposition. This,

---

* It was thought by most Western observers at the time that the Korean War was launched by the Communist powers acting in concert, but it seems more likely that it was Russian or North Korean initiative in which the Chinese did not at first participate (*China Crosses the Yalu,* by Allen S. Whiting, New York, Macmillan, 1960).

coupled with the failure of Chou En-lai at the Geneva Conference on Indochina to make much headway in establishing Peking's right to speak for China as long as the Kuomintang survived in Taiwan, led to the first of a series of sabre-rattling campaigns by Peking to recover the island. An all-party declaration in Peking in the summer of 1954 stated:

> We solemnly proclaim to the whole world that Taiwan is Chinese territory; that the occupation of Taiwan by the USA cannot be tolerated; and that it would also be intolerable to place Taiwan under United Nations trusteeship. . . .

The so-called offshore islands of Quemoy and Matsu, which were still held by the Kuomintang and were regarded by the USA as essential to Taiwan's defence, were bombarded by Communist artillery. The only important result of this was to press the Americans into their first formal commitment to give military assistance to Chiang. The USA–Taiwan Mutual Security Treaty of 1954 also contained Chiang's first formal undertaking not to attack the mainland without prior consultation with the Americans. But this did not prevent Peking's hostility to America from developing into implacable hatred against the power that thwarted her conclusion of the long civil war.

In the following year Peking sounded the war drums again, but the Bandung Conference of Afro-Asian statesmen, in which Chou En-lai was a leading participant, led to attempts to bring Peking and Washington to some kind of understanding. Talks were held in the Hotel Beau Rivage in Geneva between Alexis Johnson (for the USA) and Wang Ping-nan (for China), but they could not agree on the American demand that China should renounce the use of force in settling the Taiwan question. The furthest Chou En-lai would go was to say that:

> Conditions permitting, the Chinese people are ready to seek the liberation of Taiwan by peaceful means. If possible, the Chinese Government is willing to enter into negotiations with the responsible local authorities in Taiwan. It should be made clear that these would be negotiations between the central Government and local authorities. The Chinese people are firmly opposed to any idea of "two Chinas."

Peking insisted that it should not be asked to renounce force in what was a domestic matter, namely the final phase of the civil war: China was willing to make a mutual renunciation of the use of force in its international relationship with the USA, but not in putting down its own domestic foes.

In 1958 there was yet another "offshore island crisis," but the Kuomintang airlifted supplies to its beleaguered garrisons

and there was no change in the balance of power in the Formosa Straits. In 1962, when mainland morale was particularly low after the famine of 1960–1, Peking claimed to have
forestalled a Kuomintang invasion by securing advance information of its plan.[1] And there the matter still stands, because
China is still too poorly equipped to invade the now heavily
fortified island; Taiwan is thus a nagging reminder of the
Communists' weakness.

Politically, Taiwan abounds in contradictions, as Mao
would call them. The National Assembly and the Legislative
Council which were elected on the mainland in 1947–8 still
sit, more than twenty years later, and the Nationalist Government which derives its legal authority from these doddering
bodies prevails over the popularly elected provincial government of Taiwan. Senator Wayne Morse has called Taiwan "a
US puppet state," but Chiang has shown on many occasions
that he is no tool of the White House. In particular he makes
no concessions to the many Americans who would prefer him
to practise a little more democracy in his tiny island. The
press is government-controlled and no genuine opposition
parties are permitted. Lei Chen, the editor of a mildly critical
magazine called *Free China,* was sentenced to ten years' imprisonment for sedition in 1960, and since then even Americans call Taiwan a police state.[2]

Economically, however, the island has been made a show-
case for American aid (of which more than $4 billion has
been given in the twenty years since 1949—making an already well-provided and fertile island the most generously
aided part of the entire under-developed world). The American taxpayer has supplied two fifths of the island's gross capital formation, and the money has been well spent. Both
Chiang himself and the Americans learnt some lessons from
the fiasco of the last few years of Kuomintang rule on the
mainland, one being a better control of development funds.
For the past decade the Taiwanese economy has been growing at about seven per cent a year, which is certainly faster
than the mainland, and the average income per head is now
over $135 a year—double what prevails in the People's Re-
public. The Land-to-the-Tiller programme, completed in
1963, allows a maximum private holding of fifteen acres, and
has turned the island into a community of freeholder farmers. Textiles, steel, chemicals and many other industries have
been developed, and, if it were not for the political necessity
of maintaining an expensive army of 600,000 men, and for a
certain degree of corruption and bureaucratic inefficiency at
the lower levels of government, the economy would be in ex-

cellent shape. It is already good enough for the US to have ended its economic aid programme, Taiwan having developed economically to the point where US aid officials feel it can obtain the capital it needs through the normal channels of international private investment and loans.[3]

The political destiny of Taiwan is highly problematic. The two million mainlanders who came to the island after 1945 are growing old, and the emerging political force is the native Taiwan-Chinese community which regards these recent arrivals from the mainland almost as foreigners. But the furthest this community has yet been able to go is to elect one of its members, Kao Yu-shu, as Mayor of Taipei. If Taiwan were left alone, we should see a slow process of "Taiwanization" and a gradual transfer of power to the indigenous Chinese— who would probably grasp at independence or autonomy if it were offered them, but who have not since 1947 shed any blood for their beliefs and who might equally well settle for the anonymity of Chinese provincial status if Peking were to make it easy for them.

Chiang still rules in Taiwan, though he is now eighty-two years old and will soon hand over to his son, the sixty-year-old Chiang Ching-kuo, who studied in Moscow and lacks both the charm and the political gifts of his father. Whether Ching-kuo will be able to hold the Kuomintang Party together and avoid clashes with the increasingly impatient Taiwanese-Chinese is doubtful, and it would be rash to predict the consequences of his rule. Forward-looking Americans are already preparing the groundwork for Taiwanese independence,[4] pointing to the emergence of what Chester Bowles, the American diplomat, called "an independent Sino-Formosan nation." It would suit American interests admirably if the government in Taiwan now admitted defeat in the Chinese civil war, quietly dropped its pretensions to be the Government of the Republic of China, and accepted a new role as government of the independent state of Taiwan, entitled to its own membership in the United Nations (though not to a permanent seat in the UN Security Council) and to its own bilateral security arrangements with the allies of its choosing. The question of the political future of the island could be put to a plebiscite, possibly under UN supervision.

This line of thinking obtains ready support in Western Europe, where the plebiscite is a respected mechanism for national self-expression. It may even appeal to the Taiwan-Chinese themselves (though they have no way of expressing their genuine opinion and one cannot be certain *what* they feel), but it certainly angers the two serious contenders for power in Taiwan—the Kuomintang and the Communists. For all their ideological differences, both these groups are Chinese to the core, and both would deeply resent the creation of an independent state out of what both regard as a regular province of the motherland. We have seen their reluctance to concede independence to Mongolia after a plebiscite, and Taiwan is even more strongly attached, culturally, to the main body of China.

Dennis Bloodworth, the British correspondent, reported in the summer of 1962 that the Chiang family had negotiated a settlement with Peking under which neither side would attack the other until Chiang's death, when Taiwan would return to the national fold with provincial autonomy.[5] Everyone vigorously denied the story, but there are certainly connections between the two sets of leaders [6] and it seems the most plausible solution to the problem. Any solution which removed the fear of American attack *via* Taiwan would suit Peking, and the Kuomintang might even prefer a minor position in the Chinese body politic (one or two Ministries, a Governorship and a small place of honour, however superficial) to supreme power in a tiny banana republic vulnerable to the pressures of American businessmen, forgotten by the world as no longer controversial, and not even entitled to call itself Chinese.

Meanwhile the unresolved status of Taiwan poisons all attempts to reconcile Peking and Washington,[7] as Nehru, Sihanouk and many other intermediaries discovered. From Peking, American policy appears as an unprovoked prevention of China's reunification, while from Washington the Chinese appear as fanatics set on spreading an immoral, atheistic creed by force. The other differences between the two countries—the detention of American airmen shot down over China during the Korean war and the quarrel over the exchange of newsmen [8]—are minor matters which a basic rapprochement would settle. The Americans regard their airmen as unjustly detained, but the Chinese claim they are imprisoned after due legal process and sentence (for espionage). The Chinese say thousands of their students are unable to return home from the USA, but they agreed in 1955 that any Chinese in the USA who feels that he is being prevented from returning can apply to the Indian Embassy in Washington, and no such application has been made. China once gave visas to a group of American newsmen selected by herself, but the USA insists that what Washington regards as a representative group should be admitted. The USA, however, reserves the right to reject individual visa applications from Chinese newsmen, and so this question has become thoroughly entangled in mutual mistrust.

China's intransigence has hardened over the years, but America's has softened a little. In the early 1950s the American leaders did not even try to maintain the outward courtesies: 25,000 Americans had, after all, died in the Korean War, which most of them then assumed had been instigated by Peking. Dean Acheson told the United Nations General Assembly in 1951 that China's international conduct was "so low that it would take considerable improvement to raise it to the general level of barbarism," and at the Geneva Conference on Indochina in 1954 John Foster Dulles refused to shake hands with Chou En-lai—"leader of a regime which gained *de facto* power in China through bloody war; which has liquidated millions of Chinese; which diverts the economic resources of its impoverished people to military efforts, so that they starve by the million. . . ." [9] The Dullesian view had distinguished exponents in Western Europe also: Churchill told the British House of Commons on 10 May 1951:

> We all know they have established a reign of terror in China with hostile executions, mob butchery and merciless purges characteristic of Communist tyranny wherever it is applied, especially in the transitional stages, all over the world. We ought not to have any sympathies with Red China. . . .[10] *

This was still the era of the Cold War. After the Soviet-Western thaw, Kennedy was able to bring a more tolerant approach to China. Before his election to the Presidency he had called for "open windows between the peoples of China and the peoples of the Western nations," and his representative at the 1961 Geneva talks on Laos, Averell Harriman, even condescended to shake hands with the Chinese Foreign Minister, Chen Yi. But Kennedy's plan to work gradually towards recognition of Peking by first recognizing the Mongolian People's Republic was defeated through the efforts of the Chiang Kai-shek lobby in Washington,[11] and by then Chinese policy had become even more bitterly anti-American. The world was shocked when the *Daily Worker* of Peking published, after Kennedy's assassination, a cartoon showing his head on the ground with blood pouring from the bullet wound in his temple, and a caption reading: "Kennedy Bites the Dust." [12] The split with Russia obliges China to take a more censorious attitude toward America, since one of the major debates

---

* It ought not to have provoked surprise that China was almost the only country not to send a representative to his funeral in 1965.

within the Communist fraternity concerns the extent to which Communists should cooperate with the USA. China is the only country in the world to have organized a "Hate America Week." [13]

It is American hostility which keeps China out of the United Nations. Representatives of the Chinese Communist government did once attend meetings of the UN. In 1950, although the Security Council rejected Peking's application for the Chinese seat by thirty-three votes to sixteen (with ten abstentions), it did invite Peking to participate in its debate on the Taiwan question. General Wu Hsiu-chuan expounded the Communist case on the matter; he was fêted by Trygve Lie, Sir Gladwyn Jebb and Sir Benegal Rau, but left without having persuaded any government to change its mind. A few months later the General Assembly branded China as an aggressor in Korea, which Chou En-lai described as "an insult to the Chinese people," and since then the UN has gone through the annual ritual of rejecting the argument (put first by Russia, then, after Bandung, by India, and more recently by Cambodia and Albania) that Peking should occupy the Chinese seat. But the vote in recent years has narrowed, the result in November 1965 being actually a tie of forty-seven to forty-seven, with twenty abstentions. Only determined lobbying by the Americans keeps Peking out.

China displays mixed feelings about this annual blackball. On the one hand she occasionally reminds the world of the validity of her case for UN membership,[14] while on the other hand she affects a contempt for the whole proceedings. Since the Sino-Soviet split, which has led China to make common cause with the Afro-Asian-Latin American countries, Peking's attitude towards the UN has hardened. A secret Chinese military briefing in 1961 explained that by joining the UN, "We should lose our freedom of action"; [15] in 1960 at about the same time a *People's Daily* editorial declared flatly that, "The peoples of the world cannot put their trust, their hopes for liberation and world peace, in the UN controlled by American imperialism." [16] Peking gave verbal support to the Indonesian plan for a new world body to replace the UN, but at the same time makes it clear that it will join the UN as soon as the Kuomintang is expelled from it.[17] *

* Compromises are often canvassed, the favourite one being a separate seat for Taiwan *as Taiwan* (not as the Republic of China) to compensate it for its loss of the permanent Chinese seat in the Security Coun-

Hatred of America leads China to seek and cultivate anti-American feelings everywhere, even in Europe. One of the unique features of Chinese foreign policy is the concept of a "vast intermediate zone" between America on the one hand and the Communist world on the other, resentful of both Moscow and Washington. "France, Germany, Italy, Britain —if she can cease to be America's agent, Japan and ourselves: that is the third force," Mao explained to visiting French politicians in 1964.[18] The *People's Daily* added Canada, Australia and New Zealand, and further defined the intermediate zone by saying that, "While the ruling classes are exploiters and oppressors, these countries are themselves subjected to US control, interference and bullying. . . . Therefore, they have something in common with the socialist countries." [19]

This philosophy has some analogy with that of de Gaulle, whose diplomatic recognition of Peking in January 1964 went some way towards what Edgar Faure, the former French Premier who visited China in 1963 to negotiate the new links, called the "reintegration in the international community of a country representing nearly one quarter of humanity, and in whose absence none of the big problems of our time can be solved or even effectively approached." [20] Naturally the Chinese Communists have reservations about de Gaulle, of whom Chou En-lai said grudgingly in 1964: "as the head of the French Republic and a bourgeois statesman, General de Gaulle deserves the name of a person who is courageous in facing realities and dares to act accordingly." [21] France has not accepted the Peking point of view about Taiwan: that its international status is settled, and that any suggestion of self-determination for the Taiwanese is an intervention in Chinese domestic affairs, much as a Chinese proposal for the self-government of Texas or Scotland would be an unwarranted interference. Like Britain, France regards the ultimate status of Taiwan as still unsettled and a proper subject for international discussion, though

cil. This is completely unacceptable to either side. A recent variant on it is the proposal to create several Chinese seats, one of which could go to Taiwan and others to Inner Mongolia, Tibet or Sinkiang, on a formula similar to that by which Byelorussia and the Ukraine have separate UN seats. This is more promising, but still rich with difficulties. On 29 September 1965, Foreign Minister Chen Yi issued new conditions for Peking's entry, including Charter revision, membership review, and a cancellation of the 1950 resolution branding China as an aggressor in Korea, but these may be treated as bargaining points.

France does not go so far as to have a Consul in Taiwan.*
French recognition has not, for this reason, produced any
dramatic results.

Canada now does a substantial trade with China, selling
over $100 million worth of wheat a year and buying little
more than one tenth of this amount of Chinese products in
return. Canadian businessmen, diplomats and newspaper correspondents frequently visit China, but the Canadian Government has until recently resisted any pressure to recognize Peking.

The paucity of contact and understanding between China
and the West is alarming, and some observers hope that
Japan, now so highly westernized and American-oriented,
will ultimately provide a bridge between the two. China
shares a common culture and written language with Japan,
but Peking argues that Japan's acceptance of American military bases on her soil makes her "a colony of the USA," and
brings constant pressure on Tokyo to shake off American influence. The right-wing Japanese Government recognizes the
Kuomintang, not the Communists, and Japanese affection for
their former colony, Taiwan, makes rational attitudes even
more difficult. Trade between China and Japan is increasing,
but the Japanese do not forget that in 1958 the Chinese suddenly cut these links because of a relatively minor incident
involving disrespect to their flag on Japanese soil. Although
the Japanese would be ideal successors to the Russians as
technical advisers for Chinese industry, the possibility of their
gaining the necessary minimum of Chinese confidence seems
slight. The Chinese now trust no one.

Paradoxically, it is China's hydrogen bomb which may
bring her diplomatic isolation to an end. In 1960 the National People's Congress resolved that "any international disarmament agreement which is arrived at without the participation of the Chinese People's Republic and the signature of
its delegates cannot have any binding force on China." [22]
Now, since 1964, the Chinese have their own nuclear potential, and American officials have conceded the inevitability of
admitting Peking to the disarmament conference table. China
has blasted her way into a seat at the world's highest counsels. "The development of nuclear weapons by China is for
defence," the *New China News Agency* stated after the first
Chinese explosion, "and for protecting the Chinese people

---

* Britain maintains at Tamsui a Consul attached to the provincial government, not to the Republic of China government in Taipei: she thus
maintains a precarious representation in the island at the cost of some
unpopularity in both Taipei and Peking.

from the danger of the United States' launching a nuclear war." In its policy regarding nuclear weapons, it added, China would commit "neither the error of adventurism nor the error of capitulationism. The Chinese people can be trusted. . . ."[23] Gradually the Western powers will seek to convince China that simple declarations of good intent are not enough, and that fairly complicated machinery is needed to satisfy men's thirst for peace. One of the concessions to be offered to China, as Senator Edward Kennedy's speech on 20 March 1969 suggested, will presumably be an end to the humiliating diplomatic quarantine to which the West has condemned her ever since the Korean War.

16: HONGKONG

Window on the West

PRINCE NORODOM SIHANOUK, THE CAMBODIAN CHIEF OF STATE, once said that China was so peaceable, so non-aggressive, that she did not even use force to take possession of her "national territories" in Taiwan, Hongkong and Macao.[1] We have seen that this failure is, in the case of Taiwan, for lack of means rather than any objection to violence as such. Hongkong and Macao, the two tiny European colonies which survive in the Delta of the Pearl River, present a different case. Peking says little about them, but they play in fact a very important role in China's international relations.

The British were pleasantly surprised when the People's Liberation Army stopped at the Shumchun River in 1949, and did not immediately proceed to "liberate" Hongkong. It was supposed that Mao Tse-tung needed a breathing-space to consolidate his newly-won power over the whole of China, and did not seek a clash of arms with Britain (and possibly with Britain's ally, the USA) at such a moment. But gradually it became clear that the *status quo* in Hongkong was in Peking's interest, and is likely to remain so for the foreseeable future. The reasons are mainly economic. As a "Scheduled Territory" in the Sterling Area, and with a free money market which earns it the description "Switzerland of Asia," Hongkong pays for its imports in hard convertible currency.

With a population of almost four million (larger than Tennessee's or Norway's or New Zealand's), ninety-eight per cent of Chinese race, its daily needs are considerable, and, as a city with a 'back garden' only one third the size of Rhode Island, its natural provider is China's neighbouring Kwangtung province.

Hongkong today depends on China for about one third of its staple food supplies and one quarter of its water.* The People's Republic is, in effect, grocer to a large city of its own people—for sterling. In 1968 China sold $398 million worth of goods to Hongkong,[2] mainly food and consumer articles, but bought only $8 million worth in return. Her visible trade surplus was thus almost $390 million, and her trade officials are making every effort to increase it in future.

Besides these visible earnings, China also receives from Hongkong another sum, estimated at almost $250 million a year, in the form of banking and retailing profits, remittances by Chinese residents in Hongkong or Southeast Asia to their families in the People's Republic, and Overseas Chinese investments in the government's bonds and economic enterprises. Her total inflow in convertible foreign exchange from and through Hongkong is thus normally over $650 million a year, or about half her total inflow from all sources. If Hongkong were reintegrated into China, Peking would suffer overnight a fifty per cent cut in her hard currency earnings.

There are other advantages. The Chinese Import and Export Corporations do a large part of their business with Western merchants through the Hongkong-registered firm, China Resources Limited, their agent in Hongkong with offices in the Bank of China skyscraper which Peking also owns. It was in Hongkong that China Resources took soundings about possible Western wheat imports in 1960. Here contact can be maintained with the fifty governments which have official commercial or political representation in the Colony; only one third of these have offices in Peking, and such governments as those of Australia, Canada, New Zealand and West Germany keep up their dialogue with Peking largely through their missions in Hongkong. But the Colony is not only a convenient negotiating centre for trade. When the Communists and Kuomintang wish to hold secret discussions, it is to Hongkong that they turn. Premier Chou En-lai suggested

* The Hongkong government tries to prevent this dependence from growing to larger proportions, but in a relationship comparable to that between Long Island and the US mainland, all that can be done is artificially to maintain other sources and methods of supply—at some cost.

Hongkong in 1964 as a neutral site for exploratory discussions with Japan pending a Sino-Japanese diplomatic agreement.*

Finally, the Hongkong postmark has a value for Peking, whose propaganda services can reach, through the Hongkong Post Office, countries where a Chinese postmark is either embarrassing or unacceptable. The USA, Taiwan, South Korea, South Vietnam, Thailand, Malaysia, the Philippines and many African and Latin-American countries have for a long time been in this category, and now the Sino-Soviet dispute has widened the field. Two *Pravda* correspondents who visited Hongkong in 1964 were shown, on their journey through various countries of Europe and Asia, anti-Soviet pamphlets and books addressed to individuals and offices in the socialist countries: "As is apparent from the envelopes," they reported, "these foul concoctions had been posted in Hongkong. . . . Hongkong has from ancient times been a city of ill-fame, noted for its oppression and arbitrariness, its gambling houses and prostitution, and a refuge for gangsters and drug smugglers: now it is becoming the main foreign centre of the slanderous propaganda and subversive activity conducted by Peking against the Soviet Union and the world Communist movement." [3]

The advantages which China derives from maintaining the *status quo* in Hongkong are corollaries of her present poverty and international ostracism, and are therefore likely to retain importance in the immediately foreseeable future. The position in international law is that, by the Treaty of Nanking (1842) and the Convention of Peking (1860), the island of Hongkong and the tip of the Kowloon peninsula are ceded in perpetuity to the British Crown, while the much larger area of the so-called New Territories, lying behind the city of Kowloon, is leased for ninety-nine years under the Convention of Peking of 1898.† The lease has therefore almost

---

* Hongkong is now the only convenient piece of ideologically neutral ground in East Asia: the North and South Koreans held talks there in 1964 about a possible joint team for the Olympic Games in Tokyo (they failed), and this is the only city in the area where unofficial contacts can safely be made between the Asian Communist countries and such fiercely anti-Communist nations as Thailand, the Philippines and Malaysia.

† In practice Hongkong will stand or fall as an integrated unit: more than half of its manufacturing industry, which produces about $1¾ billion worth of goods annually and is the community's most vital source of livelihood, is now conducted on leased territory, and the big new water conservancy projects are also on leased territory. The reversion of the leased territories to China in 1998 would strike at the heart of the Hongkong economy and leave a virtually unviable pocket of ceded territory in British sovereignty.

thirty years still to run. When the Communists came to power in 1949, they declared that they would:

> Examine the treaties concluded by previous Chinese Govern-
> ments, treaties that had been left over by history, and . . .
> recognize, abrogate, revise or renegotiate them according to
> the respective contents. . . . With regard to the outstanding
> issues, which are a legacy from the past, we have always held
> that, when conditions are ripe, they should be settled peace-
> fully and through negotiations and that, pending a settlement,
> the *status quo* should be maintained. Within this category are
> the questions of Hongkong, Kowloon and Macao. . . .[4]

Peking was not allowed by London to set up any official con-
sular office in Hongkong, because the British Colonial authorities feared that such an office would inevitably become involved in domestic issues within Hongkong. But a formidable
quasi-diplomatic presence is maintained in the persons of the
senior resident representatives of the Bank of China, of China
Resources Limited, and of the *New China News Agency*—
supported by one or two local notabilities sympathetic to the
Communist cause. There is practical day-to-day cooperation
between the British authorities and the administration of
Kwangtung province on such matters as border traffic. The
relative poverty of Kwangtung provides a constant incentive
for its inhabitants to migrate to Hongkong: normally the flow
is kept down to a thin trickle by the tacit cooperation of the
two sets of border authorities, though for one brief period in
1962 it assumed unacceptable proportions (apparently as an
unexpected consequence of Peking's temporary liberalization
of the procedures relating to exit permits at that time).

People in the communes close to the Hongkong border are
naturally influenced by what they hear of the better conditions in the British Colony, and this led the local authorities
to initiate in 1963 an "anti-Hongkong" campaign against
thinking of, longing for and envying Hongkong. A Canton
journalist who visited the Shataukok Commune actually on
the border itself reported that, "All ugly ideas and decadent
life of the capitalist society spread their influences here every
minute," but that the older residents exposed the realities of
Hongkong life to counteract its subversive appeal, describing
the "stench of wine and meat inside the red doors; the bones
of the frozen dead along the roadsides. . . ."[5] But formal relations between the Kwangtung and Peking authorities on
the one hand and the British Colonial officials on the other
hand were, until 1967, correct—even cordial. A Vice-Gover-
nor of Kwangtung province joined the celebrations of his

clan in Hongkong in 1963, and the provincial administration was most helpful and cooperative in supplying emergency water during the 1963–4 drought* and digging a sixty-mile channel for the provision of 15 billion gallons of water a year to Hongkong from a Chinese river. A Vice-Minister of Trade in the Peking Government visited Hongkong for a week in 1963 and was received by the British Governor. Even the dispute over the Kowloon Walled City in the early part of 1963 was allowed to die away.†

For a revolutionary and nationalistic government such as that in Peking, it is an obvious embarrassment to continue to acquiesce in the foreign rule of small pieces of Chinese soil. If this were purely a domestic Chinese affair, it would appear as a straight conflict between pride and profit. The loss of $700 million a year would further delay China's industrialization programme, and presumably the Peking leaders feel able to swallow their pride and exercise their patience because of this. But they are also vulnerable to world opinion. The United Nations Special Committee on Colonialism regularly debates Hongkong (the list of colonies is getting very small, after all), and when it did so in 1964 the Soviet delegate insisted that Hongkong be "restored" to China.[6] India has felt obliged to rebut the Chinese charge that she is less ardently anti-colonialist than China, reminding Peking (and the world) that while the Indians have expelled the Portuguese from Goa by force, the Chinese do nothing about Portuguese and British colonialism on their soil. In the autumn of 1964 the World Youth Forum in Moscow touched on the matter: the Ceylonese delegation called for the independence of all colonies, including Hongkong and Macao, but the Chinese delegation condemned the reference to these two territories, which "the Chinese people will recover without fail at an appropriate time."

The Russians have eagerly seized this weapon against China in the ideological dispute. The Soviet Union, Khru-

---

* Hongkong households were rationed to four hours of freely running water in their taps every fourth day, for twelve months.

† The original walled town of Kowloon, which was inhabited at the time of the cession in 1842, has always provided the potential of dispute because China claimed some vestigial sovereignty there. In 1962 the British authorities began to tear down some of the old buildings as part of a slum clearance scheme: a local resident complained to Peking, and the Chinese government took the matter up, charging a "gross violation of China's sovereignty." Britain disputed the sovereignty, but quietly dropped the rehousing scheme. See Derek Davies, "The Walled City—Hope Deferred," in FEER, 31 January 1963, p. 225.

shchev told the Supreme Soviet in Moscow in 1962, had supported Indonesia's liberation of West Irian and India's liberation of Goa, yet remnants of European colonialism survived in Hongkong and Macao.[7] "The smell spreading from these areas is no sweeter than the stench given off from Goa." [8] Khrushchev's point, of course, was not that Peking ought to act on the Hongkong question, but that she ought to be as understanding about other Communist nations' apparent tactical concessions to imperialism (e.g. in Cuba) as she expected them to be about her proposed timetable for Hongkong. In 1964 *Izvestiya* gave an account of the mass crossing of 140,000 refugees from China into Hongkong two years before:

> It is hard to realize, and impossible to reconcile oneself to the fact, that these refugees are from the Chinese People's Republic. . . . When you see these exhausted people, who have only occasional earnings in Hongkong but at the same time refuse to go back, a thought strikes you. Where are the Chinese leaders leading their country, these leaders who favour ultra-revolutionary phrases but neglect the task of improving the life of their own people? [9]

In the spring of 1967 these emotional pressures on the Hongkong Communist leaders were intensified by the Cultural Revolution and by their need to prove their loyalty to Maoism after the disgrace of Tao Chu, their patron and the former Party boss of Kwangtung. Four minor labour disputes were built up into a confrontation between the local Communists and the British colonial government, in the course of which Communist journalists were imprisoned for inciting disorder. It was this which led to the burning of the British Mission in Peking in August, the deterioration of Sino-British relations that fall, and the detention of Anthony Grey, the Reuter's Correspondent in Peking. It was clear, however, that those in power in both Peking and Canton did not wish to expel the British from Hongkong (though they would presumably have welcomed an improvement in the status and power of the Communists in the Colony), and the Hongkong Communists received only half-hearted support from the mainland: a couple of cheques for the strike pay bill and verbal statements aimed at frightening the British authorities. The end result of the affair was to weaken the Communist standing in Hongkong, inflict temporary damage to the Colony's economy (hurting China itself more than Hongkong), and provoke the British administration into some much-needed reforms in labour legislation and local government.

Curiously enough the four million Chinese who live in

Hongkong constitute the least important factor in the city's future: most of them eschew politics and remain silent in the many battles of words that are waged around them. Both the Communists and the Kuomintang have small followings in the schools and trade unions, and among the intellectuals, but after the disastrous politically inspired Kowloon riots of 1956, when the police had to use tanks and fifty-one people died, the two factions have tacitly agreed not to fight each other. Half the adult Chinese in Hongkong were born there, but have branches of their families in the People's Republic: the other half are "refugees," mostly from Kwangtung province but some (and a rich and vocal "some") from Shanghai and other northern Chinese cities. No legal obligation ties these people to Hongkong. They may return to China at any time, and in the past there has always been a drift back to China when times are bad—during the 1929 Depression, for instance, and during the Second World War. So Professor E. Stuart Kirby, former Head of the Economics Faculty at Hongkong University, has likened the problem of self-government for Hongkong to "that of self-government for a railway station." [10] Most residents in the Colony, whether Chinese or not, do not feel rooted or committed to the soil of this particular political unit. They are transients hoping to move on—to Taiwan, Britain, the USA, or even back to China in the event of a change in government policy there. There is no separate Hongkong nationality.

Sinification of public life proceeds very slowly, partly because the Briton is respected as an impartial umpire between the Cantonese and the northern minority, partly because few Chinese care to bow to foreign modes and manners to the extent that joining a colonial administrative service entails, and partly because it is understood that Hongkong remains separate from China only because it is British-run. Peking would not tolerate a democratically elected government of Chinese in Hongkong, because this would threaten the Communists' authority far more seriously than a British façade which everyone knows must eventually crumble. Even the University students are slow in expressing any viewpoint which might remotely be called "Hongkong nationalism." There is a handful of small political organizations which contest the few elected seats of power for which the Hongkong constitution provides (the real power is the Governor, who controls the appointments to his advisory Councils), but they are moderate both in outlook and numbers. "We are not in favour of either political independence or self-government," said Dr. Raymond

Lee, leader of one of them, in 1964; "to advocate such views means political suicide and economic death." [11]

When China does want the situation to change, force will not be necessary. A total economic and physical boycott of Hongkong by the Chinese would scare all its sensitive capital away, ruin its economy and render it virtually unviable. But the chances are that China will not feel able to practise on her own doorstep the anti-colonialism which she preaches elsewhere until her economic development has advanced a little further. Meanwhile Hongkong will continue to offer her a window on the world (and the world a window on to China) which is one of her few channels of genuine relationship with the West. But Hongkong does not so far provide the West with clear evidence of Chinese aggressiveness. It is in Southeast Asia that we shall find more clues to China's expansionist image.

17: SOUTHEAST ASIA

What Kind of Expansionism

THE ATTITUDE OF THE CHINESE COMMUNISTS TOWARDS THE small neighbouring countries which formerly acknowledged, in some degree, the authority of the Emperor in Peking is understandably a mixed one. Their sense of nationalism makes them proud of the historical achievements of the Chinese civilizing mission, and yet intellectually they are also ashamed of the political oppression into which that mission degenerated. Their sentiments basically correspond with those of Europeans now shorn of their empires, though with the important difference that the Chinese lost their former dependencies less to the forces of local nationalism than to rival foreign imperialisms. The deepest layer of contemporary Chinese sentiment on the matter is thus a desire to expel the foreign rival and resume China's former authority; this has become overlaid by the more modern idea of accepting the self-determination of these former subject states, though the deeper layer sometimes shows through. The two layers are in harmony as long as the Chinese are assisting the local nationalists to eject their most recent, European or Japanese, overlords. But once the usurper has gone, the Chinese attitude becomes strained by the tension between emotion and intellect; a tension that seeks relief in pursuing the new Chinese mission, satisfying to heart and mind alike, of spreading Communism.

Mao Tse-tung was once (in 1939) explicit about the conquests by foreign imperialists of "a large number of states tributary to China, as well as a part of her own territory. Japan appropriated Korea, Taiwan, the Ryukyu islands, the Pescadores, and Port Arthur; England took Burma, Bhutan, Nepal and Hongkong; France seized Annam; even a miserable little country like Portugal took Macao from us. . . ." [1] * This catalogue, when read alongside Mao's earlier statement to Edgar Snow, that, "It is the immediate task of China to regain all our lost territories," [2] sends a shiver down the spine of many Southeast Asian leaders. Their fears are intensified by the "cartographical aggression" which some see China as waging. In a book entitled *A Brief History of Modern China*, first published in Peking in 1953, a map† is given which shows the "Chinese territories taken by the imperialists from 1840 to 1919": these lands comprise parts of Soviet Siberia and Soviet Kazakhstan, together with most of Southeast Asia, including the Andaman islands and the Sulu archipelago (now ruled by India and the Philippines respectively). Anyone glancing at British history books would see thirty or so present sovereign members of the United Nations there portrayed as within the British Empire of that day, yet historical maps are not cited as evidence of present British expansionism. China is now in full mutual diplomatic relationship with almost all the countries that once bent the knee to her, and has signed treaties of friendship, treaties regulating economic relations, or border treaties (sometimes all three) with every

---

* In this Mao shares the feelings of his political rival, Chiang Kai-shek (see Chiang's *China's Destiny*, London, Dobson, 1947, pp. 38–9 and *passim*). Sun Yat-sen wrote that "Annam and Burma were both formerly Chinese territory," and that "Siam paid tribute to China."

† Peking alleges that some maps quoted by foreign critics of Chinese policy are forgeries. Thus the *New China News Agency*, on 15 August 1962, declared that a map and article on the unequal treaties reproduced in New Delhi that summer as of NCNA origin were both false. Anna Louise Strong, pressed on this point by correspondents abroad (she lives in Peking), commented: "Any history that covered the Ming and Ching Dynasties and showed them on maps would have all of Southeast Asia, Burma, parts of India and the Soviet Far East in China. So what? China's present Government recognizes historic changes and has made boundary treaties with most of its neighbours. . . . Modern treaties speak louder than historic maps." (*Letter from China*, No. 11, 25 October 1963).

one of her contiguous neighbours. It is true that the Russians now allege that Mao Tse-tung once told Khrushchev that Mongolia ought to be Chinese, but Peking has so far maintained the outward diplomatic courtesies and has not formally laid claim to Mongolia.[3]

China has in fact given up these old tributary claims, though pride makes her leaders reluctant to say so in unequivocal terms. But this forbearance is qualified by four separate foreign policy objectives of the Chinese Communist Government in Asia, each one of which contributes to the image of an expansionist China.

The first of these aims is to settle China's frontiers definitively and fairly. The Chinese resent the way in which their border territories were nibbled away (by the British in the Himalayas, the French in Vietnam, the Russians in Central Asia and Siberia), but recognize the just rights of the new nation states which have inherited the creations of European imperialism. The question is: Does justice require the new states to make any amends to China for what was grabbed at a time when China was too weak to resist? The Chinese feel that the new states ought to make gestures, at least, recognizing their debt, but other Asian leaders, enabled by a happier recent history to be more forward-looking and less concerned with the historical record, do not share this premise: hence the misunderstandings which helped to turn Nehru from an eager friend to a bitter foe of the new China. China, concerned with the restoration of her pride, wanted others to express a willingness to make historical amends (which the Chinese would then politely refuse, amid scenes of joy and goodwill). India, Burma and the rest, no longer concerned with matters of pride after their liberation from European rule, and with leaders full of the doctrine of self-determination, felt that any change in frontiers ought to be justified not on historical grounds but on arguments relating to the present wishes of the local population, to current economic and communication needs and to plain good sense.

Burma affords an excellent example of this difficulty. From the end of 1953 Peking began to publish maps which included revisions of the Chinese border: they belatedly recognized, for instance, the cession of the Pamir plateau to Soviet Tadzikhstan and of the narrow Afghan corridor to Afghanistan, and made other minor adjustments which brought the Chinese maps more closely in correspondence with Western and Soviet atlases.[4] The Kuomintang maps had not given anything away; these new Communist maps at least made some concessions to the realities of the preceding century or so. In the case of Burma they acknowledged the Burmese claim to one piece of territory previously depicted in Peking as Chinese, but they took an entirely new bite out of the Wa territory shared between the two. The Wa are a large tribe which bestrides the Sino-Burmese border. This was an area to which Kuomintang troops had retreated in 1949 and where they were still spasmodically fighting against Communist forces, and it was probably in order to justify the chase that the new border claim was tacitly made by Peking.

China's southern and western borderlands are not like Belgium or Saarland, settled and beyond the disputes of geographers: they are mostly mountainous, inhabited only sparsely and then by people of small tribes not obviously belonging to any of the new nation states of twentieth-century Asia, and were in 1949 largely unsurveyed and unadministered. The hold of the central Chinese Government over these distant, almost inaccessible regions was slight (even, in the case of Tibet, non-existent) and when the Communists came to power in 1949 they had little information about their own frontiers. What had been collected by previous governments was largely lost in the civil war and was in any case out of date. Mao knew that he would need several years in which to consolidate his power in the border areas (there was not even a motorable road to Tibet from China until 1954), obtain local information about the border and its history and then formulate a specific policy for its negotiation with the foreign countries concerned. It was for this reason that the Chinese stonewalled whenever Nehru or U Nu asked for border negotiations in the early years.

The new Peking maps of 1953 caused alarm south of the Himalayas. U Nu, then the Burmese Prime Minister, said frankly at a banquet in Peking in 1954 that, "We had at one time entertained grave apprehensions about the possibility of interference by the People's Republic of China in our internal affairs." [5] Prime Minister Chou En-lai assured him, as he had assured Nehru, that a friendly delimitation of the border would take place at the appropriate time, but an incursion of Chinese Communist troops in the Wa State of Burma in 1956 brought the matter to a head. The two sides now discovered that, for all their professions of friendliness, their conflicting interests over the border made a quick and easy agreement impossible. The Chinese wanted three villages inhabited by another minority group, the Kachin tribe, because they commanded seven high mountain passes into China (which was precisely why the British had been careful to take them over); but the Kachins rejected Burmese appeals to cooperate in this transfer. The Burmese, on the other hand, badly needed a small tract, previously leased from China, which carried Burma's only road linking her Shan and Kachin States.[6]

At first U Nu thought these two mutual needs could form the basis of a bargain, but when he triumphantly went to Peking with a hard-won Kachin agreement (that the three villages go to China) in his pocket, he found that Chou wanted two other areas in exchange for the road tract, and did not regard the Kachin villages as valid bargaining counters. Presumably the Chinese had found that they urgently needed this further adjustment on their Burmese border, either for strategic reasons or for reasons of internal politics between the Chinese central authorities and the local tribes whom they administered. It would have suited Chou to have appeared at this juncture as leader of a government that could show generosity and goodwill on a matter causing such anxiety among her neighbours, and only the emergence of new local factors on the Chinese side could have led to such a rebuff. But the Burmese pressed hard for a settlement, and when Chou visited Rangoon at the end of 1956 he was met with placards, carried by Kachin students, reading "Friendships forever, cession never." At a formal speech Chou said, as if addressing his colleagues at home more than his Burmese listeners, that China must "make even more strict demands on herself to put resolutely into practice the principles of peaceful coexistence" and promised that China would not be guilty of "big power chauvinism" in her policy towards Burma.[7] Later the chief Burmese delegate at the long and involved negotiations which ultimately produced an agreed border, declared to his Chinese hosts at a Peking banquet: "If a nation takes the size of its territory, the strength of its armed forces and abundance of its natural resources as a starting point, and acts on the principle of the strong bullying the weak, this can only be called a poison that will sacrifice tens of millions of lives. . . ."[8] The Burmese border settlement was followed by others negotiated with Nepal (where the ownership of Mount Everest* could have been an insuperable difficulty), Mongolia, Pakistan and Afghanistan. In each case China formally

---

* The Chinese fail to understand why a Nepalese, if he is genuinely free from Whitehall control, would continue to use the name of an English civil servant for his sacred mountain: they themselves use the Tibetan name Cholmolungma, the Nepalese name Sagarmatha or a Chinese name which means "Nepal-China Friendship Peak." The continuing use of such names as Everest and the McMahon Line is regarded by Peking as "cultural imperialism." The border now runs through the middle of the summit.

surrendered many of her earlier claims, but vigorously argued for the points where present self-interest supported historic sentiment. It would be unjust to read into these border negotiations a deliberate policy of expansion.

The second Chinese objective in East Asia, after settling her borders, is to insist on a share of the influence exerted by the great world powers on the smaller countries of the area. If Britain and America are to assume responsibilities for the affairs of Southeast Asia or the Far East, the Chinese say, then China should also be recognized as having responsibilities there. Western powers, General Wu Hsiu-chuan told a United Nations press conference in New York at the end of 1950, were trying to deny China's "rights of expression and representation on important Far Eastern problems." [9] Sir Benegal Rau, the Indian delegate, had told the UN Security Council in its debate on the Korean War a few days earlier, that the Chinese "seem to be moving towards a Monroe Doctrine for China," by which non-Asian powers should keep out of East Asia.[10]

The Chinese take every opportunity of inflaming what anti-American feeling exists (in the Philippines, for instance, and in Japan, where the American connection sometimes appears burdensome and humiliating) and encouraging the gradual British withdrawal from Southeast Asia. China's continuing weakness prevents her from achieving parity of influence in East Asia with the USA: only when she succeeds in this shall we be able to judge whether she will then insist not only on equal but on a preponderant or even exclusive influence in the area. It would seem difficult for Americans who expect to have the last word in Latin America (and for Europeans unprepared for an Asian voice in European affairs) honestly to deny China a sphere of influence around her own borders, though the Western powers would certainly, and rightly, intervene if this influence were to take the form of outright conquest. So far there is no evidence that this is China's intention.

The third major aim of Peking in East Asia is, like the USSR, to spread the gospel of Marx and Lenin, and to promote the linked process of national liberation, democratic reform and socialist revolution. "Under the influence of the success of the Chinese Revolution," Chou En-lai told a political meeting in Peking in 1951, "the level of consciousness of the Asian people has been raised to an unprecedented degree, and liberation movements are developing more and more strongly with each passing day. The unity of the Chinese people and the peoples of Asia will certainly create a powerful and matchless force in the Far East which will rapidly push forward the great wheel of history in the movement for the independence and liberation of the peoples of Asian countries." [11] In those early years Peking policy, like the Soviet, stressed help to armed rebels against the "bourgeois" nationalist regimes in Southeast Asia. The Chinese Communists made their alignments clear in a radio broadcast on the Indonesian situation just before their final victory in China:

> The reactionary ruling classes of the [Indonesian] Republic dread the anti-imperialist strength of the people of their own country and of the people of the world. Therefore they not only cannot shoulder the great cause of national liberation but cannot preserve their "Republic" from being destroyed by Dutch aggressors. They have the same outlook as the Nehrus, Jinnahs, Luang Pibul Songgrams, Quirinos, Syngman Rhees and other feeble-minded bourgeoisie of the East.[12]

Mao had written in 1949 that it was "impossible for a genuine people's revolution to win victory in any country without various forms of help from the international revolutionary forces." [13] But after the Bandung Conference in 1955 Peking's policy became more flexible: China tried to woo neutralist opinion and gain respectability in Asian circles in spite of her ideological fervour. In India and Indonesia where the Communists had established a loose *modus vivendi* with Nehru and Sukarno, respectively, this was not difficult. In countries where the nationalist government was in conflict with the Communist Party, the new policy called for finesse. Such was the case in Cambodia (where Prince Sihanouk, who sent three of his sons to study in Peking and was until 1967 an ardent advocate of the Chinese diplomatic viewpoint nevertheless suppresses the few Cambodian Communists), Burma (where Communists have been fighting the government militarily for almost twenty years) and Nepal (whose Communists are in exile, some of them in China, while King Mahendra maintains a policy of friendship with Peking).

From time to time the Chinese leaders reassure foreign opinion about their intentions: revolution, they say is "not for export" [14] (meaning that it must originate in a local initiative) and Chou En-lai at Bandung assured his Asian audience that China did not intend to subvert her neighbours. Naturally he did not accept the advice of Sir John Kotelawala, the Ceylonese anti-Communist leader, who asked him to call publicly on all Afro-Asian Communist Parties to disband, as a "reassuring gesture" of good intention.[15] The Chinese continue to support revolutionary movements all over the globe with words, sympathy, money, arms—and, on occasion, with offers of volunteers to fight in their cause.* To put it in another way, the Chinese carry out the foreign policy of a great power, following the example of Britain, America, Russia and France, thus astounding observers who expect them to leave world politics to the Europeans. But China prosecutes her ideological aims abroad with a sense of proportion and has not so far rocked the boat unbearably. Her assistance, for example, to the Communist-backed left-wing forces struggling against Western-backed right-wing forces in Laos and Vietnam (on her own doorstep) has been limited to moral encouragement and some military and civilian supplies. She has not committed her combat troops in Indochina, and played an important role in the Geneva conciliations.

The fourth factor in China's Asian policy is her concern for the twelve million Overseas Chinese who live in Southeast Asia. These communities represent a diminishing problem, because they are gradually becoming socially assimilated under the pressure of local Southeast Asian nationalism. The Thai, Burmese, South Vietnamese, Philippine, and Indonesian authorities have all taken severe measures in the past decade or two to curb the economic power of their Chinese communities (which represent, on average, five per cent of their total population) and force them into the mainstream of their national life.[16] There is a Javanese saying that, "if you meet a snake and a *mata sipit* [slit-eye, i.e. a Chinese] kill the Chinese first and then the snake," and similar stories are told elsewhere in Southeast Asia, where the Chinese over the centuries have come to dominate the local economies by monopolizing moneylending and commerce. "For the intellectuals," an Indonesian Cabinet Minister has remarked, "our revolution was against Dutch political colonialism, but for the masses it was against Chinese economic colonialism."

Today it is estimated that only a million Overseas Chinese students are enrolled in the remaining 3,400 schools in Southeast Asia where Chinese is either the main medium of instruction or else the first "foreign" language to all pupils.[17] The majority of Overseas Chinese children are now in schools where they learn in the local language—Malay, Thai, Burmese, etc. This means that they will inevitably lose their mastery of the Chinese characters (which demand a large proportion of a student's time) and will be sucked gradually into the local national culture, as has already happened to the

---

* The success of China's clients does not necessarily make them unswerving champions of the Chinese line: national differences make the Sino-Vietnamese relationship, to take one example, a difficult one in spite of their basic community of ideology.

Chinese in America, Australia, Canada and Europe. (It is rare nowadays to find a young American-born or European-born Chinese who speaks and writes fluent Chinese.) But the *jus sanguinis* still carries weight in China, and the Overseas Chinese are still accorded honour and a special role there.[18]

The Communists' official policy is that the "overseas compatriots" should either assimilate into their adopted country or, if they retain Chinese citizenship, behave with the restraint due from a foreign resident (i.e. refrain from participating in local politics). In a joint *communiqué* signed in 1954, the Burmese and Chinese Premiers agreed to encourage their nationals residing in the other's territory "to respect the laws and social customs of the country in which they reside, and not to take part in the political activities of that country." [19] * Similar statements of policy have been made by China with respect to the Overseas Chinese in Singapore [20] and Indonesia. A Dual Nationality Agreement was signed with Indonesia in 1955, but it disappointed Indonesian opinion because it gave the Indonesian Chinese two escape routes from the responsibilities of Indonesian citizenship; they could choose which nationality they wanted, but one who chose Indonesian could automatically revert to Chinese citizenship merely by returning to China for good, and one who chose Chinese citizenship automatically passed it on to his children even if they were born in Indonesia and were in all other respects Indonesianized. If these people were Indonesian, it was said, then they ought to be subject to Indonesian law and should not seek Peking's protection against its provisions. If they were Chinese, and did not obey the laws, then they should be deportable to China. In theory Chou En-lai accepted this point of view, but as a Chinese he also felt obliged to protest if his compatriots were discriminated against or persecuted merely on account of their racial origin: he probably felt like reminding his Indonesian friends that the Chinese in Indonesia had obtained their privileged position through hard work and enterprise, and that the real answer to the problem was for the Indonesians to compete with them.

From 1957 onwards the Indonesian Government began to close the separate Chinese schools, ban local Chinese newspa-

---

* There are virtually no Burmese living in China: this formula of reciprocity is characteristic of Chinese sensitivity and desire not to appear to be the only cause of a problem. It also illustrates the practical horse-trading approach of Chinese diplomacy, which prefers an exchange of concessions, and which was so badly misunderstood by Nehru.

pers, restrict the employment of aliens (i.e. Chinese citizens) and reduce the power of the Chinese business community. In 1959 foreign retail traders in the rural areas were obliged to sell out to Indonesian cooperatives or individuals. This policy was not explicitly anti-Chinese, but the only foreign traders in the villages were the Overseas Chinese, most of whom had retained their Chinese nationality: they resisted this order, and Indonesian troops became involved in enforcing it.[21] Subsequently a number of violent incidents took place. Two Chinese women were killed in a clash with Indonesian soldiers at Tjimahi in 1960, and in 1963 a Chinese magistrate at Tjirebon sentenced an Indonesian youth to imprisonment for causing the death of a Chinese youth. His action caused a wave of anti-Chinese demonstrations and there was a fight between Indonesian and Chinese students at the Bandung Institute of Technology (because some of the Indonesian students had taken part in anti-Chinese incidents in their home towns). The government apologized to the Chinese community, but the Federation of Students' Organizations called on "a certain section of society with a privileged, strong and better economic position, particularly foreigners," to "adjust themselves to the national aspirations of the Indonesian people." [22]

In the end Peking and Djakarta reached agreement on implementing the dual nationality treaty, and Peking sent ships to bring back the tens of thousands of Chinese who opted for repatriation to China. But amity was maintained only with difficulty, especially when anti-Chinese rioting broke out again in 1967 after the eclipse of Sukarno. Peking appeared in Indonesian eyes to be protecting people who were smuggling, hoarding, evading taxes and bribing officials, all of which, as Indonesians pointed out, was not "in conformity with the socialist policy of the Government of the Chinese People's Republic." [23] When the *People's Daily* commented at one difficult moment in 1959 that 650 million people could not tolerate the oppression of their overseas compatriots, the reaction of an Indonesian Foreign Ministry official was probably typical: China, he remarked, was "just another imperialist power with expansionist inclinations." [24] But in fact Peking did eventually acquiesce in the progressive elimination of the Overseas Chinese community in Indonesia, and it would be fairer, particularly in view of the strong pressures of long-frustrated nationalism operating on Chinese policy, to commend the restraint and self-sacrifice of the Communist Government in coming to terms with Southeast Asian nationalism. The spill-over of the Cultural Revolution into the Overseas Chinese communities in 1967, which spoiled Peking's relations with Burma, Cambodia and other countries, will probably be seen later as an aberrant interlude in this complex relationship.

Chinese leaders are aware of the imperialist temptations which the past history and present size of their country pose. They have publicly acknowledged (as Sun Yat-sen did) that China was imperialist in the past and that "great-nation chauvinism" could become a serious danger: in 1956, during the debate over Khrushchev's de-Stalinization campaign, they even admitted that the first symptoms of this were already visible.[25] When Viscount Montgomery asked Mao Tse-tung in 1961 what China's aims would be, once she had regained her strength, Mao replied: "Ah! You obviously think China will then practise aggression outside her borders." Montgomery explained that he did not *want* to think so, but that this had happened to other nations, including his own. Mao then proceeded to give what would appear to be a realistic and honest answer: he could not speak for the future, but was himself very much aware of the humiliations experienced by China at the hands of foreign aggression and was exerting all his influence to prevent China's ever succumbing to such a temptation.[26]

As we have seen, the population growth in China is not of itself likely to create strong pressures for foreign expansion, but every economist in Asia knows that Southeast Asia is rich in four commodities of which China is short: rice, rubber, oil and timber. Economic temptations could conceivably combine with political ambitions in a future generation of Chinese with no personal memory of being aggressed against. There is one factor in China's case which makes it different from that of Britain, France, Japan and other previous imperialists of modern times. China is already so vast, so preoccupied with the problems of self-administration, so traditionally inward-looking, so potentially self-sufficient, that one is entitled to hope that she will prove more immune from the imperialist itch than her predecessors in modern world power. Even at the height of her former power, China preferred to seek a diplomatic *cordon sanitaire* of friendly governments around her borders than to conquer foreign peoples by force of arms, and this is probably still true. The historical maps in the Peking bookshops are in fact misleading, for no Chinese army ever stayed in Southeast Asia and the Chinese presence there fell far short of conquest.

It was possible for Nehru, all the same, to describe China in 1959 as "a great and powerful nation which is aggressive." [27] He was especially aware of the crude manner in which the Chinese Communists asserted their authority in Tibet. Understandably, China alienated many sectors of Asian opinion by her action in Tibet (not so much by her claim to sovereignty as by the way in which she exercised that sovereignty). The Nepalese socialist, B. P. Koirala (who later became Nepal's first elected Prime Minister), said that the Tibet question was "a matter for moral consideration by other Asian countries." The Rangoon *Nation* called China's actions a "gross violation" of the spirit of Bandung. The All-Ceylon Buddhist Congress denounced China, Kripalani and J. P. Narayan in India led a strenuous verbal crusade for Tibetan self-determination, and Malaya took up the cudgels for Tibet in the United Nations.[28] But when all is said and done, the charges of aggression in Tibet have a hollow ring: most Asians believe that China had *some* historical rights in Tibet; what they resent is China's brutality against one of its own minority communities, rather than a naked conquest of a completely foreign state.

The Chinese leaders are fond of reminding their critics that no Chinese combat soldier is stationed in any foreign country (which is more than can be said by Britain, America, Russia, France or Australia) and that Chinese soldiers have never crossed their border (though there sometimes is a local dispute over where the border lies). The Korean War, in which the label of "volunteers" could not disguise the official nature of the participation of thousands of Chinese troops, is the only exception. But even here, many Asians now feel that the UN's charge of Chinese aggression at the end of 1950 was too hasty: the Chinese did not in fact intervene until General MacArthur had led the American troops north of the original North-South border line in Korea. General Wu obviously had Japan in mind when he told reporters at the UN that winter, "an aggressor who invades Korea today invariably invades China tomorrow," [29] and MacArthur was known to be lobbying for freedom to strike across the Yalu into Manchuria. There is evidence that China genuinely feared an American invasion. Tibet and Korea thus fail to provide the decisive proof of Chinese bellicosity which distant observers see in them. But for many such people the attack on India, a country which had championed Chinese causes at the bar of world opinion and had apparently extended the hand of friendship to Peking, was conclusive. It becomes important to see what China did to India, and why.

18: INDIA

Whose Himalayas?

CHINA AND INDIA HAD NO GENUINE INTERCOURSE BEFORE
1949, though both countries, during their five-year honeymoon in the mid-fifties when Indians dreamily chanted the
refrain *Hindi Chini bhai bhai,** liked to dwell on the little evidence that history had left of earlier contacts—the transmis-
sion of Buddhism, the journeys of the monk Fa Hsien. China
and India were totally different worlds to each other, and
they began their modern relationship in the early 1950s
under clouds of misapprehension, particularly on the Chinese
side. Liu Shao-chi spoke in 1950 of India's "sham independence," and Mao referred to the neutralism of which Nehru
was such a burning champion as "a term for deceiving people." Nehru himself, as we have seen, was dismissed as a
"feeble-minded bourgeois" incapable of leading an Indian
revolution. China's sympathies were with the Indian Communists, who at this time were also doubtful about Nehru: Peking did, however, advertise her feelings of friendship for the
Indian people by supplying several hundred thousand tons of
precious grain during the Indian food shortage of 1951–2.[1]

The Chinese occupation of Tibet provided the first test of
this fragile new relationship. India's interest was, in Nehru's
words, a "sentimental" one, Tibet being "culturally speaking,
. . . an offshoot of India, . . . of Buddhism." [2] He accepted
the Chinese overlordship of Tibet,† but when the People's
Liberation Army was ordered into the territory in the autumn
of 1950 he officially expressed the Indian Government's "surprise and regret" at such a "deplorable" attempt to solve the

---

* "Indians and Chinese are brothers."

† India also helped China considerably by effectively blocking any discussion of the Tibetan question in the United Nations, and by withholding from the Dalai Lama the diplomatic assistance he requested in
1950. India by her naïve and inexperienced though well-intentioned diplomacy managed to get the worst of both worlds, earning the resentment of both the Tibetans and the Chinese over this question.

problem of Tibet "by force instead of by the slower and more enduring methods of peaceful approach." [3] The Chinese Communists had gained power by the use of military force, and had been betrayed and had lost ground on almost every occasion when they attempted peaceful Gandhian tactics with the Kuomintang: they were about to send a volunteer army to Korea to repel what they feared might be an imminent American invasion of China and they were in no mood for lectures on non-violence. They also saw an official Indian hand in the fact that the Tibetan delegation which was supposedly on its way to negotiate in Peking *via* India never proceeded further than Calcutta, and they accused Nehru of blocking a peaceful settlement in order to frustrate China in obtaining her rights!

But the Chinese later succeeded in establishing themselves in Tibet without violence, and in 1954 India formally accepted a diminution of the privileges she had inherited from Britain in "the Tibet region of China." By then the Chinese had been genuinely impressed, as had Stalin, by the scrupulousness with which Nehru had acted out his self-chosen neutral role in the lengthy negotiations which brought the Korean War to an end.

The Indian Communists were also coming to terms with Nehru as an unchallengeable national father-figure and a leader more acceptable than the powerful right-wing elements in the Congress Party which would otherwise have ruled India. In 1954 Chou En-lai came to Delhi, to be told by Nehru that, "We have been good neighbours and friends, and have not come into conflict with each other during these millennia of history." [4] A few months later Nehru was acclaimed by a crowd of a million Chinese in Peking. Chou responded to Nehru's mood, declaring that the solidarity of the two nations would constitute "a gigantic moral and material force in stabilizing the situation in Asia and Africa." [5] The two announced their adherence to the *Panch Shila,* or five principles of peaceful coexistence. Nehru judged, correctly, that the Communists had established themselves as a lasting government in China, that they had been isolated in their struggle for power and were mistrustful of the outside world, and that the most constructive and sensible policy was therefore to be as friendly as possible and to promote their acceptance in the world community.

It was in this spirit that he gave the limelight to Chou at the Bandung Conference of Afro-Asian leaders in 1955: this endorsement by the most trusted and respected statesman of the anti-colonial world gave Chou an entrée which he exploited with skill, although eight years later he was to reveal an irritation which few observers suspected at the time. "Nehru took me round and introduced me to one delegation after another," Afro-Asian journalists reported him as saying to them in Peking in 1963; "It appeared that he thought Chou En-lai needed introduction to other nations. He behaved like an elder statesman. After all, he is only ten years older than I am." [6] More recently, Chou has said (to visiting Ceylonese politicians in Peking): "I have never met a more arrogant man than Nehru. I am sorry, but this is true." [7] The sophistication and charm of these two statesmen could not efface the great differences of national culture and tradition which they brought to their international relations. India gained her freedom by moral persuasion, not by force, and her trust in the Western world is therefore based on experience. Her leaders are considerably westernized, mostly western-educated, well-travelled and fluent in English. Nehru himself admitted that he lived in two worlds, and there was more of Harrow and Cambridge than of Allahabad in his diplomacy. The Chinese leaders are by contrast decidedly unwesternized (save in ideology), home-educated, little-travelled and with no fluency in foreign languages. Their attitudes spring straight from the Chinese tradition, which makes them attach importance to personal relationship and to the feudal virtues of loyalty, pride and honour, rather than to abstract ideas. Nehru felt himself to be part of an open, single world; Chou feels this too, but only intellectually, his emotional reflexes being those of a man ignorant and suspicious of the world.

The Sino-Indian honeymoon came to an end with the Tibetan Rising of 1959. India's tradition of tolerance and the liberal political beliefs of her leaders obliged her to offer asylum to the rebels who began to stream into northern India. But when Nehru allowed the Dalai Lama, the acknowledged head of the Tibetan people and of their own government, to settle at Mussoorie, in the shadows of the Indian Himalayas, Peking felt that the spirit, if not the letter, of the *Panch Shila* had been broken. Nehru told the Dalai Lama (whose religious authority extended, after all, into India itself) that he would be expected not to "function on the political plane," [8] but in the course of time the Tibetan exile issued statements, addressed missives to the United Nations and acted to some extent as an *émigré* government. The presence in India of this most blatant advertisement of Chinese failure in Tibet did more than anything else to cause the Peking Communists to revert to their earlier distrust and disapproval of the Nehru Government.

As for Indian opinion, while Nehru had been able to restrain its sympathies for Tibet in 1950, no one could suppress its indignation at the way in which the Chinese troops quelled the 1959 revolt. This in turn provoked strong language in Peking, where one newspaper said that India had "expansionist" aims and wanted Tibet as a "vassal state." [9] A delegate at a political meeting in Peking declared that the Chinese people would "never allow foul dogs to poke their snouts into our beautiful garden." [10] The Chinese leaders, Nehru said, were using "the language of the cold war without regard for truth or propriety." [11]

The central point, however, was the existence of two quite different conceptions of "autonomy." To the Chinese, an autonomous Tibet was a Tibet in which the ordinary people had first been liberated from serfdom, and in which basic social and economic reforms had first been made to establish the foundation for a just society. When Chou En-lai promised "autonomy," he meant it for the ordinary people of Tibet, not for the minority of vested feudal interests. [12] When Nehru spoke of autonomy he meant, allowing social reform to proceed at the speed of the slowest, in order to avoid violence and to ensure the preservation of the Tibetan national culture. For Chou this meant autonomy for the *status quo*. It was the difference between the revolutionary and the Fabian mind. Some Chinese, particularly those who have had any dealings with Tibet, probably suspect that Nehru was right, when he said that to attribute the 1959 revolt exclusively to class reactionaries was "an extraordinary simplification of a complicated situation." [13] But Tibet represents in the Chinese Communist mind the last stage in the honourable reintegration of the Chinese state after its depredations at the hands of foreigners, and the fact that the Chinese army (given a virtually impossible task to perform) happened to behave badly in Tibet, makes it particularly difficult for Peking to admit its mistakes in this matter. But the Tibetan revolt had an even more disastrous consequence for Sino-Indian relations. It brought to a head the border differences which had been till then kept in the background.

The border between China and India has never at any point been delineated on a modern, accurate map nor delimited on the ground, in the form of pillars and posts, by accredited officials of the two governments. The reason is that the border area is mostly mountainous (and accurate geographical surveys have only recently been made of it), desolate, difficult of access, uninhabited and unadministered. The few people who live there are not "Indians" or "Chinese" in any easily differentiated sense; most are either of Tibetan origin or else quite distinct tribes whose racial affinities are with the Shans of Burma and the Nagas of India. There is no obvious racial border between India and China, nor are geographical criteria conclusive. The mountain crest or watershed along the Himalayas appears superficially as an easy physical pointer to the border, and in many sectors it is. But only in the far west (on what is now the Pakistan-China border) does the mountain range appear as a wall: for most of the Sino-Indian border it is more like the edge of a high, crumbling platform, so that the crest is neither easy to determine nor an obvious border. As for watersheds, there are three major Indian rivers (the Indus, Sutlej and Brahmaputra) which rise in undisputedly Tibetan territory well to the north of the Himalayan crest.

Thwarted by nature, one looks to history to suggest an acceptable border. Unfortunately the past was not clearly chronicled in these isolated areas, and what historical references do exist are often rendered useless by their lack of geographical precision. The 550-page report of the meetings of Indian and Chinese officials over the border claims, published in 1960, contains many references, for example, to the Kashmir-Tibet Treaty of 1842. There were in fact two different versions of this Treaty, each in two languages with variations of wording, and none of these was definitive. Not one of the four original texts is extant, and the two sets of lawyers are now quoting only the rival local chronicles of their own side. In any event, the only specific reference to the border in this Treaty is to a stream, of which the two sides are today unable to agree on the location.[14] Many of the historical arguments rest on hearsay, on unconfirmed reports of the few record-keeping travellers in nineteenth-century Central Asia, and on maps. The Indian lawyers cite, for instance, a 1919 map issued by the Chinese Post Office as confirming their case at a certain sector of the border, but all that is proved is that the Chinese postal authorities at that time did not give much thought to boundary matters. This is the background to this difficult border dispute.

The matter remained an academic one until 1950, when Chinese rule was reasserted in Tibet. Even the early 1950s were generally years of border inactivity. The two sides hardly came into contact with one another, and so the differences shown on the rival maps of Peking and Delhi respectively were still theoretical and of little urgency. The Indian

Government indeed complained to Peking about its maps, but was invariably fobbed off with the reply that the old Kuomintang maps had not yet been revised. Nehru told his Parliament: "Map or no map, that is our frontier and we will not allow anyone to cross it." [15]

In 1956, after some small border clashes, Nehru insisted on pinning Chou En-lai down on the North East Frontier Agency (NEFA) frontier question. Chou explained that the Chinese objected to the name of the McMahon Line * (just as they rejected the name of Mount Everest), that they also regarded it as unfair, and that they had never given formal agreement to it. It was now, however, an accomplished fact; India was independent and friendly to China, and China would therefore have to be realistic. Chou gave Nehru to understand (according to the Indian minutes of their private discussion) that the McMahon Line would now be broadly acceptable to China, subject to certain specific minor adjustments and subject to local Tibetan approval. But while the Chinese Premier was talking with Nehru, Chinese engineers were busy building a road across the desolate Aksai Chin triangle which lies between Kashmir, Sinkiang and Tibet—over ground which Chou well knew was regarded by Nehru as Indian. This is a most vital road for Chinese economic development and military security, for it is the only convenient route by which motorized traffic can link Tibet with Sinkiang (a more north-easterly route would have encountered the desert) and enable Tibet to be supplied by the oilfields and new industries of Sinkiang. The road was completed in 1957, and first noticed by diplomats on a Chinese newspaper map in the following year: Nehru then sent a border patrol to investigate and confirmed that the Chinese had constructed a road on what he regarded as his territory (without his knowing it—a fact tending to weaken the Indian claim). When this became public knowledge in Delhi, in 1959, Indian opinion was enraged.[16]

Then came the Tibetan Rising, and the necessity for the first time of Chinese troops' guarding all the major passes out of Tibet (to prevent guerrilla fighters from fleeing to India and Nepal or returning with new supplies). Until then there had been a long *de facto* no-man's land, in which Indian and

---

* Named after Sir Henry McMahon, chief British delegate to the Simla Conference in 1913–14, at which he drew a line to represent the India–Tibet border. The Tibetan delegation agreed to the line, though not the Chinese government. India in 1947 regarded herself as automatically assuming the borders and treaty rights acquired by the former British Government of India.

Chinese patrols only occasionally clashed. After 1959 both sides began to complete their physical administration of their border areas, and the risks of collision multiplied. It was the Chinese who made all the running in 1959–61, with the incentive of controlling the Tibetan rebels. Chinese forces expelled Indians from the border post of Longju and arrested Indian policemen at Khurnak. But in the summer of 1962 the Indian side organized a drive on a comparable scale: Nehru told his Parliament in August that part of the 12,000 square miles of Indian-claimed Ladakh occupied by Chinese forces had already been "recovered" and that the Indian Army had been instructed to "expel" the Chinese from NEFA.[17] The Chinese, faced for the first time with a concerted Indian military drive into what they regarded as their own legitimate territory, charged India with aggression and launched a fierce counter-attack (in October) which ignominiously drove the Indians right back to the southern part of NEFA.

China then unilaterally ceased fire and withdrew behind the McMahon Line. She did not go further because her military advantage would be lost as soon as she entered the Indian plains, because her supply lines were already stretched, and because her purpose was to establish her border rather than take India on in an all-out war. But if the Chinese won the fighting, India won the peace, in the sense that India's superiority in diplomacy and international public relations ensured that the world (including the Soviet Union and Eastern Europe) heard only the Indian side of the story and assumed that China, without provocation, had stabbed her former friend in the back. The Chinese, thinking along more feudalistic lines, apparently assumed that their Communist allies would support them automatically and without explanation. But Togliatti called the clash "unreasonable and absurd,"[18] and *Tass* referred to it as "regrettable" and "tragic."[19]

India has offered to take the border issue to the World Court: China, suspicious of all Western-created institutions, demands bilateral negotiation without any third party's interference. The Aksai Chin area is entirely desolate and the line here must be arbitrary: an impartial arbiter would probably divide it cleanly (and might cite a similar British Indian proposal of 1899, though it was not accepted by the Chinese, in support), leaving the road on the Chinese side.[20] The rival claims to traditional sovereignty in NEFA are equally groundless, since neither side began to administer the tribes sandwiched between the Bengalis and the Tibetans until half a century ago. Since then, the Indian side has certainly established the better possession, and the McMahon Line would probably therefore be confirmed by an impartial arbiter, subject to at least two and possibly four small local adjustments in China's favour.[21]

The mediation of the six neutral nations (Burma, Cambodia, Ceylon, Ghana, Indonesia and the UAR, who produced the so-called Colombo Cease-Fire Plan) has not been accepted by the Chinese, partly because it is militarily disadvantageous to them and partly because of their traditional distaste for arbitration.[22] Until 1959 it was India which was calling for negotiations, China which was stalling (because she had not established her power in the border regions). But when the border talks *did* begin in 1959, the Indian side (limited by its public opinion) approached them with no intention whatever of negotiating, only of convincing the Chinese by the evidence that the Indian case was correct. It is certain that the Chinese are willing to bargain, and would probably (Chou En-lai has openly hinted as much) trade NEFA * for the Aksai Chin road, but since 1959 no Indian Government has dared to make any border "concessions" to China because of the strong public feeling on the matter.[23]

What the Chinese want India to say is: "We agree that these areas underwent cartographical aggression by the British when they ruled us in India, and that this border is not ours by moral right: let us, however, take it as a convenient (but not inflexible) starting point and discuss how it can be made more fair at specific points where you feel particularly aggrieved." The tragedy is that India would probably have taken this attitude, and would probably have voluntarily given up the Aksai Chin road area, in the early 1950s—when China, because of her minimal control of Tibet, felt that to open border negotiations would place her in a weak bargaining position.

India must be blamed for under-estimating Chinese sensitivity over the British origin of the border, over the Indian interest in Tibet and over the asylum given to the Dalai Lama. Nehru was quick to remind the Western powers of the need to make allowances, in dealing with an apparently mistrustful and suspicious Chinese Government, for recent Chinese history and national pride, but he was strangely blind to these factors when it came to his own conflicts of interest with the new China (just as Indians fail to benefit from their

* It is wrong to regard China's NEFA claim as invented by Peking after 1959, perhaps to provide the basis for a bargain, though Indian officials sometimes do so. The Kuomintang protested against Indian infiltration into NEFA several times before the Communists came to power in 1949.

own analysis of Western-Asian relations when they now accuse China of ingratitude for India's friendship in the 1950s). Nehru expected Chou to treat him as a trusted friend, but the Chinese nature made them deal with him as, at best, a distant equal. The Chinese, in their turn, must accept the blame for their failure to appreciate the subtleties of India's free press, free speech and tradition of asylum; for their lack of trust in failing to take Nehru more into their confidence about their policy and problems in Tibet, their maps, and their Aksai Chin road; and for their injection of bitterness into the dispute in 1959 (presumably out of pique over the Tibetan Rising). It is most unfortunate that neither Mao nor Nehru felt able in the 1950s to put their foreign relations in the charge of a strong Foreign Minister free from the preoccupations of domestic politics and with continuous oversight of border matters. Both Chou and Nehru, who bore the brunt of the border tensions, were increasingly distracted by other issues.

A border settlement and general *rapprochement* will not be possible for many years. Indian opinion is now strongly anti-Chinese (even the Indian Communist Party has split on this issue, with only a small minority continuing to withhold blame from China) and China now appears as a convenient bogeyman whose threats fortify the slow-growing Indian sense of nationalism. The likelihood of continued tension is also suggested by the remaining ambiguities of the Himalayan border. There are still two tiny quasi-independent states, Bhutan and Sikkim, sandwiched between India and China: the Indians at the moment control them, but China will certainly seek to alter that. Nepal has established a viability and could remain a respected buffer state between the two giants, but any mistake in her diplomacy or sudden change in the delicate balance of power between them could threaten her neutrality. There is talk of independence for India's NEFA tribes, and of a Himalayan Federation which might include Tibet or Nagaland or both.[24] The political status of Kashmir is uneasy, and the Chinese are still unsure of their hold over Tibet (where rebellion simmers on). It is doubtful if the Himalayas will ever really be at peace until they are cleanly and unequivocally divided between their two rival masters.

Both sides are sincere in their border claims, and while China is doubtless envious of India's economic development and of the foreign aid she receives from both the West and the Soviet bloc (and possibly jealous of the political prestige which Nehru gained for India), there is no need to see these as ulterior motives for the Chinese border offensive in 1962.

The Sino-Indian border problem may be visualized as two intersecting circles: where the Indian circle and the Chinese circle overlap was until the 1950s a limbo that neither side controlled. Only when the forces of each side began to advance into it did the urgency of an agreed solution to the conflicting claims appear, and by then the necessary political goodwill had evaporated. It was China who decided to settle the matter once and for all by a conclusive show of force. But she halted her troops well before they reached what she had all along claimed as her true and rightful border (even withdrawing them virtually to the Indian-claimed border in the NEFA sector), and her offensive of 1962 ought not, therefore, to be pictured as a wanton act of aggression against another country (such as Hitler's attack on Poland, or Japan's on China). The confrontation over the Himalayas was more like a Greek tragedy, in which the inevitability lay in the fact that the protagonists were culturally unequipped to understand each other. The question which it raises is not so much one of China's aggressive tendencies as of her ability to conduct any significant relationship involving a special understanding across a cultural barrier. This question was a key one in the Sino-Soviet dispute, and is currently being tested in the entirely new and fascinating arena of Sino-African relations.

19: AFRICA AND BEYOND

Champion of the Oppressed

THE KING OF THE BELGIANS IMPORTED CHINESE COOLIES TO build the Congo Railway, and the enigmatic President Kasavubu is said to have a strain of Chinese blood in his veins as a result.[1] The modern Chinese connection with Africa rests on only a few such arbitrary links, although in earlier centuries there was a keen trade between the two (Admiral Cheng Ho landed in East Africa in the fifteenth century AD, and in 1414 an embassy from the Kenya coast took a giraffe to Peking as a gift to the Emperor).[2] In those days Africans were among the "barbarians" from whom the Emperor expected tribute and the respect due to the representative of a superior civilization, but even as recently as sixty years ago one of the leading Chinese intellectuals and reformers, Kang Yu-wei (whom Mao Tse-tung, in his pre-Marxist days, supported for the Premiership of China), could display an astonishing colour prejudice. He advocated, in an otherwise enlightened and rational world utopia, that the black races, "owing to their extreme ugliness and stupidity," should be taken to Canada and Scandinavia for a few centuries where they would gradually become lighter in skin colour and thus acceptable for mixed marriage (he predicted that there would ultimately be only one race in this one world). [3]

The Chinese of today are conscious of colour differences, and share many of the attitudes for which Europeans are so berated: the *China Youth Daily*, for instance, urged city girls in a recent article to overcome their fear that manual work in the village fields would darken their complexions. [4] Emmanuel John Hevi's book *An African Student in China*,* for all its hastiness of judgment, shows clearly that African students do not find China free of these prejudices. When in 1962, dissatisfied with their conditions of life and study, they staged a mass exodus from Peking,† they advertised one of the Chinese Communists' greatest diplomatic failures. The Party has tried to overcome these prejudices, and it seems fair to assume that in another generation or two more rational attitudes will become accepted to some extent: meanwhile, as in the controversial field of family planning, the Communists have to face the sad fact that a very large proportion of the Chinese people is stubbornly unreceptive to reason on a matter where social prejudice has been nursed for centuries.

This inherited colour prejudice is officially outweighed, in China's foreign policy, by the intellectual conviction of the

* London, Pall Mall, 1963. Hevi is a Ghanaian. His impassioned account of the beating up of a Somali student in the Peace Hotel in Peking by a Chinese crowd, which then turned on other resident negroes who came to his rescue, needs to be supplemented by the more restrained and coherent account of Sven Lindqvist (*China in Crisis*, London, Faber, 1965, pp. 24–6), who was also a foreign student in Peking at that time and knew the Africans.

† To my astonishment, when I asked about this in an interview with officials of Peking University in 1964, the incident was denied: "though some students may have failed to keep the regulations, and returned home prematurely." The Chinese tradition of denying (or refusing to discuss) events which put them in a bad light probably earns them more bad feeling among foreigners than anything else.

Communists that Africans are not inferior to Chinese. But an emotional substitute creeps in to take the place of the officially suppressed feeling of racial superiority: the Chinese revolution is regarded as an example for Africans to follow. "The Chinese people," the *People's Daily* declared in 1959, "who have gone through a fate similar to the African people's, fully understand and deeply sympathize with the plight of the millions of African people under colonial rule, and firmly support their heroic struggle for independence and freedom. With great elation we have seen how the people of African countries, like the people of Asia, have stood up in the past few years. Anti-colonial flames have lit up the entire 'dark continent.' " [5] This sense of political mission in Africa is fed by compliments such as that paid by Ahmed Balafrej, the Moroccan leader, in Peking in 1959: "I am convinced that China's revolution has awakened the African continent." [6] It is dramatized in the Chinese mind by the key role attributed to Africa by the Chinese Communist theorists: "The centre of anti-colonial struggle is in Africa. The centre of struggle between East and West is Africa. At present Africa is the central question of the world." [7]

It was the Suez crisis of 1956 which first drew China decisively into Africa. Although Peking was so distant from the scene of Egypt's trial, 400,000 Chinese demonstrated in Tienanmen Square, women wept for Arab honour and two million Pekinese wrote letters of support to the UAR Ambassador. The Minister of Health offered to go personally to lead a Chinese medical team in the field of battle, and Kuo Mo-jo, the poet laureate of the regime, wrote:

I wish I could be a member of a volunteer army,
And go to the river of the Nile, to the foot of the Pyramids,
To fight shoulder-to-shoulder with my Egyptian brothers. . . . [8]

Chou transferred twenty million Swiss francs to Cairo to help the UAR Government in its hour of need, and was almost disappointed when the offer of Chinese volunteers was gratefully rejected after the entry of the United Nations force into the battlefield. Later Peking's relations with Cairo went through much strain: the Chinese openly criticized Nasser for turning against the Egyptian Communist Party and thereby "betraying" his people,[9] while the Egyptian leaders were furiously angered when a Syrian Communist was permitted at a Peking rally in 1959 to describe the Nasser Government as terroristic and fascist.[10] But Chinese support in 1956 is not forgotten, and Sino-Egyptian relations remain, on the surface at least, cordial.

From their new embassy in Cairo the Chinese began to court first the North Africans (particularly the Algerian rebels, for whom their help was more wholehearted than that of Moscow, for example, and whose violent conflict with French imperialism Mao saw as a beacon to lead the rest of Africa) and then the black Africans below the Sahara. An important landmark was the tour of China in 1959 by Barry Diawandou, the middle-of-the-road Guinean leader, who wrote afterwards:

> I started out full of apprehensions and false ideas; I returned fully convinced of the efficacy of Chinese methods. I was struck by the similarities which exist between China's economic problems and those which today are problems common to all the peoples of Africa.[11]

In 1960 the Chinese mission opened in Konakry, and Chinese friendship was given material expression by the gift of 5,000 tons of rice (which *Figaro* unkindly reported as being promptly mixed in by the Guinean authorities with American gift rice).

In 1964, concluding the first visit ever made to Africa by a Chinese Prime Minister, Chou En-lai uttered his famous pronouncement that the continent was "ripe for revolution," and by the time Chou made his second and third visits, in the summer of 1965, Chinese diplomacy was active in more than a dozen African states. Peking takes its mission seriously. After having given military help to the Algerian rebels, China now provides arms, training and encouragement to the nationalists preparing to overthrow the Portuguese colonialists in Mozambique and Angola, as well as to guerrilla fighters in other territories which are technically independent but regarded by China as under Western influence. Pierre Mulele, the Congolese rebel leader, and Camerounian rebels are among those who have benefited from this assistance.[12]

China would like to play a larger role in Africa's economic relations, but is not a natural market for many African commodities (such as cocoa, coffee and oilseeds) and finds it difficult to compete against such rival suppliers of manufacturers as Japan and Hongkong. Peking has signed many trade agreements with African countries, but her commerce with Africa represents so far a negligible proportion of her own total trade and of Africa's.* She has, however, staged a number of extremely successful trade and economic exhibitions which have performed the double function of correcting the old-fashioned image of China as a non-industrial power and at the same time arousing interest in Chinese goods in new markets. Peking has dispensed something like $350 million (mostly in the form of Chinese goods and services) in loans and gifts to African countries, and has promised another like amount for future use: the principal beneficiaries being the UAR, Algeria, Tanzania, Somalia, Ghana, Guinea, Mali, and Congo (Brazzaville).[13] The Chinese are probably going to build the new railway linking Tanzania with Zambia.

The African reaction to this remarkable new interest, so startling a change from the Chinese indifference to Africa until only a decade ago, has been mixed. A number of African leaders are suspicious of China's motives and even see in her demographic pressures a potential threat to their security. Among these are the late Abubakar Balewa of Nigeria, Malagasy's Tsirinana and the Ivory Coast's Houphouet-Boigny,[14] who said in 1965 that, "The danger threatening Africa today comes from China. . . . Should we, who do not want Africa to remain under foreign domination, allow it to become Chinese?"[15] Typical of this viewpoint is the opinion of Niger's President Diori Hamani, who includes China among the nations which "decide in their distant lands that such-and-such a country is not independent, and that accordingly it is necessary to destroy it in the name of the sacred concept of struggle against neo-colonialism," and the remark of Upper Volta's President Maurice Yameogo, that "We do not detest China, but we ask her to practise her policies at home only, while we build up our independence."[16]

These might be considered the views of the African right wing, but even on the left wing a similar approach can be detected, though phrased more cordially. President Julius Nyerere of Tanzania stands for the view that the Chinese are "human" and that their dogmatism ought not to cause Africans to treat them as outcasts: on the contrary the Chinese interest in Africa deserves encouragement, and they should

* The South African Government trade statistics consistently record dealings with China, although in 1960 the Peking Government suspended "all economic and trade ties with the South African colonial authorities," in sympathy with the African nationalists' call for an economic boycott of South Africa. China continues to deny that she trades with South Africa (a denial which many African politicians take with a pinch of salt), but it appears that she may have been purchasing goods of South African origin through French middlemen.

be drawn more closely into the realities of Africa so that in time their dogmatism may rub off a little. Nyerere therefore welcomes Chou En-lai and raises his glass with him, but he does not withdraw from his famous speech about the "second scramble for Africa," where he warned that the new imperialism of the Communist powers must be resisted just as strongly as the old imperialism of the West.[17] Zanzibar is regarded almost as a Chinese base by some Western commentators, but, when Chou En-lai visited it in 1965, Vice-President Karume, the Zanzibari leader, told him to his face: "No one should come here and say that they have come to lead Tanzania. Tanzania is going to be led only by the men of Tanzania." [18]

The Chinese have a strong appeal for many Africans because of their militant anti-colonialism, which matches the African concern to liberate the white-held south of their continent. As a Kenya politician said, after the clash between Chinese and Russian delegates to the Afro-Asian Conference at Moshi in 1963, "The Russians are getting too statesmanlike. We are not yet all free in Africa, and the Chinese talk the revolutionary language we want to hear." Even an anti-Communist leader of the Mozambique liberation movement has said: "There is such a dire need that we would even take arms from the devil, let alone Russia and Communist China."

But Africa's militant anti-colonialists find China's inflexible Marxist analysis hard to stomach. President Sekou Toure of Guinea believes that Communism is inappropriate for Africa because "the class struggle here is impossible, . . . there are no classes," and has said that Guinea will not subscribe "to ideologies established without African participation." There are very few pure Marxists in Africa, and the Chinese will not easily extend their influence in this direction. Their own dogmatism, however, leads them to regard such leaders as Kenyatta, Kaunda, Nyerere and Nasser as only temporary torchbearers of the revolution, destined by the logic of history to give way before long to more radical popular leaders. The Chinese lack of finesse in the events surrounding the postponements of the Afro-Asian Summit Conference in Algiers in 1965 also offended some African leaders.

Africa is in fact only part of the world struggle as it is seen from Peking. "All oppressed nations and peoples," Foreign Minister Chen Yi declared in 1959, "see in the Chinese people their tomorrow." [19] Chou En-lai said in Cairo in 1963 that the Afro-Asian civilizations had only recently been "trampled upon" by Western imperialism, and that: "Once the Asian and African people have taken destiny into their own hands, they will catch up with Western countries and even surpass them, and contribute to a new civilization of mankind." In this endeavour, he told Egyptians, China had "a special destiny, . . . to support countries which have not yet won victory or are about to win it." [20]

This even includes Latin America, and the crusade for liberation thus extends right into Uncle Sam's backyard. In 1960 Cuba became the first country on the entire American continent to recognize the Communist Chinese Government, and Havana has since become China's base for her work in the Americas. "We Cubans," Ernesto Che Guevara told his hosts in China in 1960, "can well understand the Chinese people because both of us have been subjected to American imperialist blockade, to insult and aggression." China extended $280 million in credits to Cuba during the period 1961–5. In 1961 Peking nearly established herself in the Brazil of President Quadros, but was promptly rebuffed by the right-wing successors to that eccentric radical. Despite her lack of diplomatic recognition, China has trade officials and newsmen in a number of Latin American capitals and sends frequent visitors there.[21]

The inclusion of Latin America in the league of oppressed which China seeks to organize and lead, is perhaps a token that the crusade cuts across the colours of the world's skin. Chinese policy is far from being explicitly based on any colour criterion. Albania, because of its stout resistance to Russian dictation, is dearer to the Chinese Communist heart than North Vietnam or Mali. When Mao Tse-tung made his unprecedented personal statement on the American negro problem in the summer of 1963, he called on the vast majority of the people of the world (of all colours, including white) to unite against the minority of USA reactionaries who denied equality to the American negroes.[22] Anna Louise Strong writes that the Peking ballets staged on the USA negro problem show "progressive white people fighting heroically alongside the Negroes: this is carried on film and television to educate the Chinese peoples." [23] The Chinese state that "the Asian-African countries are not a racial concept, . . . there are also white peoples in Asia and Africa." [24] *

There are undertones of racial feeling, perhaps in such statements as that of *Radio Algiers* during the 1963 visit of Chou En-lai, that, "Linked by a common ideological basis, China and Algeria will soon jeopardize the last bulwarks of colonialist occupation in the world, up to and including the

* Presumably referring to Cyprus and to some Arab countries.

famous myth of European cultural and technical superiority"; [25] and in Chou's remark at the Bandung Conference that the people of Asia would never forget that the first victim of an experimental N-bomb explosion was an Asian. East African newspapers reported the Chinese as privately saying to the Africans at an Afro-Asian meeting in 1962, "We non-whites must get together," or even "We blacks. . . ." [26] The crusade against the European and North American monopoly of power and wealth is not meant to be of one colour (or group of colours) against another, but it so happens that most of the people on one side are white and most of the people on the other side are not white, and in the heat of the struggle the colour and ideological lines sometimes blur together. Now Mao has explicitly characterized the developing countries of Africa and Asia as the world's villages, the industrial nations of the West as the world's cities: just as he led China's peasants to victory in the Chinese revolution, so, by implication, China will now lead the developing countries to defeat their Western oppressors (ignoring the Afro-Asian preference for other methods and other leadership). This analysis was spelled out most elaborately in 1965 in the long article by Lin Piao, Mao's chosen heir, entitled "Long Live the Victory of People's War." This thesis was received by some as almost a declaration of war, but in fact it does not add anything substantial to the previous Chinese policy line, and it contains a number of important cautionary statements, of which the most important is:

> In order to make a revolution and to fight a people's war and be victorious, it is imperative to adhere to the policy of self-reliance, rely on the strength of the masses in one's own country and prepare to carry on the fight independently even when all material aid from outside is cut off. If one does not operate by one's own efforts, does not independently ponder and solve the problems of the revolution in one's own country and does not rely on the strength of the masses, but leans wholly on foreign aid—even though this be aid from socialist countries which persist in revolution—no victory can be won, or be consolidated even if it is won. [27]

So Peking waits for the world revolutionary situation to explode. The USA, Chou told reporters at the end of his first African visit:

> . . . pursues a colonial policy of interference, and adopts an arrogant attitude in an attempt to control other countries . . . [but] not only the peoples cannot be held down, but even those in power in various countries sometimes find it

unbearable.* . . . Consequently the whole thing will burst, and this is the sorrow of US imperialism.[28]

Later, reporting to the National People's Congress, the Chinese Premier concluded that, "Our revolutionary influence has become wider. . . . Our international responsibilities are becoming heavier." [29] The difficulty is that China lacks the financial resources to accelerate the stream of history. She has given away more aid than she ever received from Moscow, her generosity extending to over $1¾ billion in the past eighteen years (with another $700 million committed for future use).[30] In the earlier days the recipients were mainly fraternal Communist countries (North Korea, North Vietnam, Mongolia, even Hungary and Albania), but more recently the aid programme has concentrated on Afro-Asian neutrals.[31] Chinese aid is dispensed as a contrast both to Western capitalist aid (which attempts "to realize imperialist economic aggression by the subterfuge of passing a fish eye for a pearl," as one Chinese delegate once put it in Cairo: [32] one should not imagine "that one day the imperialists would suddenly lay down their butcher's knife and become Buddhas") *and* to Russian revisionist aid. The modern revisionists, a Chinese official told a meeting of Asian economists in 1964:

> . . . lack a sincere desire to help Asian and African countries develop their independent national economies. They demand that some of these countries become their suppliers of raw materials and even control the economy of other countries; they do not trade at reasonable and mutually beneficial prices but cut down the prices of exports. . . . They sometimes provide the machinery while holding back the key machine units and parts; sometimes they provide equipment while holding back the techniques, trying all they can to make the Asian and African countries economically dependent on them.[33]

Chinese aid endeavours to compare favourably with all this. No interest is charged on loans, and borrowers usually get a grace period of ten years before they need start repaying. Peking makes a virtue of necessity by undertaking that her technicians working abroad will not live at a higher standard than their local counterparts. Thus reporters visiting the Chinese road construction project in Nepal (which links Lhasa with Kathmandu for the first time) were astonished to

---

* A reference to the dislike for some aspects of American policy to be found among the leaders of Japan, the Philippines, Thailand, and other American allies in the Afro-Asian world.

find the *"Cheeni sahibs"* cooking their own meals, dispensing with servants and working with their hands like the other labourers.[34]

With less to give away than the rich powers, China chooses her projects carefully: she usually invests in the first serious industrial plant in a previously agrarian country. This is then identified with her name and not lost in the public mind as would the dull bread-and-butter infrastructure projects such as roads, telecommunications, water conservancy and the like. Some of the Chinese projects have not succeeded, notably the Cambodian plywood factory (for which the preparation and survey was inadequate, possibly as much by the fault of the Cambodians as of the Chinese themselves).[35] The combination of Chinese bureaucratism, the disorder of the Chinese economy since 1960, and the vast distance involved (geographical as well as cultural, scientific and linguistic) has meant unusual delay in realizing many projects, but there are many examples of successful factories put up under Chinese aid: the woollen textile mill in Ulan Bator, for instance, and the Kompong Cham cotton mill in Cambodia. A small cash outlay can thus be made to gain much goodwill, especially when it is accompanied by the sort of humility sometimes shown by Chou En-lai—"Your praise embarrasses us," he once told Prince Sihanouk, "for we do not really deserve it, as China is today still economically weak. The aid we are giving to Cambodia is, in fact, very small. . . ."[36]

If the Chinese push their theory of revolution too brutally down African and other Asian (and Latin American) throats, they will risk losing friends and provoking clashes with the West. So far they have displayed some patience; when they come to realize that the Afro-Asian situation is far too complex to be contained in their simple formulations, and that the "burst" will in fact be more a ferment than an explosion, then Mao will probably have given way to younger and less visionary leaders.

Chou En-lai remarked to the National People's Congress at the end of 1964 that Mao's statements on international events in recent years "reflect the revolutionary will of the people of the world in a highly concentrated form."[37] There are Western analysts who regard the Chinese cult of Africa and of the underdeveloped world as a product of the personal megalomania of a leader frustrated at his inability to change human beings in his own society and turning therefore to a larger forum where he can pretend to be more effective.[38] China, such observers argue, is traditionally and by temperament isolationist. There is no doubt a grain of truth in this, but it would be a sad day if China were so discouraged by her poor reception in the world as to turn in upon herself again. What we are witnessing * is the beginning of the breakdown of that traditional isolation, and every chance should be taken to exploit this and to ensure that the Chinese learn as much as possible about the reality of the world they live in. It will be a lengthy process, as will be evident from the failure of those who had the best opportunity to influence the Chinese Communist outlook on the world—the Russians.

20: RUSSIA

Uncle No Longer

THE STORY IS TOLD IN PEKING THAT STALIN ONCE SENT MAO Tse-tung a book expounding the Russian experience of guerrilla fighting in the Second World War. Mao passed it on to Lin Piao, his leading general, for comment: Lin, after reading it, remarked: "If we had had this as our textbook, we should have been annihilated ten years ago." Stalin's advice to the Chinese Communists in the years before their final victory was consistently wrong and disastrous. He doubted their ability to survive alone and counselled them to cooperate with the Kuomintang, with the result that a majority of their leaders was lost in the bloodbaths of Chiang Kai-shek. In 1949 Mao went on his first pilgrimage to Moscow and made his peace with Stalin. The Soviet Union had already impressed all shades of political opinion in China by being the first foreign power voluntarily to renounce rights conferred on it by the unequal treaties of the nineteenth century. Now Stalin agreed to give up the few surviving traces of those unequal days, including the use of the military base at Port Arthur and the management of the Manchurian railway. The two countries signed treaties of friendship and military secu-

* Until 1967, when the internal upheaval of the Cultural Revolution brought out (temporarily, one hopes) the incipient chauvinism of the Chinese.

rity, and the Soviet Union granted credits * for Chinese economic development (charging interest of "only one per cent," in view of the devastation left by the war). In cash terms, Russian aid financed only about two per cent of the Chinese investment programme in the 1950s, and China received only about one eighth of Russia's total aid outflow (less than Poland or East Germany received, and only marginally more than tiny Mongolia). Subsequently Peking dispensed to other Afro-Asian governments more than she had received from the Soviet Union. Russian help was not charity, since the goods were mostly on credit and had ultimately to be paid for by the delivery of Chinese goods to Russia, but the technical advice which led to the creation of the heavy industrial base of China's First Five-Year Plan was invaluable.

Afterwards the Russian advisers were criticized by China for living at standards too ostentatiously higher than those of the Chinese technicians; for using the Chinese-paid development programme to conduct unproved experiments; [1] for failing to adapt Soviet models of equipment to Chinese conditions (ignoring the effect of the humid climate of south China, for example, or providing costly automation in a land where labour is plentiful); for failing to make adequate surveys and preparation, and so forth. These are common grievances in almost any international aid programme (Indians sometimes make this kind of comment on Western aid), but the Chinese had nothing against which to measure Russian help.†

---

* These were less than Mao had hoped for: David Floyd suggests they were only one tenth of his request (*Mao Against Khrushchev*, New York, Praeger, 1964, p. 12).

† Suslov, the Soviet leader, gave the following account of the difficulties of the Russian experts during the Great Leap Forward, "which unbalanced economic development and led to violation of accepted technical standards. The Soviet specialists could not help seeing the dangerous implications of this policy. They warned the Chinese organizations against violating technical standards. But their advice fell on deaf ears. Due to the fact that the recommendations of the Soviet specialists were ignored and that the Chinese officials grossly violated technical standards, large breakdowns occurred, some of them involving loss of life. This happened on the building site of the Hsinantsien hydro-power station, where thousands of tons of rock crashed down because technical requirements were disregarded, and work on the project was considerably delayed. At the Hsinfungtsien hydro-power project the dykes burst and the pit was flooded for the same reason. In both cases there was loss of life" (Report to the Soviet Central Committee of 14 February 1964, published in *Pravda* on 3 April and *New Times* on 15 April). The Chinese, for their part, accused the Russian experts of conservatism and insensitivity to the different conditions of China—of being "fuddy-duddies."

In the early 1950s the Soviet example was often slavishly imitated, Russia being officially regarded as a utopia where all the right answers had been found. When Russian boys and girls were separated in secondary schools, China followed: when the USSR switched to coeducation, China also followed —but without the debate over the merits of the two systems which had preceded the Russian change.[2] "Articles on geography published in Russia are read in China as if they were the Bible," a Chinese geographer complained in 1956; "if, later on, these articles are criticized [in Russia] the devotees here are non-plussed." [3] The Soviet system of giving young people strenuous physical endurance tests was faithfully copied, and only when two Chinese students died of exhaustion after a six-mile bicycle race, in which they carried a 20-pound load on their backs, was this changed.[4] But from about 1956 onwards a sense of proportion was restored, and the automatic acceptance of things Russian ceased. That was the year in which Russia itself, after all, moved decisively from the Stalinist to the Khrushchevite era.

Khrushchev's denunciation of the crimes of Stalin was a turning point in Sino-Soviet relations as well as in the history of world Communism. Mao and his Chinese colleagues were astonished that the Soviet leadership should announce such far-reaching policy changes, affecting the whole international Communist movement, without consulting the other Communist Parties. Stalin was much more than a dictator of Russia: he had led the world Communist cause through three eventful decades, and such men as Mao surely deserved the courtesy of advance warning that the Russian Party was now to turn its back on Stalin's memory? The Chinese disagreed with much that Stalin did, and were among the major victims of his mistakes, but they also found much to quarrel with in the Khrushchev platform. The Chinese and the Russian Communists were in true harness together for only seven years, from 1950 to 1956: they had won and maintained power by totally different methods and faced completely different problems, and even during their seven-year marriage they failed to create a genuine working relationship. Khrushchev was equally put out and angered when the Chinese, two years later, announced startling new ideological claims (for the Leap Forward and the People's Communes) without any reference to the Kremlin.

The Sino-Soviet argument over methods of constructing socialism in a country where the Communist Party had already won power (how fast to collectivize, how to deal with the bourgeoisie, how to develop the material base of the economy) was less important, because a good deal of local differentiation in domestic policy is acceptable in the post-Stalinist Communist world. But the differences over how to bring the Communists to power in the West and in the uncommitted Afro-Asian world could not be so easily suppressed. The Chinese leaders are active revolutionaries: every one of them has led armies in the field and conducted uprisings and strikes against the class enemy. Though old in years, they are young in ardour, and believe that the natural world drift towards socialism could be greatly accelerated by the wise but firm exploitation of the Communist states' power. The Russians are now led by technicians who do not remember the fighting, and in any case the Russians never had to fight for their revolution in the way the Chinese did. The Russian outlook on the world is much more cautious, more anxious about the consequences of violent action, wiser but less exciting. The Russians have built their state up so that they have something to lose by world instability, while the Chinese have only just arrived and see less reason for not lighting the flames of revolt everywhere.

When Moscow acquired its first Inter-Continental Ballistic Missile and sent up the first space satellites in 1957, the Chinese assumed that the scales had been turned and that the Communist camp, at last superior in power to the capitalists, could begin to assert itself. As Mao told the assembled leaders of world Communism in Moscow at the end of 1957:

> I am of the opinion that the international situation has now reached a new turning-point. There are two winds in the world today: the East Wind and the West Wind. . . . I think the characteristic of the situation today is the East Wind prevailing over the West Wind. That is to say, the socialist forces are overwhelmingly superior to the imperialist forces.*

This was a technical misassessment: the Russian advance in modern weapons still left the balance of military advantage

* As published in the *Peking Review*, 13 December 1958. The Russians have since charged Mao with attaching a racial meaning to this famous phrase about the East Wind, and many Western commentators have followed suit: Michael Field has based the title of his book, *The Prevailing Wind* (Methuen, London, 1965), on this misconception (pp. 378–9). The origin of the phrase is in the eighteenth-century novel *Dream of the Red Chamber*, where a character remarks: "If it is not the eastern wind crushing the western wind, then it is the western wind crushing the eastern"—a phrase usually taken as a cynical comment on the fickleness and valuelessness of politics. West and East had at that time no racial or cultural connotations in China. By East, Mao here means the Communist camp, including the Soviet Union, as he makes clear in the passage quoted in the text. See CQ 10, 1962, p. 154.

with the USA, and the Russian leaders themselves never claimed (or acted on the assumption that they possessed) actual military superiority.[5] They were in any case anxious to consolidate a tactical accommodation with the US—which the Chinese opposed, because any deal with the imperialists was like asking "a cat to keep away from fish." [6] The Chinese argued that the new weapons justified a tougher policy towards the West. It was in this mood that they prepared seriously to scare the Americans out of Taiwan in 1958 (but refused Russian help to do so),[7] and that they counselled physical Soviet intervention in the Middle East crisis of 1958 (when a nationalist, anti-Western *coup d'état* succeeded in Iraq, and British and American troops landed in Jordan and Lebanon, at the request of the right-wing governments of those countries, to bolster them against possible revolution). Peking was willing, in the encouragement of these "wars of national liberation," to walk closer to the brink of nuclear war than the Russians.

Moscow has since accused China of advocating nuclear war, and of discounting the cost to mankind of a nuclear holocaust. Suslov quotes from Mao's speech in Moscow in 1957 a blood-curdling excerpt:

> Can one foresee the number of human lives that a future war may take? It may be one third of the 2 billion inhabitants of the world, that is, a mere 900 million people. . . . I had an argument over this matter with Nehru. He is more pessimistic in this respect than I. I told him that should half of mankind be destroyed, the other half would survive, and what is more, imperialism would be wiped out completely and there would be only socialism in the world. In half a century or a whole century, the population would grow again —even by more than half. . . .[8]

This remark shows Mao in a characteristic mental pose, that of the man faced with overwhelming odds (as the Chinese Communists were in their early days), but determined to rally his companions' spirits by drawing attention to the good side of things however bad the immediate prospect appears. Mao is not so insane as to argue that the Communist powers should, at a favourable moment, make a nuclear strike against the West, and indeed he later criticized Khrushchev for his initial "adventurism" in supplying missiles to Cuba. The Chinese have recently reaffirmed that they would never be the first to use a nuclear weapon.[9] Mao does, however, apparently believe that the leaders of Western capitalism might, in a moment of desperation, use their nuclear weapons against a surging tide of world socialist revolution, and that

Communists ought to be mentally prepared for this: it is a very Chinese gesture outwardly to make light of the bad things that one's enemies could do to one. Mao also believes that to dwell on the gloomy side of things diminishes a man's revolutionary spirit and his ability to assert the maximum control of his environment. "Even if the Americans are crazy enough to start a nuclear war," he is saying, "that doesn't necessarily mean the end of the world." [10] As with many issues in the Sino-Soviet dispute, this is a difference of emphasis rather than of substance.*

The area of policy affected by these different attitudes about war is chiefly that concerning the uncommitted world, for which China regards herself as the chosen torchbearer of Marxism. In the mid-1950s the Russians and Chinese jointly wooed the Afro-Asian neutrals, with financial aid and political sympathy, in the belief that the cause of socialism would thereby be promoted. The Chinese were less convinced of the logic of this than the Russians; they had grave reservations about the ideological dependability of such bourgeois leaders as Nehru, Nasser, Sukarno and Nkrumah (remembering how Chiang Kai-shek had taken advantage of Stalin's trustingness to turn on the Chinese Communists), and they also felt that the financial resources of the Communist camp ought to be put to work within the camp. As in other aspects of the Sino-Soviet dispute, the Chinese viewpoint is best expressed in an Albanian newspaper article (in 1961), asking why the Russians were giving economic aid to neutral countries before the socialist states themselves had become "showcases of prosperity."

Mao gave the "Bandung spirit" a trial, only to find that the hold of the West on the Afro-Asian neutrals was in no serious way dislodged, and that indigenous capitalist elements were being boosted in such countries as India. From 1958 onwards the Chinese urged a more constant application of pressure on the neutral world. They helped the embattled Algerian nationalists at a time when Russia thought it a better prize to woo de Gaulle away from the American camp. They aided the left-wing Congolese rebels against Tshombe when the Russians were still in diplomatic relations with him. They may have encouraged the Iraqi Communists in 1959 to bring their differences with the Kassim Government to a head before they were ready to face a show-down (and thus

---

* The same goes for Mao's celebrated characterization of nuclear bombs, of all reactionaries and of all enemies, as "paper tigers." His purpose is to minimize the enemy's strength tactically, while acknowledging it strategically: in short, the phrase is a morale-boosting slogan.

contributed to their defeat). They argued that the Kremlin ought not to have withdrawn its missiles from Cuba (though they also said that it would have been wiser never to have installed them there in the first place), and that the Russians should have taken a tougher line in Brazil. All this is a debate over tactics more than basic aims: both powers agree that their objective is to spread Communism everywhere as fast as possible. But they are competing for the prestige of being regarded as the best steward of Marxism and the cleverest general of its armies. China thus fights bitterly to exclude Russia from the Afro-Asian organizations, which she regards as her own responsibility. Russia was not invited to the original Bandung Conference of 1955, in spite of the Asian Republics within the USSR, but the competition for the mantle of Marx now drives her to seek membership of the Afro-Asian club. She is met by such remarks as that allegedly made to the Soviet delegation at Moshi in 1963 by Liu Ning-yi, the chief Chinese delegate to the Afro-Asian Solidarity meeting there: "East European countries should not interfere in Asian and African affairs. . . . We regret the fact that you have come at all. Who wants you here? It is an insult to the solidarity movement of the Afro-Asian countries." [11] The battle still continues over Russian membership of the various Afro-Asian organizations.

In November 1960, eighty-one Communist Parties met in Moscow and agreed on a Declaration of principles which both Peking and Moscow signed: it was a compromise document, which both sides later used to support their differing views.[12] The polemics were hard-hitting. The *People's Daily* referred to Khrushchev as "a Bible-reading and psalm-singing buffoon," [13] and Suslov called the Chinese "hysterical." So doctrinally sure of themselves are the Chinese that they defend open polemics as promoting the world's education in scientific Marxist debate (whereas the Russians would have preferred secret exchanges). In 1963 lengthy letters were exchanged between the two Parties: one of the Chinese replies was read five times on all domestic radio stations, an exercise which took thirteen hours. For Peking this was the "great debate" of the century, taking precedence over such minor affairs as the Indian border quarrel and the economic crisis. At last China was again a leading participant in the international forum of the human mind. As the purer theorists, they gained supporters among intellectuals everywhere. Two East German philosophers spoke for many in 1959: "Khrushchev is just an economic pragmatist," one remarked, "but Mao is a thinker." The other commented: "We need ideals, and the only place you can get them today is from Mao, . . . not from Khrushchev." [14] The Asian Communist Parties initially threw their support behind Peking (save for Mongolia and the pro-Soviet Dange faction of the Indian Party), and so did the New Zealand Party and strong factions of the Australian, Belgian, Brazilian, and other Parties. Some Parties broke into two or even three splinter groups: the "Split" has been compared with the Bolshevik-Menshevik debate of Communism's early days, and with the schism in the Christian Church of Europe in the middle ages. Russia tried to hold another world meeting in 1965, but only nineteen Parties attended.* Peking declares that it might take eight or ten years to prepare for a successful world Communist conference.[15] When Khrushchev fell, the Chinese felt at first vindicated in their criticism of him, but soon accused the new Soviet leadership of ousting him "because Khrushchev himself had become a serious obstacle to carrying out Khrushchevite revisionism." [16] Later they roundly accused the Russian leaders of "accelerating the restoration of capitalism" in the Soviet Union.[17]

There is a strong element of national rivalry, independent of ideological considerations, in the dispute. President de Gaulle may be too forward in predicting that China will ultimately take over Soviet Asia with its tempting economic resources, but there is certainly tension over the Sino-Soviet border. Japanese politicians reported in 1964 that Mao told them that:

> The Soviet Union occupies an area of twenty-two million square kilometres, while its population is only 20 million. It is time to put an end to this allotment. . . . About a hundred years ago the area east of Baikal became Russian territory and since then Vladivostok,† Khabarovsk, Kamchatka and other areas have been Soviet territory. We have not yet presented our account for this list.[18]

The Russian reply to this was:

> Naturally we will not defend the Russian czars who permitted arbitrariness in laying down the state boundaries with neighbouring countries. We are convinced that you too do not intend to defend the Chinese Emperors who by force of

---

* Chinese students in Moscow led demonstrations against the American Embassy, much to the embarrassment of the Russians, during this meeting, which coincided with a worsening of the Vietnam war. The *People's Daily* was thus able to print a photograph of Asian students being manhandled by Soviet police (next to another picture of American police manhandling negroes); see CNA 567, 4 June 1965.

† The name Vladivostok means "Rule the East," in itself offensive in Chinese ears.

arms seized not a few territories belonging to others. . . .

To which the Chinese counter-replied:

> Although the old treaties relating to the Sino-Russian boundary are unequal treaties, the Chinese Government is nevertheless willing to respect them and take them as the basis for a reasonable settlement of the Sino-Soviet boundary question. . . .[19]

Border negotiations were in fact held, in close secret, in 1965, but clashes on the Ussuri River took place in March 1969.

In the summer of 1960 the Russians recalled all their experts from China and cancelled many contracts for the delivery of key equipment to China. The Chinese economy was dealt a blow from which it took many years to recover. Some trade was still carried on, but at a lower level than before, and in 1965 China finally paid off all her debts to Moscow. When the Russians tried recently to resume their economic aid, hoping thereby to regain political influence in China, the Chinese rejected these new approaches:

> To be frank, the Chinese people cannot trust you. . . . You have insisted on providing large amounts of goods which we do not really need. . . . For several years you have used the trade between our two countries as an instrument for bringing political pressure on China. . . . The prices of many of the Soviet goods . . . were much higher than those on the world market.* . . . Soviet aid to China, mainly in the form of trade, was far from *gratis*. . . .[20]

In view of the appalling gap between Soviet and Chinese living standards, Khrushchev was cruelly insensitive in his taunts about the Chinese philosophy that "to drink watery soup is Communism, but to labour for a better life is capitalism." His 1961 long-term programme for the USSR boasted of creating for the Russians "a cup of plenty which would always be full to the brim," and the Soviet attitude is, in Edward Crankshaw's phrase, "prosperity for the Soviet Union —and good luck to the rest of the comrades." The Chinese were always critical of the Soviet leaders' stress on raising Russian living standards,[21] and the gap between the two standards of living is undoubtedly widening, just as it is between the industrialized West and the undeveloped nations of the capitalist world. National income per head is estimated by

* Yet the Minister of Foreign Trade, Yeh Chi-chuang, had declared in his report for 1956 that, "the prices governing the Sino-Soviet trade are fair and just, and we have not suffered any loss" (speech of 11 July 1957, quoted in Li, Chapter 7, p. 192)!

Pick's, the American authority, at about $1,300 in Russia, compared with only $75 or so in China. A booklet by the Soviet leader Ponomarev recently accused China of demanding equal distribution among socialist countries, as if this were quite improper.[22] Some of the Russian leaders doubtless feel that their interest lies in securing a decisive breakthrough in Chinese economic development, otherwise the growing gap between the two economic levels will cause tensions liable to provoke Chinese violence and thus threaten the higher Soviet standards. But less farsighted Russians presumably feel that to help China too much would be to hasten the day when she will dictate to Russia by virtue of her numbers.

The sad thing is that the Russians wasted a golden opportunity in 1949 to shepherd a long-lost China back into the stream of international life. Privately they will now admit that they were not sufficiently prepared for the difficulties of a relationship with China. They had ignored the study of Chinese history and culture which might have allowed them to understand Chinese ways of thought and action. Instead they assumed that their own European tradition was a sufficient basis for understanding. Even in 1960 George Sherman found that Muscovite intellectuals regarded the West as better informed about China than they were themselves, and complained that the Chinese were apparently retiring into their shells just as the Russians were beginning to emerge from theirs.[23] There was fault on both sides: the Chinese were equally unprepared for the Russian embrace. But the senior partner always owes more to the enterprise, and it will always be a matter of profound regret that the Sino-Soviet honeymoon was so brief, so unhappy and so infertile. Those in the West who welcome China's estrangement from Moscow have a short-sighted view of the problems posed by China's isolation.

21: THE WORLD

Lamb into Lion

"CHINA . . . IS NO LONGER A LAMB THAT COULD BE SLAUGHtered at people's pleasure," the *People's Daily* declared proudly in 1961.[1] Some of its foreign readers might be pardoned for thinking that the lamb had turned into a remarkably uncooperative and noisy lion. China's foreign policy can be reduced to one basic objective: to reassert herself as a great world power. Paradoxically it is easier to achieve this in the wider world of Africa, Europe and the United Nations, where Chairman Mao already casts a long shadow, than in China's immediate neighbourhood. Her efforts to establish a kind of "Monroe Doctrine," which would acknowledge her general hegemony in East Asia, collide with the stone wall of American power.

Chinese leaders frequently express their fear of American encirclement. Foreign Minister Chen Yi told the General Manager of *Reuter's* in 1961:

> US military bases in Taiwan, Okinawa, Japan, South Korea, South Vietnam and the Philippines are all directed against China. How can we escape fear? The US has nuclear weapons. We have none. We have our fears. They are always in our minds. We cannot sleep easily at night.[2]

There is also a genuine apprehensiveness among the Chinese about a possible revival of Japanese militarism. They foresee a right-wing government in Japan openly abandoning its pacifist constitution and rearming to become America's policeman in East Asia, controlling South Korea, Taiwan and the Philippines. Peking therefore seeks by all practicable means to expel American power from the area and extend her own influence there. Michael Field, the British correspondent, reports that Chou En-lai once told Prince Sihanouk bluntly that the Chinese were not concerned about the French military instructors in Cambodia, because France could not threaten China, but "if you bring the Americans in, we shall be obliged to attack you." [3] In the pre-Bandung days of 1950, a Chinese official warned that U Nu, the Burmese leader, had become (because of his vote against North Korea in the UN debate, his retention of British advisers, his admission of American private capital and his rumoured agreement to the establishment of foreign airfields) "a springboard of aggression against the People's Republic of China." [4] Peking would like to be surrounded by states that are strictly neutral and help her to feel secure against foreign invasion: this would restore her former status as the dominant power of East Asia, but she is thwarted by her continuing military and economic weakness *vis-à-vis* America. She dare not press too hard against the American wall in East Asia in case she provokes an American attack.

Snubbed by the West, the Chinese have now turned their attention to the Afro-Asian bloc, but it is most unlikely that they sincerely identify themselves with the so-called "coloured" nations. Like the Japanese and the Koreans, they feel instinctively that they are the equals of the Europeans, and, jointly with them, superior to the Africans and to the darker-skinned people of South Asia. Andrew Corsalis wrote to his patron, Lorenzo de' Medici, in 1515 that the Chinese were a skilful race, *"di nostra qualità."* [5] The Chinese in those days characteristically jibbed at according formal equality to the Europeans, but acknowledged that the Europeans (and Arabs) were at least nearer to the Chinese level of civilization than were the barbarians of the South Seas. Although Europeans' respect for China was largely destroyed by their nineteenth-century discovery of her effeteness, the Chinese sentiments survived. If once China were to be accorded an equal place in the world's highest counsels, along with the USA, Western Europe and Russia, she would probably conduct a gradual disengagement from her temporary, tactical identification with the have-nots of the Afro-Asian world.

The Afro-Asian idea is thus one vehicle for the reassertion of China's power in the world: the Communist movement is an even more important one. It was through her membership in this club that Chou En-lai was able in 1956 and 1957 to appear in Eastern Europe as a mediator among the quarrelsome heirs to Stalin, that Molotov paid her the compliment in 1955 of calling her "co-leader" of the club above the smaller European members, and that Peking assumed the role of diplomatic rich uncle to the Hungarians and Albanians [6] in their hours of need. Now the Chinese have broken out of their joint harness with the Russians and astonished the world by offering an alternative world leadership for the Communist movement, one that is accepted not merely by some Asian Communists but also by a number of sincere and idealistic Marxists in Europe and America.

The Chinese feel intensely proud of their ideological integrity. When Anna Louise Strong expressed to a Chinese leader in Peking her concern over the withdrawal of Russian economic aid in 1960, he said to her: "We do not thus regard it. An economic setback can be relatively soon overcome. A mistaken 'line' could curse our children's children." [7] The North Korean publication *Rodong Shimoon* spelled out in April 1963 what the Chinese themselves undoubtedly feel, but cannot express without seeming immodest, the view that the leadership of international Communism would, as Lenin predicted, pass to Asia. China believes herself to have a new civilizing mission. Our work, the *China Youth Daily* told its readers in 1963, is not finished with the liberation of China from feudalism, capitalism and imperialism, for two thirds of humanity remain in bondage: our task is no less than "the liberation of mankind." [8]

The West sees China as reaching the phase of nineteenth-century imperialism which Europe itself experienced; but the Chinese see themselves as conducting a crusade for a better world, as coming in from a "new" world to redress the inequities of the "old." It is really cultural recognition which China seeks, even above material or military power. She wants her cultural tradition to be respected by foreign powers, but by the application of their intelligence rather than her bayonets, and because Europeans rejected her indigenous culture a century ago she presents her claims now in the guise of an ultra-Western mission—Marxism.

The other civilizations have long ago bent the knee to Europe: the Arabs, the Hindus, the Amerindians, the Africans, the Malays are all culturally subverted by the sheer grandeur of Europe's intellectual and technological achievement. So, incidentally, is Japan, an offshoot of Chinese civilization now entering a phase of acute cultural schizophrenia as a result of Mao's challenge to the Westernization which it accepted in 1945. True, the Chinese are supporting their cultural comeback by the use of a distinctively European ideology, but their split with Moscow heralds the transformation of Chinese Marxism from a vehicle by which China might have become culturally assimilated into European or Western civilization, to an instrument by which she proposes to challenge the West's claim to have provided a model for the whole world. China is thus the apostle of a genuinely polycultural world with institutions which make more than superficial concessions to the "quaint" customs of non-Western peoples. Bertrand Russell sensed this when he wrote, in his *History of Western Philosophy*:

> I think that if we are to feel at home in the world . . . we shall have to admit Asia to equality in our thoughts, not only politically but culturally. What changes this will bring about I do not know, but I am convinced that they will be profound and of the greatest importance.[9]

One area in which such an accommodation could take place is that of law. In the Graeco-Roman-Judaic tradition of the West, law is sacrosanct, but the Chinese have always despised law, attaching greater importance to personal and intrafamilial relations. Law has never been a favourite course of study in Chinese universities, and the Chinese courts exercise more a parental than a judicial kind of authority: in a society still so familial, where individuality is relatively little advanced, the judge is a conciliator who seeks to convince both parties to accept his judgment. The idea of the judge merely holding an arena in which two equal adversaries must fight under agreed rules is quite alien to China.[10] It is in this light that sense can be made of the Chinese antipathy for the legalistic Indian arguments over the border dispute, their apparently obstructive attitude towards the prolonged legal wrangles in which the Korean War involved them with the United Nations, their under-estimation of the complexity of international disarmament procedure and their fury over the Hongkong court sentences on Communist journalists in 1967. Where America and Russia require a formidable array of checks and arbitration machinery before they will trust each other to honour a disarmament pledge, Peking appears to believe that a summit meeting of heads of all world governments could achieve "the complete, thorough, total and resolute prohibition and destruction of nuclear weapons." [11]

The *People's Daily* once declared quite squarely that: "International law is one of the instruments in international problems. When this instrument is useful to us, we use it; when this instrument is of no use to us, we use other instruments." [12] China's attitude towards what little machinery the Western nations have constructed to maintain international discipline is thus one of immense suspicion.

When the British Courts threatened to deprive the Peking Government of some seventy civil aircraft which an American firm (in partnership with the Kuomintang) had brought to Hongkong on the eve of the Communists' victory, the Chinese responded by requisitioning British property in Shanghai worth approximately the same value: the impersonal workings of English law seemed to them a trick to deny them their political rights as the new Government of China.[13] But where there is no room for cultural misunderstanding over the nature of the judicial authority, the Chinese display the traditional good dealings for which they have become so famous among Western traders (who have come to know that once a Chinese has given his word he will never renege on it despite the absence of legal documentation). Thus when a Skymaster belonging to Cathay Pacific Airways was shot down by Chinese guns off Hainan Island in 1954, Peking acknowledged its fault, apologized and promptly paid over $1 million in compensation.[14]

But any form of third party arbitration remains abhorrent

to the Chinese, who refused to accept an International Red Cross investigation into the alleged use of germ warfare by United Nations troops in Korea in 1952, or the Dalai Lama's suggestion for international arbitration of the dispute between Tibet and Peking over the definition of "autonomy" in 1959, or the six-power Colombo proposals for a cease-fire on the Indian border in 1962. Two Western states would agree to refer a dispute (as France and Britain referred their disagreement over sovereignty of one of the Channel Islands) to the World Court without considering themselves involved in any humiliating subjection to the lawyers who happen for the time being to occupy the chairs on the World Court. For Western states this kind of arbitration is a convenience, enabling a popular government to make a concession to a foreign state without appearing to give way: it is the court that may be blamed for the loss of national interest or pride, not the government of the losing side. For the Chinese there is no substitute for a genuine bilateral agreement which neither side can afterwards dishonour without total disgrace. It is possible that in the coming decades, while the Chinese draw nearer to accepting the Western-initiated world system, the West may at the same time come to see the utility of an approach to international law which places a premium on conciliation and voluntary compromise. It is in this kind of way that Russell's idea of cultural accommodation between the West and Asia (of which China is the most serious spokesman) might well be realized.

The Western reaction to the Chinese challenge for cultural and material parity falls into two categories. The first is one of total opposition to what is regarded as China's budding national aggressiveness on the classic Western model. This was the viewpoint of General Douglas MacArthur, who told a joint session of the American Congress, after his dismissal from the Korean command in 1951, that the Chinese Communists' "aggressiveness recently displayed not only in Korea but also in Indochina and Tibet, and pointing potentially towards the south, reflects predominantly the same lust for the expansion of power which has animated every would-be conqueror since the beginning of time." [15] It is from this standpoint that Dulles and his successors at the State Department have justified their policy of boycotting and isolating China. Recognition of the Communist Government, they say, would discourage Mao's domestic opposition, disappoint the Overseas Chinese who look for a non-Communist China, betray the population of Taiwan, demoralize the anti-Communist Asian states and destroy the United Nations.[16] Anyone who

sees the current world situation as primarily an urgent struggle to the death between the ideologies of capitalism and
Communism might agree with the Dullesian view, but there
is now a preference in the West for the view that capitalism
would be better served by a gradual and unspectacular sub-
version of Communism (which would be hastened by an increase in contacts) than by a violent confrontation. It is difficult to envisage within the foreseeable future a world with a
non-Communist China, and the Dullesian position has become increasingly unrealistic.

Some observers saw in the Cultural Revolution of 1966–8
a confirmation of the worst fears of the Dulles-MacArthur
school. Chinese foreign policy was certainly a victim of the
Cultural Revolution, the tensions of which inevitably over-
flowed into the Chinese communities overseas and were even
injected into the various diplomatic and commercial missions
of the Chinese abroad. At one point groups of young Red
Guards attacked the Chinese Foreign Ministry in Peking and
stole or burnt some of its documents, and for five days the
Ministry was under the control of a group of extreme leftist
officials: it was during this interregnum that the British mission was set on fire. But Chou En-lai quickly re-established
his authority over the Foreign Ministry and reinstated Chen
Yi as its head. By 1968 more normal relations were re-established with many of the countries which had been
offended by the chauvinistic extremism evinced at the height
of the Cultural Revolution. The eventual acceptance of the
Paris peace talks on Vietnam, which Peking had initially opposed, and the early approach to sound out the incoming
Nixon administration about its East Asia policy, suggested
that these excesses had been an aberration in China's foreign
relations.

The second attitude towards China discernible in the West
(especially in Western Europe and the Commonwealth) is
that more or less peaceful coexistence with Peking is both
possible and desirable. Many of the arguments which led to
the Western-Soviet "thaw" in the mid-1950s are applicable to
Sino-Western relations, with the added difficulty, however,
that China (unlike Russia) is an unsatisfied state. That Mao's
consummation of his own Chinese revolution is now thwarted
by the American support for the Kuomintang on Taiwan, or
that China's natural yearnings for a major say in East Asian
affairs are totally frustrated by the presence in the area of
American power, are not, for the Chinese, matters of ideology. It was nationalistic rather than ideological considerations
which led Peking into the engagements which earned her

(not entirely fairly) the reputation of being aggressive—in Korea, Tibet, the Indian border and the Taiwan Straits. This second Western view holds, therefore, that a degree of accommodation to Chinese national self-interest (probably involving a Western disengagement from Taiwan, together with China's admission to the United Nations, and possibly also some visible recognition of her right to have a voice in East Asian affairs) would make possible a relationship with Communist China not substantially more difficult than that which the West already enjoys with the Soviet Union. It is possible that such a relationship could involve tacit agreement over the existence of non-Communist (but neutral) states in East and Southeast Asia. The official American view is, however, that no Chinese Communist is to be trusted to keep such a tacit bargain, and that only American support can prevent the spreading of Communism throughout the area. There is also a joint resolution of Congress on the record, dating from early 1955, which unequivocally states: "The secure possession by friendly Governments of the Western Pacific island chain, of which Formosa is a part, is essential to the vital interests of the United States." [17] It is idle to argue that the same logic would allow China to claim similar rights in Hawaii and the eastern Pacific, because the Congressional position is based bluntly on American national interest, and for the foreseeable future the United States will be the dominating power in the Pacific by virtue of her wealth.

There is evidence that American policy has succeeded in making the Chinese feel isolated, especially since their quarrel with the Soviet Union. *Red Flag,* the Chinese Communists' own magazine, referred in 1963 to the 'Holy Alliance' against China, formed by Kennedy, Nehru, Khrushchev and Tito.[18] At the same time the *People's Daily* was publishing a series of letters to the editor under the headline: "Our Friends and Comrades Fill the Whole World"—a sign that some Chinese comrades needed reassuring.[19] The Chinese sometimes explain to visitors that they are now threatened on every side: by US-backed forces to the east (Taiwan), south (Laos-Vietnam) and west (India), and by the USSR to the north. It is indeed this extraordinary vulnerability which makes any serious military adventures by Peking so unlikely. It must also serve as a warning, to Chinese and non-Chinese alike, that the meeting between the newly reinvigorated China and a world accustomed to her absence is a highly difficult one. No doubt the next generation of Chinese leaders will have formed reservations about a policy which has succeeded in leaving China with no friends in the world worth the name, and will begin to move towards a greater understanding of how the rest of us, the non-Chinese three-quarters of humanity, work and think and live. As Professor C. P. Fitzgerald has said:

> When to later generations the expectation of world-wide Communism is no more real than the millennium has become to the Christian, the sharp hostility towards the unregenerate part of the world will also fade. . . . The future Chinese Communist, assured of the stability of his own system and no longer deluded into the belief that it is about to be accepted by others, will be ready to understand and practise toleration.[20]

But the rest of the world must also prepare for its part in that accommodation. It is too visionary to expect, what Per Haekkerup, the Danish statesman, and Cyrus H. Peake, the American diplomatist, have advocated: a world-wide pledge, backed by both Moscow and Washington, to help China move decisively out of her material poverty and her spiritual isolation into the broad stream of the modern world.[21] But it is a matter of great urgency that the rest of the world should increase its studies of Chinese history, culture and language so that it is better prepared than it was in 1949 for the challenging new relationship *inter pares* which the Chinese demand.

CONCLUSION

The Future

WHEN THE COMMUNISTS BEGAN TO RULE CHINA IN 1949 THEY enjoyed considerable goodwill. An American General spoke for many, both Chinese and non-Chinese, when he called the Kuomintang in 1948 the "world's worst leadership," [1] and Li Tsung-jen, the middle-of-the-road figure who tried, as President of China for a brief period in mid-1949, to reconcile the Kuomintang and the Communists, said afterwards that Mao came to power "not because of the merits of Communism, but because the regime of Chiang Kai-shek was rotten to the core." [2] A clean break was made with the past in 1949, and power was taken by people who had a coherent and clear political philosophy of some international reputation, were reasonably honest and incorrupt, enjoyed close links with the ordinary people and had forged the habit of working together as a team. There were many thoughtful Chinese who felt that Communism, under these leaders, might not be a bad instrument for the drastic surgery that was needed to modernize the country.

The Communists' handicap was their guerrilla training, which was essential for their slow march to power but hardly relevant to running a nation of hundreds of millions of people. Mao recognized this: soon after taking power he observed: "A serious task of economic construction is ahead of us. Things in which we were well versed will soon be needed no longer, and we shall have to do things in which we are not versed. This is our trouble." [3] Teng Hsiao-ping, then the rising

235

light in the Politburo, shed a tear at the Eighth Party Congress in 1956 for the good old days when "soldiers carried water for the people, and the army officers covered the soldiers with blankets." [4] But this simple idealism had become corrupted, and many of the Party's ideas about administration, arts, science and the economy proved old-fashioned, philistine and ineffective. Hu Feng, the writer, referred to the "crypto-feudalist" elements of the Chinese Communist Party: [5] these are the men, the hard core of the few thousand survivors of the Long March of thirty years ago, who try to industrialize by "cavalry charges," who treat Doctors of Science like office-boys, who regard novels and Western music as frivolities, and who believe that the inhabitants of a quarter of the globe can be rallied to make steel or become literate or change their morality by the blowing of bugles, the shouting of slogans and the reading of sermons.

It is this handicap which prevented Communist rule from being as successful as its early admirers had hoped. In 1954, when China's new Constitution was adopted, Mao Tse-tung defined the five tasks of his government: to unite the Chinese people, win the support of its friends in all nations, build a great socialist state, defend peace and further human progress.[6] None of these goals has been attained.

Unity was almost won: Taiwan remains the only gap on the Communist map. Even Taiwan might be closer to reintegration in the Chinese family if Mao had been less mistrustful of the Americans, followed Khrushchev's advice and negotiated the neutralization of the island. But the unity of the greater Chinese family has been bought at the cost of immense strain between the Hans and the minority races, and it may be doubted whether Tibet will ever become reconciled to Chinese rule.

Friends abroad have been estranged by the apparent inflexibility and crudeness of Chinese diplomacy. Some of the blame for this must be attributed to cultural misunderstanding, but when things go against them the Chinese tend to sulk and bluster (as they did over the Algiers Conference in 1965, and at some of the stages in their dispute with the Soviet Union). They have given the impression of being bad losers. China has fewer friends in the world today than she had in 1949 (when such leaders as Nehru and Attlee showed much sympathy towards the new government).

Socialism remains a dream in China, as it does elsewhere. Mao has shown the world that China possesses unique social techniques for reducing tension between classes, but even he has failed to persuade the ordinary Chinese to think collectively and work unselfishly for the social good. Individualism has not been stamped out among the peasantry, and the bourgeoisie looks suspiciously as if it is biding its time for better days. China is in some ways more socialist than Russia, but paradoxically this is largely a legacy from her recent feudalism. As the individual becomes liberated by education and by the forces of socio-economic change, the attainment of socialism will become even more difficult, as Mao acknowledged in launching the Cultural Revolution. Socialism also depends on material economic progress, and while the Communists have done better than their predecessors in developing the economy, their efforts still fall short.

There has been more peace during the Communist administration than under previous regimes, but China in the past sixteen years has become involved in fighting United Nations forces in Korea and Indian troops on the Himalayan border. Neither of these incidents was caused by Chinese aggressiveness, but Peking has shown itself less interested in world peace than in global revolution.

Human progress will undoubtedly be furthered by developments in China, but not until her scientists, intellectuals and administrators shed their nervousness and go some way further towards resolving their domestic tensions. In recent years Communist China's art has been too stifled, her science too shackled, her political message too rudely broadcast, to make any serious impact on the world at large.

The catalogue of failures may sound depressing. They are an improvement on the Kuomintang period, however, and there is hope for more success in the future. A new group of technocratic-nationalist leaders can be expected to emerge during the 1970s. By then a younger generation, born under the red flag and taught the glimmerings of modern science in the schools, will be taking its place in adult society, and the first signs of radical social change ought to become apparent. John Foster Dulles declared in 1957 that:

> We know that the materialistic rule of international Communism will never permanently serve the aspirations with which human beings are endowed. . . . Communism is repugnant to the Chinese people. They are, above all, individualists.[7]

Possibly the premature resurgence of individualism in China might jeopardize the collective discipline which radical social change requires, but there can be little doubt that in the end it will assert itself again.

By then Chinese society will be very different. Its familial basis will have been fatally undermined and modern rational attitudes will have become established as the new ideal. To take one example: no foreign observer can hope to understand contemporary China or the Chinese tradition without studying the concept of "face," so important in a society where sanctions are based on shame rather than guilt. Yet the official fictional literature of contemporary China studiously avoids the go-between so beloved of traditional life and literature, and portrays adversaries who face each other squarely, without middlemen to render their personal relations or dealings safe from a direct and overt loss of reputation.[8] The consequences of this are profound, though they will not be seen for many many years. One can safely predict that the Chinese will become, not more difficult, but more easy for outsiders to understand, as their social behaviour turns slightly towards what one might call the modern universal norm.

The Chinese will also become better informed about the world. Of the seven old men who form the inner circle of the now divided Politburo, four have never been in any non-Communist country at all (Mao himself has been outside China only twice, to visit Moscow in 1950 and 1957), two have not seen any non-Communist country for the past forty years, and only one (Chou En-lai) has any recent personal experience of modern capitalism. Even he has not visited any of the giant Western cities since his student days in Paris forty-five years ago: Geneva and Cairo are the largest capitalist centres he has seen in recent years. No senior Chinese leader has been to post-war America, Britain, France, West Germany or Japan. The first Western politician whom Mao met was Clement Attlee, during his visit to China in 1954, when Mao was already over sixty. The official Chinese press maintains an image of the West that is at least one generation out of date. The only Western film deemed worthy of dubbing for Chinese audiences during the first few years of Communist rule was Oliver Twist,[9] and the London correspondent of the People's Daily in 1959 actually penned the words: "The conditions described by the great English writer Dickens a hundred years ago have not changed." [10] The slanted view of the world purveyed by the People's Daily does not mislead the Communist leaders themselves. Reasonably informed and objective digests of the foreign press are circulated to Party and Government officers and intellectuals. Mao Tse-tung reads modern Western books and periodicals, especially in the field of military strategy: but just as Chinese scientists, aware by reading of developments in contemporary Western science, somehow betray a sense of being cut off from its "feel," so Chinese political leaders appear to lack the "feel" of Western politics in spite of their being well-informed through reading. Even the official press sometimes gives a glimpse of external reality: Chien Hsun, for example, argued in *Scientific Journal,* the Peking periodical, a few years ago that wealth, technique and employment were increasing in the West as a matter of objective fact, so that the decline of Western capitalism was not inevitable (as the ortho-dox Party view insists).[11] Sometimes a foreign statesman tries to deepen the Chinese understanding of the outside world. U Nu of Burma told his hosts at a Peking banquet in 1954:

> As a people, the Americans are very generous and brave. In the sphere of scientific knowledge, the Americans have devel-oped to such an extent that they can make this world a happy and prosperous place to live in. The Chinese people are also very generous and brave. They enjoyed a high de-gree of civilization at a time when the rest of the world were barbarians. Therefore we have a great affection and regard for both these people. . . .[12]

These remarks were published in the Peking press, the Chinese Communist attitude being that to publish something unfavourable to yourself proves that you are aware of it and implies that you do not fear it but, on the contrary, are pre-pared for it. A good deal of domestic and foreign criticism of the Party's policy is thus printed in the Chinese newspapers (where readers could see, for example, the Dalai Lama's complaints against Peking after his flight, as well as the Rus-sian Party's side of the ideological dispute).*

But the average view in China is that things outside are not as good as foreigners claim: I have met a Scandinavian woman who failed to argue intelligent Chinese in Peking out of their fixed belief that photographs of Scandinavian ports busy with ships were faked, in order to cover up the decline of capitalism. The Russians used to provide a tiny window on the world for China, which sent over 10,000 students and trainees to the Soviet Union and received about the same number of Russian specialists on loan. Now the number of Chinese students in the European Communist countries is very small, and the gap is not filled by the despatch of a few dozen Chinese students to the Ealing Technical College in London or the recruitment of a few dozen Britons to teach English in Chinese cities. The exchanges used to be numbered

---

* Russian readers were not given the same privilege of reading the Chinese case in *Pravda,* a fact of which Peking likes to remind us. Unfavourable items in the Chinese press are always, of course, accompa-nied or followed by an official refutation.

in hundreds and thousands: now they can be counted in tens.

China has been traditionally suspicious of foreigners and foreign cultures. Andrew Corsalis explained to his patron, Lorenzo de' Medici, in 1515 that Portuguese traders reaching the Chinese coast "were not permitted to land, for they say it is against their custom to let foreigners enter their dwellings." [13] Even today a visitor cannot easily strike up an impromptu acquaintance with a strange Chinese met in the street, nor visit his home unless by previous arrangement and after adequate preparation by the Party authorities. But there is no officially inspired hatred of foreigners. Toddlers may play in their kindergartens beneath crude caricatures of Lyndon Johnson, but when the Canadian doctor Norman Bethune died in 1939 from a disease contracted while treating wounded soldiers of the People's Liberation Army, Mao Tsetung composed a poem in his memory and wrote: "A man with such an unselfish spirit is great, is noble, is virtuous." [14] The flaw in the Chinese world view is a genuine cultural distaste for things foreign, not an artifically inflamed and officially endorsed Hitlerian hatred for other races. "The Chinese people," a book published in Peking in 1958 hopefully stated, "now occupy a place in the world along with all other nations and no longer live isolated in a tightly closed circle." [15] It is indeed the universalism of Communism that allows the wider-horizoned of China's leaders to encourage the breakdown of her former isolationism. The enthusiasm that greets Cuban dancers, Guinean trade unionists or Albanian writers is a new thing in China: it is artificial, perhaps, but it is part of a new opening up that will eventually change Chinese attitudes profoundly.

It is possible after only twenty years to observe the first signs of erosion by Communist rule of the two most famous Chinese characteristics: patience and pride. A country in which it is officially stated that the "traditional curse of poverty" will take three hundred years to overcome, where cities are urged to plan their construction needs for centuries ahead,[16] and where the continuation of the class struggle is taken to mean that "after 10,000 years there will still be a difference between the advanced and the backward groups in society": [17] this is a country in which patience remains a virtue.

But impatience is also found: many are the occasions on which a complacent officialdom has been shocked into precipitate action by the needlings of an impatient leadership. The acceleration of the collectivization campaigns in the early

1950s, the Great Leap Forward itself, the constant efforts to telescope the timetables for industrial development, the Cultural Revolution of 1966–8: all these betray a strong impatience. The mood is suggested in the exchange of poems between Kuo Mo-jo and Mao Tse-tung in 1963, when the full consequences of the dispute with Russia had struck home to the Chinese leadership. Kuo wrote:

> Only among the cross-currents of this vast sea
> Does the greatness of men become manifest.
> The six hundred million,
> Having consolidated their unity,
> Hold fast to their tenets.
> When the sky falls, raise it;
> When the world goes wrong, right it.
> Listen to the cockcrow
>
> As dawn breaks in the east
> . . . pure gold
> Is never consumed by flames . . .
> It is absurd that a rogue's dogs should bark at a saint,*. . .
> Unfurl the red flags into the east wind
> To turn the world scarlet.

To this attempt to rally the Chinese leaders' spirits in the face of extreme adversity, Mao replied:

> There have always been
> Many things that were urgent.
> Although the world spins on,
> Time is short.
> Millennia are too long:
> Let us dispute about mornings and evenings. . . .[18]

This is the Mao who wrote, on the eve of the first People's Commune in 1958:

> The former exploiting classes are reduced to mere drops in the ocean of working people, and they must change whether they want to or not. There are undoubtedly some who will never change and would prefer to remain wooden-headed till their dying day, but this does not affect things in general. All degenerate modes of thought and other unsuitable parts of the superstructure are daily crumbling. It still takes time to clear this refuse away completely, but there is no doubt that these things will break up. . . . China's 600 million people are . . . poor and . . . blank. This seems a bad thing, but in

---

* An obvious reference to Khrushchev's attacks on Mao.

fact it is a good thing. . . . A clean sheet of paper has nothing on it, so that the newest and most beautiful words can be written and the newest and most beautiful pictures painted on it. . . .[19]

This breathtaking vision of effecting hurried social change on such vast scale, this extraordinary optimism, are unique to Mao and his close associates. Their successors will be far too heavily swamped by the immediate administrative problems of modernizing China to indulge such awe-inspiring daydreams. But they will be less patient with the *status quo* than any previous generation of Chinese leaders. The idea of change has been popularized for the first time, and this will in time transform the traditional Chinese attitude of composure and studied self-control.

Pride is more difficult to destroy. Impatience is a natural attitude for a man who desires change, but humility is hardly to be expected of a man who believes that his culture has been unjustly scorned by others. Sun Yat-sen, father of the Chinese Revolution, set the tone by writing: "What we need to learn from Europe is science, not political philosophy. As for the true principles of political philosophy, the Europeans need to learn them from China."[20]

The knowledge that they possess millenary cultural treasures, which astounded the world and were religiously absorbed by their neighbours, has developed in the Chinese a sense of cultural superiority which hinders their acceptance of elements of other cultures,* and makes them hyper-sensitive to cultural comparisons. They feel impelled, if someone lets them down, to assert that, far from being inconvenienced, they can do the thing better themselves: adversity is always turned to advantage. The Russian walk-out in 1960 was a good thing: "Some comrades think we should offer Khrushchev a medal for the spur he gave to our self-reliance."[21] A third world war would have its bright side: "The Chinese people believe that if imperialism dares to start an atomic war, its result will be the extinction of imperialism, and on its ruins will be constructed a brilliant future for the people."[22] This philosophy is summed up by a Marxist

---

* Chinese are pleased when foreigners make a special study of Chinese culture, but take offense at the separate classification of this into "Sinology" or "Orientalism"—terms which imply a lack of parity between East and West, because there is no comparable place for "Europology" or "Occidental Studies" in world scholarship. Thus China boycotted the 25th International Congress of Orientalists in Moscow in 1960, and Gafurov, its Chairman, observed that some Asians felt that Orientalism was a reactionary study.

theoretician thus: "At times temporary losses may occur owing to lack of experience in fighting the imperialists and the reactionaries, but losses help you to learn. As the Chinese saying goes, 'A fall in the pit, a gain in wit.' And that is why bad things can be turned to good account." [23]

Chinese national pride is particularly aroused by any suggestion of foreign charity. A visit to Peking by an American ear surgeon to demonstrate a new technique was cancelled in 1965 because the Chinese resented the American Government's justifying their giving permission for the journey on the grounds of its "humanitarian" purpose.[24] One reason for the Chinese cancellation of a large purchase of French wheat a few years ago was the suggestion in the French newspapers that the sale (subsidized by the European Economic Community under the agricultural arrangements of the Common Market) was a "humanitarian gesture" on the part of EEC taxpayers. But the most pointed example of this sensitivity over foreign aid is a passage in the Chinese Party's letter to the Kremlin on 29 February 1964: "We would like to say in passing that . . . we are very much concerned about the present economic situation in the Soviet Union. If you should feel the need for the help of Chinese experts in certain fields, we should be glad to send them."

Another aspect of this sensitivity concerns the reputation which the Chinese used to have in Europe for softness. The early European visitors to China in the sixteenth century reported that the Chinese people were unwarlike, unvaliant and even effeminate. "It appears to me," wrote Matteo Ricci, the Jesuit, in 1584, "the most difficult thing in the world to regard the Chinese as warriors. . . . They spend two hours every morning in combing and plaiting their hairs. . . ." [25] Today the queues have gone, China is led by a man who almost makes a fetish of a spartan programme of physical self-toughening, and the whole nation parades daily for calisthenics. When two young Chinese and a Tibetan stood together on the summit of Mount Everest at 4:20 in the morning of 25 May 1960, and solemnly deposited a plaster bust of Chairman Mao wrapped in the Chinese flag, they symbolized a new self-image for the Chinese, just as the "heroes" of the Korean War changed every Western General's notions about the quality of Chinese fighting men.

The Chinese still refuse to countenance failure. When Mao told Edgar Snow in 1936 that Mongolia would "automatically become a part of the Chinese federation at their own will," [26] the apparent lack of logic simply meant that he could not conceive or admit the possibility of the Mongo-

lians' not wanting to join China. Again, when Mao told artists and writers that they "must, for long periods of time, unreservedly and wholeheartedly go into the midst of the
masses . . . before they can proceed to creation," [27] he revealed his reluctance to consider the possibility of their being
unwilling to join the masses. The Tibetan problem is rendered
ten times more difficult than it need be by this Chinese distaste for admitting to failure. But the seeds of change have
been planted. Every visitor, when he goes to a commune or a
factory, is earnestly asked to comment and criticize the arrangements he has observed. It is evident that this goes
against the grain of many a manager or commune director,
but it is Party policy and so it must be done. Gradually it will
sink into the collective mind that some of the suggestions are
helpful, and that one can live with other people's awareness
of one's imperfections. Clement Attlee found the official
Chinese humility about their problems "a most refreshing
contrast with the Russians, who are always telling the world
that it is lagging behind." [28] So far the official attitude has not
struck root in people's minds, but it will eventually do so.

Communist China is not an impossible country, a nation
condemned to perpetual mistrust and isolation. There are
forces at work there which will hasten her eventual reconciliation with the world by the same token that they will render
her a more modern and more rational society (though not,
for all that, a mere carbon copy of Europe). And the
Chinese themselves are lovable people, wise, diligent and artistic. Sven Lindquist, despite the rigours of Communist
Chinese student life in the early 1960s, admits that Peking
"touched my heart" more deeply than any other foreign
city; [29] and Mikhail Klochko, the Soviet scientist who spent a
year in China before opting for life in the West, cannot disguise his affection for the Chinese people and Chinese ways.
This is perhaps the most difficult time for the Chinese relationship with the rest of the world. China is like a clever
child who has been bullied, and whose circumstances are
poorer than other children's: her present actions often betray
the continued painfulness of those old wounds and her sense
of insecurity in her newly reasserted independence. Western
policy has fed the pain and insecurity, rather than sought to
overcome them, and it will be many years before the Chinese
are able to put reason before emotion in their international
dealings. But time is on the side of reconciliation. The leaders
who now appear to us as so belligerent and uncooperative are
also the men who administered to an almost dying country
the drastic surgery which enables it to resume a major role in

world history. The patient lies on his bed, weak, nervous, irritable and confused. He will certainly revive, and his new life will most likely be one which the rest of us can more easily understand and share.

APPENDIX

The Chinese Puzzle

CHINA IS A CLOSED SOCIETY, MORE TIGHTLY CONTROLLED BY A single political Party than any other country in the world, and totally unfamiliar, culturally, to foreigners. So little information about China reaches the outside world, and that little seems so contradictory, so exaggerated, so particular and ungeneralized, that many people have despaired of ever forming a satisfactory impression of what is happening in the world's largest state.

The newspapers in China are informative in many respects.[1] "The instructions of the Party and the direction and policy of the Party," said the *People's Daily* (the principal organ of the government) in 1961, "are conveyed to the public through the newspapers."[2] There has never been any mention in the Chinese newspapers of the import of Western grain that has been going on for the past nine years, or of the defection to England of the pianist Fou Ts'ong (such things come to be known, among people who are interested, by surreptitious listening to the Voice of America, the BBC and Radio Australia, or orally through returned Overseas Chinese). Nor is the press in any way free to express different viewpoints: as an editor once said, when returning the manuscript of a poem submitted to the *People's Daily*, if that newspaper were to give equal treatment to divergent views, "that would turn it into a storehouse of bourgeois class freedom."[3] But some criticism is recorded in the daily and weekly press (especially in the provinces), and more can be inferred.

Reading the *People's Daily* is like listening to one side of a debate: the other side may not be audible, but you can reconstruct the gist of it from what its opponents have said. This requires, however, a number of unusual qualifications: the ideal foreign reader and interpreter of the Chinese press needs to be fluent in the Chinese language, well versed in the Chinese cultural tradition, and also knowledgeable about the jargon and concepts of Marxism. Very few people combine these gifts. Nor is it possible, even for a foreign resident of Peking, to obtain all the Chinese publications. Some are not available to foreigners, many are not allowed to be sent out of the country. The five national newspapers may be subscribed to anywhere (though there was a period in the early 1960s when even these were sometimes difficult to obtain [4]). Some of the prohibited provincial or technical publications are smuggled into Hongkong, where they fetch inflated prices from frustrated diplomats and researchers (a forbidden four-page newspaper costing a cent or two in its city of origin can sell for $35 in Hongkong [5]). Observers can also listen to Radio Peking and the occasionally more revealing provincial radio stations (the British Broadcasting Corporation puts out a daily monitoring report in English which includes many Chinese broadcasts).

Peking puts out a great quantity of well-produced and intelligently edited propaganda material in foreign languages. The New China News Agency puts out two lengthy daily bulletins in English and French; the *Peking Review* offers a weekly round-up of official Chinese news and opinions in several languages; and the Chinese perspective on world affairs is summarized in a steady flow of pamphlets in all major languages of the world. But items chosen for publication in these foreign-language media are naturally those which serve the Party's purpose of projecting abroad the image it wants China to have, and they are no substitute for the Chinese-language press.

In addition to the Chinese sources themselves, there are resident foreign journalists in Peking, notably those representing *Reuters, Agence France-Presse, Tanjug, Tass, Kyodo*, the *Toronto Globe and Mail*, several Japanese newspapers and *Pravda*. Their despatches are not censored, but if they display an "unfriendly" attitude towards their hosts they are deprived of the little cooperation they normally receive from the authorities and are usually not given any extension of their residence permit. Most of these journalists are openly frustrated and bored, with little to do save attend empty formal ceremonies and paraphrase official hand-outs (the reading of wall posters during the Cultural Revolution provided a short-lived break in this routine in 1966–8). They are dependent on the Foreign Ministry for everything they do, and regard a visit to a school or a factory as a triumph of diplomacy. It is rare for them to interview any senior Ministers (who reserve their occasional charms for the fleeting, more impressionable visitor) and even their minor factual queries are often left unanswered. They think themselves lucky if they can obtain permission to go outside Peking once a year.

There are two other kinds of resident foreigner in Peking. The diplomats suffer from the same frustrating lack of information and restriction on their movement: they are usually taken on a provincial trip once a year as a conducted group guided by the Foreign Ministry, but are otherwise more or less confined to Peking. As one well-educated Chinese who fled from Peking to Hongkong recently remarked: "Who would ever dare to talk frankly to a foreign diplomat?" [6] The third category of foreigner is the one employed by the Chinese Government, either to advise it on some technical matter, or to do a specific professional job such as teaching or translating. This list includes such well-known writers as Rewi Alley (the New Zealand poet who has lived in China for over forty years and loves the country passionately), Israel Epstein, Anna Louise Strong (the American Marxist whose occasional printed *Letter from China* gives a picture of China more easily understandable to Western readers than the official literature) and Solomon Adler (the Cambridge economist). But these people are not easy to meet, for the other resident foreigners any more than for visitors, and some of them fell into disgrace during the Cultural Revolution.

Chou En-lai told the Afro-Asians at Bandung in 1955 that there was no "bamboo curtain." "Come and see us," he cried.[7] But only a proportion of applicants are rewarded by a visa. Americans are not considered, unless their political views are of the kind that would in any case lead the State Department in Washington to deny them passports on security grounds. Tourist groups of almost any other nationality are admitted, for previously specified tours, and the only apparent obstacle to their admission in substantially greater numbers is the shortage of Western-style hotel accommodation and domestic transport facilities. Foreigners wishing to travel to China alone, and with particular objectives, find entry more difficult: partly because there are not enough guides and interpreters available. More important is the apparent Chinese need for some kind of assurance of a prospective visitor's friendly motives (or at least his lack of *un*-friendly motives), indications of which may be sought in his nationality, job, political views and personal relations with Chinese officials or other foreigners known to be friendly to China. The Chinese display a noticeable preference for visitors who do not understand the Chinese language, and none of the British correspondents who have made a special study of Chinese affairs has been given a visa for China for the past six or seven years (the *Reuters* representative knows no Chinese).

Certain parts of China are taboo for all but very privileged visitors (Sinkiang, for example, or Lanchow where the uranium plant is), and a traveller must resign himself to being taken to the same communes and factories which previous visitors have seen. Certain institutions and enterprises are prepared for a flow of visitors: someone there has the Party line at his fingertips, the cadres have cast about and failed to find anything which a foreign visitor might find disgraceful or discreditable, and there is, if possible, a Western lavatory available (even specially built for the purpose). Of the 70,000 communes in China, only a few dozen have been visited by foreigners and these are naturally the more successful and better-provided ones.

Great pains are taken to satisfy a visitor's wishes. The old-style painter Li Ku-chan was dismissed from his teaching post at an art school and reduced to selling cinema tickets: one day Russian visitors to the school asked to see his works, so they were hurriedly displayed—"but were taken down immediately the guests had gone." [8] This kind of experience is common, and anxious-to-please comrades in Shanghai have even arranged for a foreign writer to be "recognized," as if by accident, by a passing admirer in the street.[9] On the other hand most of what a traveller does see cannot be completely contrived. The trouble is that no visitor has any way of measuring or estimating the representatives of his experiences. No one comes away with the whole picture: the only difference is that some admit it and others do not.

In Peking itself, most of the non-committed foreign residents say that they would know more about China by living in Hongkong, which is certainly the best listening post for China. Almost all the official Chinese materials are available there as easily as in Peking, and they are supplemented by three things impossible for foreigners to obtain in China itself: smuggled publications not supposed to reach the hands of foreigners, a full range of interpretations of Chinese happenings from every political point of view (the American, the Russian, the Kuomintang, the Japanese and so forth), and the testimony of refugees. There are more diplomats, scholars, businessmen and journalists who follow Chinese affairs in Hongkong than there are in Peking or in any other city, and they can work and debate their findings in a free society that is also, culturally, Chinese. The disadvantages of Hongkong as a window into China are two: its temptation to be over-impressed by what the latest refugees from neighbouring Kwangtung province are saying (which is like judging America exclusively from what the Texans say about it in Europe), and its inability to sense the "feel" or atmosphere of life in China. The ideal observer would live in Hongkong but visit Peking fairly frequently.

The processing of information about China has become a minor industry in Hongkong. The American Consulate-General has a gifted staff of Chinese-speaking scholars who pore over the Chinese newspapers, interrogation reports of refugees and all other available data, and who maintain a continuous and complex record of their conclusions. They put out a mimeographed series of English translations of selected items from the official Chinese press which are prized by many university libraries around the world. They are probably better-informed about China than any other group or organization in the world (though this does not mean that one must necessarily agree with the conclusions they draw from the data). There are also other offices where similar work is conducted, on smaller scale, by other governments and enterprises—religious, commercial, academic and so forth.

A refugee's story is always suspect: just as he tells one tale on the Chinese side of the border, to assist his escape, so he tells another on the Hongkong side in order to gain acceptance and cooperation in his new life. The ritual by which frontier-crossers in Macao would go (before its closure in 1967) to the Kuomintang consulate there on arrival, record statements about the miserable and oppressive conditions which they have escaped, and be duly rewarded in cash for their contribution to Kuomintang propaganda, became a standing joke. But skilful detailed interrogation can yield information which, subject to independent confirmation and with all due reservations, can help to build up a fuller and more convincing picture of contemporary China than could otherwise be obtained. Sometimes a man comes to Hongkong who was a foreman at a steelworks: what he says about his work there can supplement what foreign visitors to it were told by the Party representatives on their guided tour and what the local newspaper has been reporting—provided every allowance is made for the man's motives, powers of observation and tendency to exaggerate (all of which can be subtly tested by an experienced questioner). To take another example: seventeen million Party members were given details in 1959 of the reasons for the dismissal of Peng Teh-huai (the Defence Minister) far more revealing than any of the newspaper accounts. Sooner or later one of these seventeen million, or a confidant of one of them, crossed the border and made these details known.[10] It is in this way that the scrupulously careful use of refugee evidence can assist an observer to interpret truly the passing Chinese scene.

There are now many non-Chinese periodicals carrying regular material about contemporary China. The *China Quarterly* of London is the chief academic publication, patronized by most Amrican experts. *China News Analysis,* a weekly put out in Hongkong by a Jesuit priest with a long experience of China and a strong love for the country, combines short extracts and digests of the official Chinese press with an illuminating comment that is, of course, anti-Communist. The weekly *Far Eastern Economic Review* of Hongkong, which is not exclusively about Chinese affairs but covers them well, takes a more middle-of-the-road position and is largely non-political. The American-sponsored *Current Scene,* also published in Hongkong, is helpful. There is no ideal interpreter of China; those who are either sympathetic or hostile tend at best to be naïve, at worst politically biassed, while those who maintain a healthy scepticism and are simply interested to know what is happening without caring too much whether the outcome proves or disproves any particular political philosophy are very very few. The same could be said of the books. Authors who have the ear of Peking, and gain access to more information and material than other visitors, are also so concerned to have the world approve the many creditable things which the Chinese Government has done that they prefer to play down some of the darker parts of the picture. Similarly those who are mainly anxious that the world should not overlook the price which China pays for her unity and strong government are also those who have least to say about that government's achievements.[11]

It must be obvious from all this that statistics about China are especially suspect. We have seen that some foreign demographers question the reliability of the 1953 Census: after people, the most vital statistic in China is the grain harvest, and yet the counting of this is also highly controversial. An Indian delegation in 1956 found that the system of estimating the harvest was less reliable than the Indian,[12] and the difficulty is enhanced by the political pressure on the cadres to raise output and exceed targets. To take one example: in Tunghsien county in Hopei province the Party Committee summoned the cadres and leading farmers in 1956 and explained that since the previous year's grain yield had been 242 pounds per *mou* of land, it proposed to begin the discussion of the proper target for the current 'high tide' campaign with a suggested 825 pounds. Everyone present wanted to avoid being labelled as a "conservative," so one Cooperative representative bid 1,430 pounds, and another raised it to 1,980 pounds, as if in a poker game. The county Committee finally settled for 1,100 pounds, noting, however, that "many cadre workers and the masses thought that this was too high, but did not dare to voice their doubts. . . ." Afterwards the older Committee members realized that even this was over-ambitious, and they prudently lowered the target to 352 pounds, but some cadre workers did not tell the peasants in their charge in case they relaxed their efforts.[13]

It was in this kind of atmosphere that the Great Leap Forward was launched, and in 1958 it seems that there was a general tacit agreement to inflate local harvest figures by about forty per cent, so that even the leadership was deluded into believing that the crops had been doubled in one year. A check was made on this in 1959, but it is likely that since 1960 the exaggerations have crept back.[14] Some serious foreign observers tend to deduct some twenty per cent from the officially claimed figures because of what has become known about these local problems in assessing the harvest accurately.

The comparability of the statistics has also been called in question: it was only in 1954 that a nationally coordinated system of estimating crops was organized, and in the light of this the statistics for the earlier years of the First Plan (1952 and 1953) were revised. This rendered them in turn impossible strictly to compare with 1949 or previous years. One American agronomist even argues, with some plausibility, that average grain production during the first decade of Communist rule was lower than in the decade preceding the Japanese war! [15] The excessive enthusiasm of the Leap and the reorganization of cooperatives into communes ruined the patient work of the statisticians. "Brilliant figures," exclaimed one (non-Communist) delegate discussing the Leap results at a political meeting in 1960, "a piece of brilliant poetry." [16] But the poetry could not be sustained, and since 1960 even the few regular production statistics which Peking used to announce each year have been dropped. Early in 1961 the stocks of the official book *Ten Great Years* which had splashed in diagrammatic form the exaggerated early result of the Leap, were quietly withdrawn from bookshops all over the world.

This new total silence merely worsens what was already a murky situation. The guerrilla mind does not appreciate the value of a free flow of current data, and scholars in China have not been able to obtain even innocuous information on which to work. Almost everything was a state secret even before 1960. One Professor wrote in a Shanghai newspaper in 1957: "The joke of the whole matter is that one can find in foreign books and magazines, especially from capitalist countries, information about China which cannot be found here." [17] The Professor of Economics at Peking University revealed: "I always feel embarrassed when I receive foreign visitors. They ask questions about prices, foreign trade, the standard of living, and are astonished when I cannot reply." [18]

The Head of the Statistical Office himself admitted, in those free-speaking days of the Hundred Flowers: "It is indeed ridiculous: even empty forms are kept secret." [19] But now the blanket is complete, all-embracing. All that is said about the harvest each year is that it is "better."

In 1959 a new man was appointed to head the Statistical Bureau: "If statistical material does not express a clear political idea but merely reflects real conditions," he declared, "then obviously it will be used by the enemy. . . . Our statistical reports must reflect the great victory of the Party's general line. . . . They certainly should not be a mere display of objective facts. . . . Statistical work . . . must be something which when the Party is using it does not cause embarrassment and annoyance. . . ." Victory, he added, is nine fingers, defeat is only the tenth: "This tenth is also part of reality, but . . . the question is from what standpoint this one finger is presented and to whom it is presented." [20] To those who argue that actual figures are needed in print, the question is posed: "Is it conceivable that the reactionaries and imperialists are asleep?" [21] There is a genuine fear lest foreigners (especially Russians) come to know the intimate details of the Chinese economy and thereby acquire the means of damaging it more easily. China is run like a country under siege.

Actually it is easy to imagine sometimes that the government itself must be insufficiently informed to act properly. In

1959 a Newspaper Clipping Corporation was established in Peking, cutting forty papers throughout China for the benefit of 580 subscribers. Even the Ministry of Light Industry based its *Comprehensive Report on Leap Conditions in the Leather Industry* on these cuttings,[22] which suggested that the basis for economic planning and administration was flimsy indeed.

So we have to guess at China's statistics. The broad outlines of China's foreign trade can be reconstructed without serious distortion from the published figures of her principal partners: China is the only country in the world, except for North Korea and North Vietnam, not to publish any foreign trade figures.[23] The partner statistics tend to overstate China's export values and understate her import values, because of the differences in freight, and some observers adjust the figures by ten per cent to allow for this.[24] Production figures are harder to guess at, but this is by now a skilled science among the diplomats of Hongkong. There is in fact a good deal of scattered information available about both agricultural and industrial production from the official press. Hints are often dropped about trends in output, and concrete facts are sometimes given about individual enterprises or counties or even provinces. Some of the factors affecting production, such as the weather, are reported, and an experienced observer who has all these references brought together on his desk, and who understands the psychology of the Peking administration, can usually make an estimate (projected from the years when figures were published) to his own satisfaction. It is on this kind of intelligent guesswork that some of the figures in the following Table are based.

CHINA'S PLACE IN THE WORLD

	CHINA	JAPAN	INDIA	BRITAIN	FRANCE	USSR	CANADA	USA
Vital statistics								
Population (millions, mid-1969)	775?	102	540	56	51	243	21	206
Population growth p.a. (%)	+2?	+1	+2½	+1	+1	+1½	+2	+1½
Area (thousand sq. miles)	4,300	183	1,175	93	213	8,649	3,560	3,554
Wealth in 1966								
Gross National Product ($ billion)	62?	98	44	100	102	320	58	740
Income per head ($ p.a.)	65?	790	74	1,466	1,534	1,380	2,143	2,940
Economic growth rate (%)	+4?	+10	+2	+1	+5	+7	+11	+5
National Budget ($ billion)	18?	12	8	27	22	118	8	138
Production in 1967								
Electricity (billion kwh)	50?	238	38	207	112	589	165	1,314
Steel (million tons)	12?	62	6	24	20	102	9	115
Coal (million tons)	250?	47	68	175	47	600	9	517
Foodgrains* (million tons) (1966)	160?	15	62	14	92	171	30	202
Trade in 1967								
Exports ($ billion)	2.0	10.4	1.6	13.9	11.4	9.6	10.6	31.2
Imports ($ billion)	2.2	11.7	2.7	17.2	12.4	8.5	10.1	26.8
Total trade ($ billion)	4.2	22.1	4.3	31.1	23.8	18.1	20.7	58.0
Foreign aid ($ million) (1966)	−50	−285	+1,000	−501	−721	−905?	−208	−3,634

* Rice, wheat, barley, oats and miscellaneous grains: not potatoes.
Note: these figures are rough-and-ready guides for the curious non-expert reader, and they cannot provide a satisfactory basis for further calculation: they are mostly derived from UN sources.

NOTES

The following abbreviations are used:

PERIODICALS

CNA: China News Analysis.
CQ: China Quarterly.
FEER: Far Eastern Economic Review.
Keesing: Keesing's Contemporary Archives.

BOOKS

Chao: Chao Kuo-chun, *Agrarian Policy of the Chinese Commu-
    nist Party 1921–59* (London, Asia Publishing House, 1960).
Hudson: G. F. Hudson, *Europe and China* (London, Edward Ar-
    nold, 1931; Beacon Paperback, 1961).
Li: Choh-ming Li, *Economic Development of Communist China*
    (Berkeley and Los Angeles, University of California Press,
    1959).
MacFarquhar: Roderick MacFarquhar, *The Hundred Flowers
    Campaign and the Chinese Intellectual* (New York, Praeger,
    1960).
Snow: Edgar Snow, *The Other Side of the River* (London, Gol-
    lancz, 1963).
Szczepanik: *Symposium on Economic and Social Problems of the
    Far East,* edited by Edward Szczepanik (Hong Kong University
    Press, 1962).
Wu: Yuan-li Wu, *The Economy of Communist China* (New
    York, Praeger, 1965).

INTRODUCTION

1 *New China News Agency*, Peking, 24 January 1960 (cited in CQ 4, 1960, p. 85). The film was called *Lin Tse-hsu*.

2 *People's Daily*, Peking, 27 June 1958.

3 Chou Ku-cheng. See CNA 557, 26 March 1965.

4 See CNA 306, 1 January 1960.

5 Quoted with disgust in *Kuang Ming Daily*, Peking, 17 April 1955. See CNA 101, 23 September 1955.

6 *People's Daily*, Peking, 23 October 1954. See CNA 60, 19 November 1954; and 68, 21 January 1955.

7 See e.g. *People's Daily*, Peking, 25 February 1958, and the discussion in CNA 233, 20 June 1958.

8 Professor Joseph R. Levenson in CQ 12, 1962, p. 8. But some observers detect a renewed interest in the classics in the past two or three years. An article in the *Kuang Ming Daily* (Peking, 8 August 1962) notes that "the number of people who become acquainted with classical works is ever increasing," and this may be a product of the growing sense of isolation in Chinese intellectual circles. See CNA 443, 26 October 1962.

9 *Kuang Ming Daily*, Peking, 23 May 1957.

10 *People's Daily*, Peking, 10 January 1951.

11 See CNA 219, 7 March 1958.

12 In *Philosophic Research*, Peking (cited in FEER, 5 December 1963, p. 493).

13 *Kuang Ming Daily*, Peking, 14 November 1956.

14 See CNA 398, 24 November 1961.

15 Liu Chieh, in *Kuang Ming Daily*, Peking, 17 and 18 August 1963.

16 Cited in Szczepanik, p. 353.

17 *Wen-yi Pao*, Shanghai, 17 April 1961.

18 See *New China News Agency*, Peking, 10 February 1956; and the article by Wu Yu-chang, architect of the language reform, in the *People's Daily*, Peking, 7 March 1956. The proposals are reported and examined in CNA 108, 11 November 1955; and 136, 15 June 1956.

19 Summarized in CNA 183, 31 May 1957. Tan Lan's counter-proposal was published in the *People's Daily*, Peking, 18 April 1957.

20 *Wen Hui Pao*, Shanghai, 30 October 1957.

21 *People's Daily*, Peking, 13 January 1958. For a résumé of the simplification of characters see CNA 85, 27 May 1955; 345, 21 October 1960; and 443, 26 October 1962. Scholars expressed

alarm at the proliferation of amateur simplifications and abbreviations which caused great confusion, for instance in the Post Office. For a discussion of the debate on how to pronounce the Latin letters, see CNA 366, 7 April 1961.

22 See the discussion and citations in CNA 102, 30 September 1955. Historiography in contemporary China was the subject of a conference in England in September 1964; see the articles by Harold Kahn and Albert Feuerwerker in CQ 22, 1965.

CHAPTER ONE: THE PEASANTRY

1 By Ho Ching-chih and Ting Yi, Peking, Foreign Languages Press, 1954. See Chao, p. 25.

2 Chou Ching-wen, the democratic politician who cooperated with the Communists for their first ten years, says in his book *Stormy Decade* (Hongkong, 1959) that two million people were killed in the land reform movement (see CQ 3, 1960, p. 107). But he tends to exaggerate. The so-called "Warsaw" version of Mao's famous speech "On Contradictions," made on 27 February 1957, says that up to 1954 a total of 800,000 "enemies of the people" were liquidated and that since then terror had been dropped and only persuasion was used (*New York Times*, 13 June 1957). Mu Fu-sheng, in his book *The Wilting of the Hundred Flowers* (London, 1962) cites a different figure from the same speech of Mao: 500,000 up to 1957, and he contrasts this with the twenty million claimed by critical Hongkong newspapers (p. 128). Both these figures, 800,000 and 500,000, include counter-revolutionaries, who were active, either on the Kuomintang's behalf or out of general opposition to the new government, in the early years of the Communist administration, but not necessarily or exclusively concerned with the land reform. Half a million seems a fair figure. See also Chapter Nine.

3 *Selected Works* (London, 1954), Vol. 1, p. 27.

4 *The Agrarian Reform Law*, Peking, Foreign Languages Press, 1950.

5 Passages cited in Keesing, p. 14404.

6 *People's Daily,* Peking, 1 July 1956.

7 See the discussion in CNA 78, 8 April 1955; and the article by Ma Ping-chiu in *Kuang Ming Daily,* Peking, 4 January 1955.

8 Ma Ping-chiu, *ibid* (footnote 7).

9 Cited in CNA 78, 8 April 1955.

10 14 February 1956.

11 *People's Daily,* Peking, 1 October 1957

12 *New China News Agency,* Canton, 14 May 1957 (cited in MacFarquhar, p. 232): similar reports came from other provinces.

13 *New China News Agency*, Chengtu, 6 August 1957 (cited in MacFarquhar, p. 239).

14 See CNA 79, 15 April 1955.

15 See CNA 79, 15 April 1955: and 109, 18 November 1955.

16 See Colina MacDougall, "Evolution in China's Communes," in FEER, 3 August 1961, p. 217. In 1962 Brigade officials were complaining of having nothing to do (accounts and agriculture having gone down to the Team, public works and industry being retained at the commune level), and the Minister of Agriculture wrote in *Cuba Socialistica* (Havana) in October 1963 that some communes had abolished the Brigade level altogether. See FEER, 21 November 1963, p. 382.

17 Henry Lethbridge, "The State of the Communes," in FEER, 17 January 1963, p. 113.

18 *The People's Communes Forge Ahead*, first published in *Red Flag* on 26 February 1964, then in the *Peking Review* in two instalments on 27 March and 10 April 1964 and finally as a separate pamphlet by the Foreign Languages Press, Peking, in 1964. The upshot of Tao's exposition is that when the material base is strengthened and commune funds built up, responsibility will again shift upwards to the Brigade, the commune, and ultimately to federations of communes.

19 Cited in *Teacher's Daily*, Peking, 29 January 1958. An almost identical table is cited in Chao (pp. 268–9), taken from a report by Tan Chen-lin in the *People's Daily*, Peking, 5 May 1957, and said to refer to 1956, not 1958. Chao notes that the cost of the items listed would be two to three times larger in Peking or Shanghai. In some of the communes in the early days the peasants were given free meals in the mess-halls and a regular monthly salary. The Finance Minister, after touring some communes in 1958, remarked that "To have free meals while drawing monthly wages is an event of world significance" (*Peking Review*, No. 11 of 1958). This high standard could not be maintained, but the objective is to restore it when it can be afforded. Although ambitious plans were published in 1958 for commune building programmes, very few communes could afford any substantial new building and this is one reason why the idea that new dormitories were going up everywhere at that time was so absurd. The average peasant lives in the same miserable hut he had in 1949, and probably sleeps five or six to a room. New housing is envisaged, and in the "showpiece" communes the visitor can see examples of actual new construction, but it will take many years to realize these dreams widely. As for the "typical budget," it has doubtless improved since 1956 (or 1958) but not by a large margin.

20 See Joan Robinson in *Eastern Horizon*, Hongkong, Vol. 3, No. 5, May 1964, p. 7.

21 This summary of the work point system is derived from Andrew Nathan's "Paying the Chinese Farmer," in FEER, 27 Febru-

ary 1964, p. 457. See also Chen Mae Fun's "Paying the Peasants," in FEER, 3 November 1966.

22 See Joan Robinson, *op. cit.* (footnote 20), pp. 8, 10.

23 See CNA 539, 6 November 1964.

24 Cited in FEER, 3 August 1961, p. 218.

25 *Ta Kung Pao*, Peking, 13 October 1959.

26 CQ 11, 1962, p. 21. Most observers assume that the current average calorie intake is around 2,000: see the discussion by W.K. in CQ 7, 1961, p. 121.

27 See, e.g., CNA 364, 17 March 1961, and 382, 28 July 1961; and CQ 22, 1965, p. 189. In the middle of 1961 food parcels from relatives in Hongkong and Macao were entering China at the rate of two million a month (Ng Wing Bo's "Parcels to China," in FEER, 14 September 1961, p. 496).

28 See CNA 507, 6 March 1964.

29 See CQ 18, 1964, p. 231.

30 See FEER, 18 February 1965, p. 295.

31 *People's Daily*, Peking, 30 July 1963.

32 Report of An Tzu-wen, *People's Daily*, Peking, 26 February 1953.

33 *People's Daily*, Peking, 6 June 1956.

34 *Kuang Ming Daily*, Peking, 8 July 1956.

35 Editorial of 29 July 1963. See the discussion in CNA 344, 14 October 1960.

36 See FEER, 18 February 1965, p. 295.

37 *Hupei Daily*, 20 December 1964 (cited in FEER, see footnote 36).

38 *The Rise of the Chinese People's Communes*, Peking, New World Press, 1959, p. 118. The best description of a Commune is that given in Isabel and David Crook, *The First Years of Yangyi Commune* (London, Routledge & Kegan Paul, 1966), all the more valuable because it provides a sequel to the same authors' *Revolution in a Chinese Village: Ten Mile Inn* (London, Routledge & Kegan Paul, 1959).

39 This was an issue between Liu Shao-chi and Mao which came out in the Cultural Revolution. See *Current Scene*, Vol. 6, No. 17, 1 October 1968.

40 Quoted by Mao in his *Report on an Investigation into the Peasant Movement in Hunan*, published in *Selected Works* (London, 1954).

41 *People's Daily*, Peking, 12 May 1958.

CHAPTER TWO: THE PROLETARIAT

1 Li Li-san, speaking on 21 November.

2 See the discussion in Charles Hoffman's "Work Incentive Policy in Communist China," in CQ 17, 1964, p. 92.

3 See CNA 161, 14 December 1956.

4 See CQ 22, 1965, p. 189.

5 Provisional Measures for City and Town Grain Supply, 25 August 1955, Section 2, Article 5. The figures are set out in Durand's *Le Financement du Budget en Chine Populaire* (Hongkong, Sirey, 1965), p. 395.

6 See CNA 382, 28 July 1961.

7 *People's Daily*, Peking, 14 August 1953.

8 18 September 1953.

9 *People's Daily*, Peking, 9 March 1956.

10 *People's Daily*, Peking, 18 March 1956.

11 *Daily Worker*, Peking, 30 May 1957.

12 *Daily Worker*, Peking, 15 August 1957: the lecturer was Ko Pei-chi.

13 *Daily Worker*, Peking, 23 July 1958.

14 31 December 1954, Regulation on the Organization of City Residents' Committees.

15 Chao Kuo-chun, "Urban Communes: A First-hand Report," in FEER, 29 September 1960, p. 715. See also Janet Sulaff's "The Urban Communes and Anti-City Experiment in Communist China," in CQ 29, 1967, p. 82.

16 Yang Liu in *Amoy Daily*, 9 October 1958 (cited by D.E. T. Luard in CQ 3, 1960, p. 79).

17 According to wall posters cited in a Bulgarian broadcast on 2 March 1967 (*BBC Summary of World Broadcasts*, Far East, 2407/C/1 of 4 March 1967).

CHAPTER THREE: THE BOURGEOISIE

1 *New China News Agency*, Peking, 30 December 1964 (also quoted in CQ 22, 1965, p. 72).

2 See Keesing, pp. 12785–6.

3 Cited in the *People's Daily*, Peking, 23 February 1955.

4 See the discussion in CNA 118, 3 February 1956.

5 *Ta Kung Pao*, Tientsin, 19 January 1956.

6 17 January 1956.

7 In February 1960 (cited in FEER, 29 September 1960 p. 707).

8 Quoted in the *People's Daily*, Peking, 12 May 1957.

9 See CNA 193, 16 August 1957, and MacFarquhar, p. 261 *et seq*.

10 30 October 1954.

CHAPTER FOUR: THE INTELLIGENTSIA

1 *Kuang Ming Daily*, Peking, 11 May 1957.

2 The total number of intellectuals is usually estimated at between three and a half and four million.

3 In his speech on contradictions, 27 February 1957 (cited in Keesing, p. 15682).

4 *Kuang Ming Daily*, Peking, 5 June 1957.

5 *People's Daily*, Peking, 19 January 1955.

6 *People's Daily*, Peking, 8 December 1951.

7 Quoted in CNA 241, 15 August 1958, and 244, 12 September 1958.

8 *Philosophical Research*, Peking, September 1961.

9 CNA 395, 3 November 1961, p. 7.

10 See CNA 458, 1 March 1963; 488, 4 October 1963; 423, 1 June 1962; and 505, 21 February 1964.

11 Quoted in CNA 313, 26 February 1960, p. 6.

12 See CNA 248, 10 October 1958.

13 Quoted in CNA 306, 1 January 1960.

14 Keesing, p. 15233.

15 *People's Daily*, Peking, 20 April 1957.

16 *Kuang Ming Daily*, Peking, 10 May 1957.

17 Lo Lung-chi, in a speech to a political meeting on 18 March 1957 (*People's Daily*, Peking, 23 March 1957).

18 See the instances cited in CNA 185, 21 June 1957.

19 See Chapter Three.

20 *Wen Hui Pao*, Shanghai, 27 May 1957.

21 Rene Goldman, "The Rectification Campaign at Peking University, May–June 1957," in CQ 12, 1962, pp. 142 and 146.

22 *Ibid* (footnote 21), pp. 149–150.

23 *People's Daily*, Peking, 31 May 1957.

24 *People's Daily*, Peking, 8 June 1957.

25 *Kwangsi Daily*, Nanning, 3 October 1957 (quoted in MacFarquhar, p. 162).

26 Including a strengthened legislature, improvement of the legal system, and the Communist Party's abandonment of control over the universities. See MacFarquhar, p. 38 *et seq.*

27 *New China News Agency*, 5 August 1957.

28 See MacFarquhar, p. 264.

29 *People's Daily*, Peking, 19 June 1957.

30 Goldman, *op. cit.* (footnote 21), p. 151.

31 *Wen Hui Pao*, Shanghai, 16 May 1957.

32 *Daily Worker*, Peking, 4 March 1964.

33 See CQ 22, 1965, p. 188.

34 *Wen Hui Pao*, Shanghai, 28 April 1958.

35 *Literary Criticism*, Peking, No. 2 of 1962 (quoted in CNA 466, 3 May 1963, where there is also a good discussion of poetry trends). For the "million-poem" movement of 1958 see CQ 3, 1960, p. 1.

36 *Red Flag*, Peking, No. 12 of 1964 (quoted in CQ 20, 1964, p. 174).

37 *People's Daily*, Peking, 24 August 1960.

38 *People's Music*, Peking, No. 11 of 1963 (quoted in CNA 523, 3 July 1964).

39 *Ibid* (footnote 38).

40 *Kuang Ming Daily*, Peking, 18 March 1964.

41 *People's Music*, Peking, No. 6 of 1964 (quoted in CNA 523, 3 July 1964).

42 *Kuang Ming Daily*, Peking, 29 March 1964.

43 *People's Daily*, Peking, 22 September 1964.

44 *Hwa Seung Daily*, Hongkong, 7 April 1949 (quoted in CNA 381, 21 July 1961). A piano is, after all, an extremely heavy and costly instrument for a country such as China (or India) to popularize, and it occasioned surprise that Mao's wife championed it so energetically during the Cultural Revolution in 1968.

45 *Kuang Ming Daily*, Peking, 9 January 1961.

46 *People's Music*, Peking, No. 12 of 1964 (quoted in CNA 559, 9 April 1965).

47 *People's Daily*, Peking, 14 March 1957.

48 *People's Daily*, Peking, 9 March 1957.

49 See CNA 186, 28 June 1957.

50 Keesing, p. 12117.

51 *Ibid.*

52 CNA 173, 22 March 1957.

53 On 17 June. It held a second conference in January 1962.

54 *People's Daily*, Peking, 29 July 1955.

55 On 17 and 18 March 1960 (Keesing, p. 12117).

CHAPTER FIVE: THE FAMILY

1 Cited in *Contemporary China* (edited by E. Stuart Kirby), Vol. 3 (Hongkong University Press, 1960), p. 213.

2 In a conversation with Edgar Snow (*Red Star Over China*, London, Gollancz, 1937, pp. 144–5).

3 *Women of China*, Peking, No. 4 of 1959 (cited in *Current Scene*, Vol. 3, No. 10, 1 January 1965, p. 10).

4 See CNA 5, 25 September 1953.

5 See CQ 9, 1962, p. 141.

6 *People's Daily*, Peking, 11 October 1951.

7 *Women of New China*, Peking, November 1954; December 1954; and February 1955 (quoted in CNA 83, 13 May 1955).

8 See Chang-tu Hu *et al.*, *China: Its People, Its Society, Its Culture* (London, 1960), p. 177.

9 On 26 September 1951.

10 *People's Daily*, Peking, 19 November 1953.

11 See Chang-tu Hu, *op. cit.* (footnote 8), pp. 176–7.

12 *China Youth Daily*, Peking, 30 August 1956 (cited in CNA 215, 7 February 1958).

13 1 December 1956 (No. 23), cited in CQ 22, 1965, p. 177.

14 20 January 1962 (quoted in CNA 416, 13 April 1962).

15 *The Guardian*, London, 6 January 1967. See also Christopher Lucas, "The Top Woman of China," in *Current Scene*, Vol. 3, No. 10 (1 January 1965), p. 2 and *passim*. Typical of the many stories told about the behaviour of Chinese women abroad is the experience of an opera troupe, the female members of which were issued with handbags to sport on their visit to Hongkong (where a handbag is *de rigueur*). But the young women left their handbags at the first ice-cream stall they came to, being so unfamiliar with carrying them.

16 29 August 1964 (cited in CNA 537, 16 October 1964).

17 See e.g. *People's Daily*, Peking, 3 September 1964; and *Ta Kung Pao*, Peking, 25 August and 10 September 1964.

18 *People's Daily*, Peking, 14 November 1964.

19 *Theoretical Learning*, Peking, No. 12, December 1963 (I derive this from Eastern European sources in Peking).

20 *Ta Kung Pao*, Peking, 21 April 1964.

21 But refugee reports tend to suggest that prostitution continues

in a small way in private circles in cities and major towns, as one would imagine: such phenomena cannot be abolished overnight.

22 Cited in CNA 66, 7 January 1955.

23 *Communist Youth*, Peking, 16 October 1964 (quoted in CNA 66, 7 January 1955).

24 *Nanfang Daily*, Canton, 3 September 1963 (quoted in *Current Scene*, Vol. 3, No. 9, 15 December 1963, p. 7).

25 *People's Music*, Peking, No. 4 of 1961 (cited in CNA 381, 21 July 1961).

26 See CNA 491, 1 November 1963.

27 *Wen Hui Pao*, Shanghai, quoted in the *Kuang Ming Daily*, Peking, 3 September 1963.

28 *Literary Criticism*, Peking, No. 4 of 1963 (quoted in CNA 491, 1 November 1963).

29 *Kuang Ming Daily*, cited in footnote 27 above.

30 *Literature*, Peking, 11 August 1963 (quoted in CNA 491, 1 November 1963).

31 *People's Daily*, Peking, 26 February 1964.

32 See Ezra F. Vogel's "From Friendship to Comradeship: The Change in Personal Relations in Communist China," in CQ 21, 1965, p. 46. One of the saddest sentences ever written by a refugee is: "Only now do I really see how we were compelled to cover up continually our inner thoughts and feelings, how we were brought up to be insincere" (CNA 259, 9 January 1959, p. 7).

CHAPTER SIX: YOUTH

1 *People's Daily*, Peking, 19 May 1960.

2 Quoted in H. G. Creel, *Chinese Thought* (London, Methuen, 1962), p. 132.

3 See Robert D. Barendsen, "The Agricultural Middle School in Communist China," in CQ 8, 1961, p. 106; also Munemitsu Abe, "Sparetime Education in Communist China," in CQ 8, 1961, p. 149.

4 *People's Education*, Peking, February 1960 (quoted in Barendsen, footnote 3).

5 Chou's report to the National People's Congress, *New China News Agency*, Peking, 30 December 1964, and *Peking Review*, 1 January 1965.

6 Quoted in René Goldman, "The Rectification Campaign at Peking University: May–June 1957," in CQ 12, 1962, p. 144.

7 *Ibid.*, pp. 144–5.

8 *Kuang Ming Daily*, Peking, 6 May 1957.

9 *People's Daily*, Peking, 10 May 1958.

10 *New China News Agency*, Peking, 26 August 1963.

11 2 September 1958. See CQ 10, 1962, p. 113.

12 Quoted in CNA 259, 9 January 1959.

13 Lu Chi-fang, President of Hofei Industrial College, in 1963 (quoted in Sally Backhouse, "Some Problems of Chinese Education," in *Eastern Horizon*, Vol. 3, No. 10, October 1964, p. 24).

14 19 January 1965 (cited in CNA 561, 23 April 1965).

15 *People's Daily*, Peking, 21 November 1964.

16 Liu Fung, in *Hsui-min Wen Pao*, Shanghai, 7 May 1964.

17 *People's Daily*, Peking, 28 February 1964.

18 *China Youth Daily*, Peking, 25 January 1964 (an article by a Hunan youth leader, quoted in CNA 521, 19 June 1964).

19 *Youth of China*, Peking, 1 September 1961; also *Kuang Ming Daily*, Peking, 3 September 1961 (quoted in CNA 393, 20 October 1961).

20 Editorial in the *People's Daily*, Peking, 3 August 1964.

21 *China Youth Daily*, Peking, 22 August 1964 (quoted in *Current Scene*, Vol. 3, No. 12, 1 February 1965, p. 7).

22 Quoted by Lord Lindsay of Birker, in Szczepanik, p. 227.

23 *Youth of China*, Peking, No. 5 of 1960 (quoted in CNA 332, 15 July 1960).

24 *Kuang Ming Daily*, Peking, 3 May 1961.

CHAPTER SEVEN: THE NATIONAL MINORITIES

1 The Indian resolution supporting the West on this question of repatriation was carried by 54 votes to 5 in the UN General Assembly on 3 December 1952 (see Keesing, p. 12721).

2 See CNA 159, 30 November 1956; 198, 27 September 1957; and 232, 13 June 1958 for discussions of the Southwestern minorities.

3 *Kuang Ming Daily*, Peking, 15 February 1962.

4 See CNA 232, 13 June 1958. The first Kuomintang Congress in 1924 promised self-determination for minority races.

5 Edgar Snow, *Red Star Over China* (London, Gollancz, 1937), pp. 102–3.

6 Chang-tu Hu *et al.*, *China, Its People, Its Society, Its Culture* (London, Mayflower, 1960), p. 212.

7 *People's Daily*, Peking, 29 June 1956.

8 Chou Fang, in *State Organs*, Peking, December 1957 (quoted in CNA 232, 13 June 1958).

9 *People's Daily,* Peking, 21 December 1958.

10 On 22 April 1956, see Keesing, p. 14942.

11 *Kuang Ming Daily,* Peking, 15 February 1962. For Ulanfu's fall, see *Current Scene,* Vol. 6, No. 20, 15 November 1968.

12 *People's Daily,* Peking, 22 August 1958.

13 Liu Chun, Deputy Chairman of the Nationalities Affairs Commission, in *Red Flag,* Peking, No. 12 of 1964 (quoted in CQ 20, 1964, p. 175).

14 Lu Ting-yi, writing in *Folklore Literature,* Peking, No. 6 of 1964 (cited in CNA 563, 7 May 1965).

15 *People's Daily,* Peking, 6 November 1959.

16 Tung Ying, in *Solidarity of Nationalities,* Peking, February 1962 (quoted in CNA 431, 3 August 1962).

17 *Red Flag,* Peking, 30 June 1964 (quoted in CNA 563, 7 May 1965).

18 *People's Daily,* Peking, 13 January 1958.

19 *People's Daily,* Peking, 22 June 1958.

20 See P. H. M. Jones, "Scripts for Minorities," in FEER, 12 April 1962, p. 63.

21 Quoted in CNA 265, 20 February 1959.

22 *People's Daily,* Peking, 6 August 1952.

23 See CNA 226, 2 May 1958.

24 See CNA 312, 19 February 1960.

25 *Ibid.*

26 *Modern Buddhism,* Peking, August 1955 (quoted in CQ 22, 1965, p. 147).

27 *Modern Buddhism,* Peking, No. 5 of 1951 (quoted in FEER, 4 April 1963, p. 15).

28 *Modern Buddhism,* Peking, No. 8 of 1958, cited in Holmes Welch, "Asian Buddhists and China," in FEER, 4 April 1963, p. 15.

29 *New China News Agency,* Peking, 8 September 1956.

30 *New China News Agency,* Shenyang, 2 August 1959.

31 See Holmes Welch, "Buddhists in the Cold War," in FEER, 8 March 1962, p. 555; and his "Buddhism after the Seventh," in FEER, 12 March 1965, p. 433.

32 FEER, 21 November 1963, p. 381.

33 This is eloquently argued by Holmes Welch, *op. cit.* (footnote 28 *supra*).

34 See P. H. M. Jones, "Sinkiang—The Road to Communism," in FEER, 17 November 1960, p. 280.

35 The suggestion that Khrushchev made this promise to Mao was

first published, from Indian sources, in a despatch from New Delhi by C. L. Sulzberger in the *New York Times*, 14 February 1955.

36 *Montsame*, Ulan Bator, 16 May 1964: see CNA 534, 25 September 1964.

37 *Pravda*, Moscow, 2 September 1964.

CHAPTER EIGHT: TIBET

1 Quoted from Keesing, p. 11103.

2 See, for example, the arguments in Li Tieh-tseng, *The Historical Status of Tibet* (New York, 1956), and the counter-arguments in H. E. Richardson, *Tibet and its History* (London, Oxford University Press, 1962).

3 On 7 September 1958.

4 See Richardson, *op. cit.*, p. 116.

5 D. L. Snellgrove, in CQ 12, 1962, p. 250. See Alfred P. Rubin, "The Position of Tibet in International Law," CQ 35, 1968, p. 110.

6 *Radio Peking*, 22 May 1950 (quoted in Keesing, p. 11101).

7 Keesing, p. 11101.

8 *My Land and My People:, The Autobiography of H.H. The Dalai Lama* (London, Weidenfeld, 1962), pp. 80–1.

9 The Tibetans thus regarded Chinese occupation as temporary. See George N. Patterson, *Tragic Destiny* (London, Faber, 1959), p. 133.

10 See CQ 1, 1960, p. 93; and Patterson, *op. cit.*, pp. 82–93.

11 Lamaistic Buddhism, with its headquarters in Lhasa, has an influence among the Mongol communities, and the Chinese remember that a former Dalai Lama sixty years ago sought Russian help in uniting Tibet and Mongolia as a sovereign independent state which, if it fell under Russian or British or other foreign influence, would have made the Chinese feel extremely unsafe on their vulnerable western border. For continuing Soviet interest in Tibet in the early 1950s, see Patterson, *op. cit.*, p. 93.

12 *Nationalities Research*, Peking, No. 2 of 1959 (cited in CNA 270, 3 April 1959).

13 Robert Ekvall, in *Current Scene*, Vol. 3, No. 11, 15 January 1965, pp. 3 and 8.

14 *People's Daily*, Peking, 25 April 1956.

15 Dalai Lama, *op. cit.*, pp. 102–3.

16 In his speech to the National People's Congress, Peking, 18 April 1959 (quoted in Keesing, p. 16801).

17 CQ 12, 1962, p. 246.

18 Richardson, *op. cit.*, p. 27 (see also p. 213).

19 Lok Sabha, 8 May 1959. Nehru advised the Bhutanese to go slowly into their development plans.

20 Richardson, *op. cit.*, p. 130. The same opinion is reported by Stuart and Roma Gelder in their *The Timely Rain, Travels in New Tibet* (London, Hutchinson, 1964), p. 137.

21 Announcement of 3 July 1959, quoted in Keesing, p. 17094.

22 See P. H. M. Jones, "Tibet on the Threshold," in FEER, 9 July 1964, p. 53; and George Moseley, "Tibet: Tradition versus Reform," in FEER, 7 October 1965, p. 13.

23 Patterson, *op. cit.*, p. 178.

24 In a telegram to the UN Secretary-General, 9 September 1959, quoted in Keesing, p. 17091.

25 *Tibet and the Chinese People's Republic,* A Report to the International Commission of Jurists by its Legal Inquiry Committee on Tibet (Geneva, 1960).

26 Professor L. C. Green, in CQ 5, 1961, pp. 158–9.

27 Even the Gelders (*op. cit.,* footnote 20, pp. 140–1) on their brief visit to Lhasa in 1962, dependent on official Chinese interpreters, found Tibetan criticism of Chinese policy.

28 *Hindusthan Times,* Delhi, 26 July 1964, cited in CNA 534, 25 September 1964. See also FEER, 9 July 1964, p. 54.

29 See e.g. Madame Alexandra David-Neel's *Le Vieux Tibet Face à la Chine Nouvelle,* cited in P. H. M. Jones, "Tibet and the New Order," in FEER, 2 March 1961, p. 356.

30 Patterson, *op. cit.*, p. 129.

31 See e.g. Richardson, *op. cit.*, p. 193. The Gelders saw the first scientifically trained Tibetan doctor perform an appendectomy near Lhasa in 1962: he had studied in China in the 1950s (*op. cit.,* footnote 20, p. 96). Dr. Hatem, the American doctor working in China, told Edgar Snow that Chinese anti-VD teams were able to start work in Tibet only after 1959; until then the Dalai Lama had "opposed examination and treatment there on religious grounds" (Snow, pp. 277–8).

32 FEER, 16 February 1961, p. 288.

33 Patterson, *op. cit.*, p. 179.

34 Dalai Lama, *op. cit.*, p. 140.

35 Dalai Lama, *loc. cit.*

CHAPTER NINE: COMMUNISM

1 See CNA 215, 7 February 1958.

2 23 February 1962.

3 See CNA 496, 6 December 1963, p. 7.

4 Szczepanik, p. 223.

5 See David A. Charles, "The Dismissal of Marshal Peng Teh-huai," in CQ 8, 1961, p. 63.

6 See Howard L. Boorman, "Liu Shao-chi: A Political Profile," in CQ 10, 1962, p. 1.

7 See Ellis Joffe, "The Soldier's Role," in FEER, 1 September 1960, p. 477; his "Contradictions in the Chinese Army," in FEER, 11 July 1963, p. 123; and John Gittings, *The Role of the Chinese Army* (London, Oxford University Press, 1967).

8 See FEER, 1 August 1963, p. 287, for examples.

9 24 September 1955.

10 See the secret PLA *Work Bulletins* cited in CNA 510 and 511, 3 and 10 April 1964; and Samuel B. Griffith's "The Military Potential of China," in *China and the Peace of Asia,* edited by Alastair Buchan (London, Chatto & Windus, 1965), p. 65. On the Army generally, see John Gittings' *The Role of the Chinese Army* (London, Oxford University Press, 1967).

11 See Donald W. Klein, "The 'Next Generation' of Chinese Communist Leaders," in CQ 12, 1962, p. 57.

12 Teng Hsiao-ping in September 1956 (Keesing, p. 15232).

13 Hu Ko-shih, *People's Daily,* Peking, 8 July 1964.

14 *New China News Agency,* Peking, 14 October 1959.

15 26 March 1964.

16 Quoted in CNA 146, 31 August 1956.

17 *The New Society is a Great School,* October 1951 (quoted in CQ 8, 1961, p. 56).

18 An interesting study is Dr R. J. Lifton's *Thought Reform and the Psychology of Totalism: A Study of "Brainwashing" in China* (New York, 1961): twenty-five Western civilians and fifteen Chinese intellectuals who had been through thought reform were interviewed by an American psychiatrist and psycho-analyst. For accounts of "struggle meetings" see Chou Ching-wen's *Ten Years of Storm* (New York, 1960), especially passages excerpted in CQ 5, 1961, pp. 145–9.

19 See CNA 83, 13 May 1955.

20 See Chou Ching-wen, quoted in CQ 3, 1960, p. 108. It was alleged that in the Ministry of Finance, during the 1957 Rectification campaign, the proportion of delinquents had been fixed in advance, twenty-five per cent in the 1952 *sanfan* campaign and five per cent in the 1955 *sufan* campaign (*People's Daily,* Peking, 19 May 1957). For the *wufan* and *sanfan* generally, see Keesing, pp. 11419 and 12785.

21 See CNA 214, 31 January 1958.

22 Ma Tse-min, reported in *Kuang Ming Daily,* Peking, 8 May 1957.

23 *New China News Agency,* Peking, 30 December 1964.

24 *People's Daily*, Peking, 7 February 1963.

25 Hu Yao-pang, quoted in CQ 19, 1964, p. 182: see also *People's Daily*, Peking, 3 August 1964.

26 15 August 1964 (quoted in CNA 537, 16 October 1964).

27 e.g. *People's Daily*, Peking, 4 May 1963.

28 An Tzu-wen, in *Red Flag*, Peking, Nos. 17–18 of 1965 (quoted in CQ 21, 1965, p. 202).

29 *Red Flag*, Peking, No. 15, 31 July 1964 (partially quoted in CQ 20, 1964, p. 172).

30 David Chipp, 13 April 1957.

CHAPTER TEN: AGRICULTURE

1 Quoted in Chiang Kai-shek, *China's Destiny* (London, Dennis Dobson, 1947), p. 329.

2 Doubts have been expressed about the absolute validity of some of these figures, e.g. by John Lossing Buck in *Food and Agriculture in Communist China* (New York, Praeger, 1966), but at least their relationship to each other is probably reasonably correct. The best collection of Chinese agricultural statistics of recent years is in *Current Scene*, Vol. 5, No. 21, 15 December 1967. See also the Appendix above.

3 Li, p. 73.

4 See Robert Michael Field, "How Much Grain Does Communist China Produce?" CQ 33, 1968, p. 98.

5 Liao Lu-yen, *Red Flag*, Peking, 1 September 1960.

6 Including the extension of multiple-cropping on the same physical plot.

7 *Sixth Plenary Session of the Eighth Central Committee of the Chinese Communist Party* (Peking, Foreign Languages Press, 1958).

8 21 January 1958.

9 *Handbook on Current Affairs*, Peking, 10 September 1955 (cited in FEER, 1 October 1959, p. 530); see also Chao, p. 180.

10 See *People's Daily*, Peking, 7 November 1955 and 18 April 1960.

11 *People's Daily*, Peking, 10 May 1960.

12 See Denis Elliot, "China's Water Ways," in FEER, 14 January 1965, pp. 30–1.

13 See CNA 484, 6 September 1963; also 330, 1 July 1960; 383, 4 August 1961; 415, 30 March 1962; and 562, 30 April 1965.

14 Cited in C. H. G. Oldham, "Science and Superstition," in FEER, 1 April 1965, p. 17.

15 See CNA 478, 26 July 1963.

16 Hsiang Te, in July 1963 (quoted in P. H. M. Jones, "One Million Tractors," in FEER, 3 September 1964, pp. 431–3).

17 The official Peking statistic is expressed in "tractor units" of 15 horsepower each, and the average tractor is about twice that size. The usual figure of 100,000 units probably means about 50,000 actual tractors, therefore.

18 *Economic Research*, Peking, No. 6 of 1963 (cited in CNA 492, 8 November 1963).

19 24 October 1957.

20 See Henry Lethbridge, "Tractors in China," in FEER, 21 March 1963, p. 616.

21 Teng Tzu-hui, in March 1957.

22 *People's Daily*, Peking, 21 January 1958. The Party also encouraged small-scale village chemical fertilizer production, though with misgivings on the part of the technical experts: see CNA 262, 30 January 1959. For a recent survey see Alexandra Close's "Down to Earth," in FEER, 8 December 1966.

23 Ma Yin-chu's *New Theory of Population*, 1957; and the author's *Chemicals for the Communes*, in FEER, 11 June 1964, pp. 533–5.

24 *People's Daily*, Peking, 17 April 1962.

25 Keesing, pp. 14943 and 13800; Chao, p. 174; CNA 314, 4 March 1960; CNA 342, 30 September 1960; and Jerome Ch'en's *Mao and the Chinese Revolution*, p. 349.

26 *Kuang Ming Daily*, Peking, 25 August 1957; and *People's Daily*, Peking, 18 March 1959.

27 Henry Lethbridge, "Trends in Chinese Agriculture," in FEER, 30 May 1963, p. 499.

28 Cited in P. H. M. Jones, "Creeping Modernisation," in FEER, 12 November 1964, p. 350. See also *Daily Worker*, Peking, 12 February 1963; and CQ 18, 1964, p. 231. Yang Po warned in the *People's Daily* of 6 June 1964, however, that this policy could cause a deterioration in the other areas, and that it would be better first to stabilize production *everywhere* even if this took three to five years. The Marxist objection is that it is socially unfair to favour one community with more investment than another. The same debate has gone on in India in the past four or five years, and a similar decision has been made there.

29 Derek Davies, "A Kwangtung Commune," in FEER, 17 December 1964, p. 564.

CHAPTER ELEVEN: POPULATION

1 The 1930 Census produced a figure of 475 million, but was hardly thorough. The Japanese War cost twenty million Chinese

lives, and the Kuomintang estimate in 1947 was 460 million. Since the Chinese are tempted to over-emphasize the importance of their country and the vastness of its population, some critics feel the 583 million census total of 1953 to be an exaggerated figure, but others suspect an *under*-count. See John S. Aird's *The Size, Composition and Growth of the Population of Mainland China*, US Department of Commerce, Washington, 1961. What is not questioned is the fact that the 1953 Census was more thorough than any previous Census. It has recently been suggested that the actual population may be as small as 425 million (Russell Warren Howe in *The Statist*, 3 September 1965, p. 621). But this places too much weight on yet another official Chinese statistic, that of 170 million recorded live births in the fifteen years 1949–64.

2 Derek Davies, "A New Census," in FEER, 9 July 1964, p. 41. See also the second edition of Dr S. Chandrasekhar's *China's Population* (Hongkong, Oxford University Press, 1960).

3 In Conakry, 23 January 1964 (*Candide*, Paris, 6 February 1964).

4 See e.g. CNA 364, 17 March 1961.

5 Pai Chien-hua in *People's Daily*, Peking, 1 November 1954.

6 Chou En-lai said, in the interview quoted in footnote 3 above, that: "Our present target is to lower the rate of increase to below two per cent. For the future, we envisage an even lower rate. But I do not believe it will be possible to rival the Japanese rate (of one per cent) before 1970. . . ." Even this seems sanguine.

7 *New China News Agency*, Peking, 2 February 1956; and *People's China*, Peking, 16 March 1956.

8 14 November 1957.

9 See Dr S. Chandrasekhar, "China's Population Problems," in FEER, 4 June 1959, p. 783.

10 21 February 1957 (quoted in CQ 3, 1960, p. 66).

11 Report by John Strohm, the American correspondent, in the *Washington Daily News*, 16 October 1958.

12 *Wen Hui Pao*, Shanghai, 12 February 1957 (cited in CNA 172, 15 March 1957).

13 FEER, 21 February 1963, p. 353.

14 No. 9 of 1958.

15 *Selected Works of Mao Tse-tung*, Peking, 1961, Vol. 4, pp. 453–4.

16 Kao Hsiang, in *Ta Kung Pao*, Peking, 11 February 1963.

17 *Ta Kung Pao*, Peking, 5 February 1958.

18 See CNA 172, 15 March 1957; and H. Yuan Tien, "Sterilisation, Oral Contraception and Population Control in China," in *Population Studies*, March 1965, p. 215.

19 China has three persons per cultivated acre, compared with Japan's nine, Britain's five, India's two and Russia's .5.

20 See CNA 95, 12 August 1955; and CQ 16, 1963, p. 74.

21 "What could China obtain through the conquest of the region that she cannot now get through the normal processes of international trade?" (Alexander Eckstein, *Communist China's Economic Growth and Foreign Trade*, New York, McGraw-Hill, 1966, p. 247).

22 See CQ 7, 1961, p. 80; and Li, pp. 203–4.

CHAPTER TWELVE: INDUSTRY

1 January 1953.

2 See CNA 62, 3 December 1954.

3 Li, p. 47.

4 11 April 1957.

5 *People's Daily*, Peking, 3 July 1957.

6 *People's Daily*, Peking, 17 November 1957.

7 *People's Daily*, Peking, 13 March 1957.

8 *People's Daily*, Peking, 4 April 1957.

9 *People's Daily*, Peking, 12 and 17 October 1958.

10 Hsia Yi-hun, *People's Daily*, Peking, 30 April 1959.

11 Wang Chih-hsi, *People's Daily*, 8 May 1959.

12 Lushan Communiqué of Central Committee, 26 August 1959.

13 *People's Daily*, Peking, 2 December 1958.

14 Stanley Karnow, "The GI Who Chose Communism," in the *Saturday Evening Post*, 16 November 1963, p. 106 (the foreigner was Albert Belhomme).

15 Chen Pei-chen, *Kuang Ming Daily*, Peking, 25 July 1958.

16 Wang Po-chin, *Shenyang Daily*, 16 November 1959 (quoted in CNA 387, 1 September 1961).

17 *People's Daily*, Peking, 9 April 1960.

18 15 August 1961.

19 Anna Louise Strong, *Letter from China*, No. 13, 30 December 1963.

20 See Harald Munthe-Kaas, "China's Mechanical Heart," in FEER, 27 May 1965, p. 398, for a general survey.

21 *Peking Review*, 11 October 1963.

22 See CNA 541, 20 November 1964.

23 See CNA 220, 14 March 1958; 406, 2 February 1962; 490, 18 October 1963, p. 5; and also Brian Heenan, "China's Petroleum

Industry," in FEER, 23 September 1965, p. 565, and 14 October 1965, p. 93.

CHAPTER THIRTEEN: SCIENCE AND TECHNOLOGY

1 Joseph Needham, *Science and Civilisation in China*, Vol. 1 (Cambridge University Press, 1954), p. 5. See also Vol. 4:1 (1962), p. xxv.

2 See Morton H. Halperin, *China and the Bomb* (London, Pall Mall, 1965), chapter 3; and his "China and the Bomb—Chinese Nuclear Strategy," in CQ 21, 1965, p. 74; and Lewis A. Frank's "Nuclear Weapons Development in China," in *Bulletin of the Atomic Scientists*, (Chicago), January 1966, p. 72.

3 See Dr Han Suyin, "Acupuncture—the Scientific Evidence," in *Eastern Horizon*, April 1964, p. 8; Dr Felix Mann, "Chinese Traditional Medicine: A Practitioner's View," in CQ 23, 1965, pp. 32–6; and Snow, pp. 306–16.

4 *People's Daily*, Peking, 31 July 1957.

5 *Ta Kung Pao*, Tientsin, 12 October 1955.

6 March issue (quoted in CNA 385, 18 August 1961).

7 *People's Daily*, Peking, 23 June 1955.

8 Mr Sun Ting, speaking in Shanghai on 5 May 1957, quoted in *Kuang Ming Daily*, Peking, 10 May 1957, and in MacFarquhar, p. 64.

9 *Theatre Journal*, Peking, No. 17 of 1958. The text of the play is in *Drama*, Peking, 3 October 1958 (both cited in CNA 253, 14 November 1958). For the original true story see *China Youth Daily*, Peking, 28 November 1958 (cited in CNA 264, 13 February 1959).

10 *People's Daily*, Peking, 22 March 1962; and Dr C. H. G. Oldham in the *Saturday Review* of 6 March 1965, pp. 45–6.

11 28 September 1958 (quoted in CNA 485, 13 September 1963).

12 *People's Daily*, Peking, 30 June 1958.

13 Professor Chien Hsueh-sen, in *Kuang Ming Daily*, Peking, 10 June 1961.

14 John M. H. Lindbeck in CQ 6, 1961, pp. 105–7 and 114. See also C. H. G. Oldham on "Science and Education in China," in Ruth Adams' *Contemporary China* (New York, Pantheon Books, 1966).

15 Mikhail A. Klochko, *Soviet Scientist in China* (London, Hollis and Carter, 1965).

16 Kao Chih-kuo, in *Kuang Ming Daily*, Peking, 14 April 1961.

17 April 1962 (quoted in FEER, 27 September 1962, p. 577). An

article in the *People's Daily* of 13 July 1961 by Ta Ko reminded the Party that, "Indeed, abroad among bourgeois scientists there is free discussion and habitual mutual respect between different schools. . . ."

18 CNA 696, 16 February 1968; C. H. G. Oldham, "Science Travels the Mao Road," *Bulletin of the Atomic Scientists,* February 1969.

19 See FEER, 1 November 1962, p. 270.

CHAPTER FOURTEEN: GROWTH

1 Lung Yun, confessing in the *Kuang Ming Daily,* Peking, 31 May 1957. For earlier reluctance to accept Russian aid see citations in CNA 6, 2 October 1953.

2 See Choh-ming Li in CQ 1, 1960, pp. 36–7; and Wu, pp. 88 and 203.

3 *People's Daily,* Peking, 25 November and 12 December 1953.

4 *People's Daily,* Peking, 1 October 1958. Chairman Liu Shao-chi's definition of the Leap was the "General Line of going all out and aiming high to achieve greater, quicker, better and more economical results in building socialism."

5 *People's Daily,* Peking, 19 May 1958.

6 *Finance,* Peking, 5 August 1958 (quoted in CQ 17, 1964, p. 9).

7 Mayor Ko elaborated in February 1959 the theme that "the whole country is one chess board" (i.e. that national planning strategy involved control of developments in every locality), and Chen Yun wrote in the *People's Daily* of 1 March a plea for rational planning. Ko is now dead, Chen in the political shadows.

8 *Liberation Daily,* Shanghai, 18 November 1959 (quoted in CNA 327, 10 June 1960).

9 *Red Flag,* Peking, 1 February 1961. Po was later disgraced in the Cultural Revolution.

10 Anna Louise Strong, *Letter from China,* No. 13, 30 December 1963; but see Wu, pp. 98–102.

11 Speech on 30 June 1961. The disarming viewpoint of the guerrilla economists in the Party was well put by Lin Wei in the *People's Daily* on 13 October 1959: "The objective law cannot be known *a priori,* but only by trial and error: therefore a certain confusion and muddle is inevitable if we want to change the 'poor and blank' state of the country. . . . This does not mean that we are approving of the muddle, but that revolution is necessarily confused."

12 *Liberation,* Shanghai, reprinted in *People's Daily,* Peking, 13 August 1960.

13 Nos. 13–14 of 1963, quoted in CQ 17, 1964, p. 66.

14 See Durand, *Le Financement du Budget en Chine Populaire*, (Hongkong, Sirey, 1965), pp. 293–6.

15 See Durand, *op. cit.* (footnote 14), pp. 302–4; Szczepanik, pp. 117–118; and FEER, 4 July 1963, p. 6.

16 *People's Daily*, Peking, 6 September 1963.

17 *New Construction*, Peking, March 1958 (cited by Audrey Donnithorne in Szczepanik, p. 57).

18 *Liberation Daily*, Shanghai, 7 May 1958 (cited by Audrey Donnithorne in Szczepanik, p. 63).

CHAPTER FIFTEEN: TAIWAN AND THE WEST

1 *China Youth Daily*, Peking, 4 May 1963 (cited in CNA 489, 18 October 1963).

2 See e.g. John Israel, "Politics on Formosa," in CQ 15, 1963, p. 5.

3 Sheppard Glass, "Some Aspects of Formosa's Economic Growth," in CQ 15, 1963, p. 12; see also P. H. M. Jones, "Taiwan —The Cash Nexus," in FEER, 26 November 1964, p. 462.

4 See Maurice Meisner, "The Development of Formosan Nationalism," in CQ 15, 1963, p. 91, and George A. Kerr's *Formosa Betrayed* (London, Eyre & Spottiswoode, 1966). The Conlon Report, prepared for the US Senate Foreign Relations Committee in 1959, recommended the internationalization of Taiwan pending a plebiscite.

5 *The Observer*, London, 12 August 1962. See also Snow, pp. 327 and 765–6.

6 See Lewis Gilbert, "Peking and Taipei," in CQ 15, 1963, p. 56. Many families are split between the two administrations, e.g. a Taiwan Minister's sister teaching in Peking and another's aunt working as a senior health officer on the mainland. Since 1955 the Communists have waged a "letter offensive," inviting people in Taiwan to visit China, and from time to time emissaries of each side (from the Soong family, for example, which claims both Madame Chiang Kai-shek and her sister, Madame Soong Ching-ling, a Deputy Chairman of the People's Republic) are said to meet in Hongkong. On 7 August 1961 the *Ta Kung Pao*, Peking, published without comment a *Washington Post* story on these lines.

7 The Olympic Games provide an illustration of the diplomatic problem. In 1952 the International Olympic Committee invited both China and Taiwan to send teams to Helsinki. Peking regarded its invitation as equivalent to diplomatic recognition and "we hoisted the red flag with emotion." The Taiwan team, discomforted, soon withdrew (Peking had sent twenty-six sportsmen). In 1954 the IOC recognized both the All-China Sports Association in Peking and the Olympic Committee in Taipei, and Avery Brundage wrote to Peking explaining that Taiwan had a *de facto* separate

government. He was called an "imperialist" and an "American tool" for his pains. Peking selected ninety-two athletes for the 1956 Melbourne Games, but the IOC insisted on two Chinas (China Peking and Formosa China), and when the Kuomintang flag was hoisted Peking refused to take part in the Games. She ignored the subsequent Games in Rome and Tokyo. See CNA 339, 9 September 1960.

8 See Snow, pp. 8–12.

9 UN General Assembly, 6 November 1951 (Keesing, p. 11869); and Dulles' speech at Berlin, 28 January 1954 (Keesing, p. 13439).

10 10 May 1951 (Keesing, p. 11479).

11 Washington refused permission in 1962 for a sale of over ten million tons of wheat and barley to China and North Korea, but on a technicality which left it open for a different decision on another application. See Pearl Buck's letter in the *New York Times,* 11 March 1962. In March 1963, a Committee for Review of Our China Policy was set up by West Coast interests which resented the Chinese grain orders going north of the border to Canada: see Daniel Wolfstone, "The Envious Oregonians," in FEER, 17 October 1964, p. 143. Washington seems, however, to be if anything less rigid in its China policy than general American opinion would justify. See Daniel Tretiak, "Sino-American Impasse," in FEER, 7 January 1965, p. 14.

12 24 November 1963.

13 In the summer of 1960, aimed at the revision of the US-Japan Treaty and Eisenhower's projected visit to Japan.

14 e.g. *People's Daily,* Peking, 22 September 1961, arguing that revolution did not deprive a new government of its predecessor's UN seat in the case of the UAR, Cuba, Iraq, etc.

15 *PLA Work Bulletin,* 25 April 1961 (cited in CNA 511, 10 April 1964).

16 19 October 1960.

17 e.g. *People's Daily,* Peking, 4 December 1964.

18 *L'Humanité,* Paris, 21 February 1964.

19 21 January 1964.

20 See FEER, 6 February 1964, p. 305.

21 23 January 1964 (quoted in FEER, 2 July 1964, p. 14).

22 21 January 1960 (Keesing, p. 17344).

23 16 October 1964 (quoted in *New York Times,* 17 October 1964, and in CQ 21, 1965, pp. 76 *et seq.*). For China's policy towards nuclear disarmament, including her proposal for a world summit meeting to ban nuclear weapons, see Hungdah Chiu, "Communist China's Attitude Towards Nuclear Tests," in CQ 21, 1965, p. 96.

CHAPTER SIXTEEN: HONGKONG

1 *UPI*, Phnompenh, 29 December 1963; *China Mail*, Hongkong, 30 December 1963.

2 According to official Hongkong Government statistics: some observers would add between ten and twenty per cent to this figure in the knowledge that the Chinese exporting authority and the Hongkong importer have a common interest in underdeclaring values and quantities to the British customs. For figures on China's earnings in Hongkong, see L. F. Goodstadt's "Profit and Loss" in FEER, 6 July 1967, p. 41.

3 *Pravda*, Moscow, 27 May 1964 (article by M. Domogatskikh and L. Pochivalov).

4 *Daily Worker*, Peking, 8 March 1963 (an editorial also printed as a pamphlet entitled *A Comment on the Statement of the Communist Party of the USA*).

5 *Nanfang Daily*, Canton, quoted in FEER, 30 January 1964, p. 189.

6 P. F. Shakhov on 20 April 1964.

7 What is said of Hongkong in this chapter could mostly be equally said, on smaller scale, of miniscule Macao. There was a border clash with Portuguese troops in the summer of 1952, but this was resolved and the Chinese paid compensation (Keesing, p. 12567). In 1955 the Portuguese proposed to celebrate the 400th anniversary of Macao's accession to Portugal, but this was an "outrageous attempt to show off," and the *People's Daily* said: "The Chinese people have never forgotten Macao, nor have they forgotten that they have a right to demand the recovery of this territory from Portugal. . . . The fact that Macao has not been returned to China does not mean that the Chinese people can tolerate the continued occupation of Macao. Apparently the Portuguese authorities in Macao mistake the Chinese people's peace policy for a sign of weakness." (25 October 1955, quoted in Keesing, p. 14535). The celebrations were cancelled. *Pravda* alleged on 8 July 1964 that Portugal was transferring troops from Macao to keep her African colonies under control, to which the *People's Daily* replied on 28 July 1964. Portugal is so oblivious of the delicacy of her position that until the late 1950s she used African troops to patrol the Macao–China frontier. Then at the end of 1966 China successfully backed local discontent against a minor incident of Portuguese misrule, and forced the Macao Government to sign a humiliating pact giving the Communists a decisive say in the territory's administration.

8 *Reuter*, Moscow, 12 December 1962; *Guardian*, Manchester, 13 December 1962.

9 29 April 1964.

10 FEER, 12 March 1964, p. 589.

11 14 March 1964, address to the Reform Club (seen generally Daniel Wolfstone, "Conspiracy of Silence," in FEER, 4 May 1961, p. 211).

CHAPTER SEVENTEEN: SOUTHEAST ASIA

1 In *The Chinese Revolution and the Chinese Communist Party*, 1939, (as translated in Stuart R. Schram, *The Political Thought of Mao Tse-tung*, London, Pall Mall Press, 1963, p. 257).

2 Edgar Snow, *Red Star Over China*, 1936, p. 102.

3 See Chapter 7 above.

4 See the citations in CNA 129, 27 April 1956.

5 10 December 1954 (Keesing, p. 14037).

6 See Daniel Wolfstone, "Fast Work on the Sino-Burmese Border," in FEER, 18 August 1960, p. 368.

7 11 December 1956 (Keesing, p. 15334).

8 Brigadier Aung Gyi, *New China News Agency,* Peking, 1 August 1960 (quoted in Wolfstone, *op. cit.* in footnote 6, p. 372). B. P. Koirala, then Premier of Nepal, told ten thousand Chinese in Peking on 14 March 1960 that, "If any power-mad nation, however big and powerful, nurtures the feeling, or attempts to control or occupy even an inch of the territory of any of the Asian nations, such measures will certainly lead to a complete disturbance of global peace." (*New China News Agency,* quoted in FEER, 31 March 1960, p. 693).

9 16 December 1950 (Keesing, p. 11202).

10 12 December 1950 (Keesing, p. 11201).

11 *New China News Agency,* Peking, 2 November 1951.

12 Quoted in CQ 11, 1962, p. 185.

13 *Selected Works,* Vol. 4 (quoted in CQ 11, 1962, p. 235).

14 See e.g. Chen Yi's speech at the National People's Congress, Peking, in September 1956 (Keesing, p. 15233).

15 Keesing, p. 14182.

16 See Victor Purcell's *The Chinese in Southeast Asia*, Oxford, 1965 (2nd ed.), *passim*.

17 Douglas P. Murray, in CQ 20, 1964, p. 70.

18 Returned Overseas Chinese are accorded privileged treatment in housing, education, rationing, finance and general discipline; life is in every way a little easier for them than for the general body of Chinese. New housing estates have been built for them (including luxury air-conditioned apartment blocks in Shanghai and Canton). See FEER, 25 October 1962, p. 226. The Overseas Chinese were neglected under the Empire, but because of the cru-

cial support they gave to Sun Yat-sen they have a special place in Republican China, being included in the Censuses and sending delegates to the National People's Congress.

19 14 December 1954 (Keesing, p. 14037).

20 See the report on Chou En-lai's discussions with David Marshall, former chief Minister of Singapore, in October 1956, in Peking, in the *Guardian*, Manchester, 13 October 1956 (cited in Purcell, *op. cit.* in footnote 16, p. xvi).

21 See Purcell, *op. cit.* (in footnote 16), pp. 480–91.

22 See FEER, 30 May 1963, pp. 463–4.

23 Indonesian statement of 13 December 1959 (Keesing, p. 17186). The Chinese replied that it was unfair, because of the "small number" of misbehavers, to penalize the Chinese community as a whole (letter of Chen Yi to Dr Subandrio, 26 December 1959, quoted in Purcell, *op. cit.*, p. 490). Indonesians also felt that the Indonesian Chinese had not, on the whole, helped their political fight against the Dutch but had in many cases hindered it. For more recent developments see John Hughes, "China and Indonesia," *Current Scene*, Vol. 6, No. 19, 4 November 1968.

24 Quoted in CQ 11, 1962, p. 195.

25 *People's Daily*, Peking, 29 December 1956.

26 Viscount Montgomery's *Three Continents*, (London, Collins, 1962), pp. 69–70. Marshal Chen Yi, the Foreign Minister, said in the *Peking Review*, 15 June 1962: "Unlike the imperialists, we will never try to solve our difficulties by sending troops abroad."

27 In the Indian Parliament, 12 September 1959.

28 All these reactions to the Tibet crisis are cited from Keesing, p. 16802.

29 16 December 1950 (Keesing p. 11202).

CHAPTER EIGHTEEN: INDIA

1 Keesing, pp. 11538, 11978 and 12248.

2 Speech on 5 April 1959 (Keesing, p. 16801).

3 Indian note of 26 October 1950 (Keesing, p. 11102).

4 Speech on 26 June 1954 (Keesing, p. 13661).

5 December 1956 (Keesing, p. 15463).

6 In May (quoted in FEER, 20 June 1963, p. 635).

7 *The Times*, London, 12 October 1964.

8 See footnote 2 *supra*.

9 *Ta Kung Pao*, Peking, 25 April 1959.

10 A National People's Congress delegate, reported by the *New China News Agency* and quoted in Keesing, p. 16801.

11 Speech in the Lok Sabha, 27 April 1959 (Keesing, p. 16802).

12 A good exposition of this is given by Foreign Minister Chen Yi in Stuart and Roma Gelder's *Long March to Freedom* (London, Hutchinson, 1962), pp. 189–91.

13 See footnote 11 *supra*.

14 See Alastair Lamb's *The China-India Border* (London, Oxford University Press, 1964), pp. 49–50. This is the best short, impartial summary of the border dispute: it is not on sale in China and is not allowed to be sold in India.

15 20 November 1950 (Keesing, p. 11103).

16 A good summary of these events is by P. H. M. Jones, "Passes and Impasses," in FEER, 28 February 1963, p. 443.

17 Speech in Rajya Sabha, 22 August 1962.

18 *People's Daily*, Peking, 31 December 1962. European Communist opinion, concerned to maintain good relations with India, mostly felt that if China had a legitimate grievance, she ought not to have settled it by force.

19 9 September 1959. On 20 December 1962 the Russian newspapers took the view that they could not believe that India had wanted to start a war with China. See CNA 496, 6 December 1963.

20 See Lamb, *op. cit.* (footnote 14 *supra*), pp. 100–5 and 173–4; and Jones (*op. cit.*, footnote 16 *supra*), p. 451. The Indian case in Ladakh is well expounded in Margaret W. Fisher, Leo E. Rose and Robert A. Huttenback, *Himalayan Battleground* (London, Pall Mall Press, 1963).

21 See Lamb, *op. cit.*, pp. 168–70; the author's "Who's Right in the Himalayas," in FEER, 18 March 1965, p. 485; and G. F. Hudson in CQ 12, 1962, p. 203. In a mimeographed study called *The India-China Border Question* (Center for International Affairs, Harvard University, April 1963), a Western scholar notes that India made unilateral extensions of the McMahon Line after Simla (pp. 30–1 and 72): this study makes it clear that Nehru was himself well aware of the equivocal basis of parts of the Indian case.

22 See FEER, 3 January 1963, p. 17; and 7 February 1963, p. 242.

23 In January 1959 Chou wrote to Nehru that he would not insist on every inch of the Chinese territory shown on the Chinese maps, but would need local consultations and surveys before modifying them. Nehru declared: "So far as we are concerned, the McMahon Line is the frontier—firm by treaty, firm by usage and right, and firm by geography" (Lok Sabha, 13 August 1959, Keesing, p. 17115); and on 12 September 1959, he told the Lok Sabha that the Chinese claims were "absurd," meaning "handing over the Himalayas to them as a gift—a thing we are not prepared to consider" (Keesing, p. 17119). A little later Nehru told a crowd at

Bichpuri that, "The Himalayas are the crown of India," part of her "culture, blood and veins" (Keesing, p. 17121).

24 See George N. Patterson, "Recent Chinese Policies in Tibet and Towards the Himalayan Border States," in CQ 12, 1962, p. 191.

CHAPTER NINETEEN: AFRICA AND BEYOND

1 See Arslan Humbaraci, "Peking's African Limits," in FEER, 17 December 1964, p. 572.

2 Basil Davidson, *Old Africa Rediscovered* (London, Gollancz, 1959), pp. 158–9; the giraffe was sent by the old city of Malindi and was pictured on silk by a fifteenth-century Chinese artist.

3 See *Ta Tung Shu, The One-World Philosophy of Kang Yu-wei*, translated by Laurence G. Thompson (London, Allen and Unwin, 1958), pp. 141–8. In the USA, Kang wrote, "the negroes' bodies smell badly, and so it is difficult for the racial barrier to be levelled" (pp. 143–4). Later he observes that, "The appearance of the negroes—with their iron faces, silver teeth, slanting jaws like a pig, front view like an ox, full breasts and long hair, their hands and feet dark black, stupid like sheep or swine—brings fear to [one who] beholds them" (p. 144). Sven Lindquist (*China in Crisis*, London, Faber, 1965) describes how Chinese students in Peking in 1960–1 confided to him their dislike of the smell and prominent features of Africans (p. 26). For another comment on Chinese colour feelings, see Tarzie Vittachi, "We Have Our Own Colour Bar," in *The Asia Magazine* (Hongkong), 28 June 1964. J. Tuzo Wilson (*One Chinese Moon*, London, Michael Joseph, 1960, p. 149) saw posters in China showing Chinese with pink, Caucasians with *puce* faces!

4 *China Youth Daily*, Peking, 21 April 1964 (cited in CNA 521, 19 June 1964). An example of contemporary Chinese attitudes, though one for which the Communists are not responsible, was the fact that when South Africa altered its *apartheid* regulations a few years ago to accord "white" status to Chinese in certain circumstances, certain (non-Communist) Chinese political circles in Hongkong put it about that the change was due to their lobbying (via the South African Trade Commissioner in Hongkong): they professed a theoretical concern for the victims of *apartheid*, but emotionally they could not suppress satisfaction at the Chinese being at last put on the white side of the fence.

5 *People's Daily*, Peking, 5 October 1959.

6 Speech on 17 November.

7 *People's Liberation Army General Political Department Work Bulletin*, 25 April 1961 (published in Washington, cited in CNA 501, 24 January 1964).

8 *People's Daily*, Peking, 21 September 1956.

9 *Red Flag,* Peking, 1 April 1959 (cited in CNA 320, 22 April 1960).

10 See *New York Times,* 12 October 1959. W. A. C. Adie, "China and Africa Today," in *Race* (London), April 1964, presents a lucid summary of China's relations with the North African —and with other African—countries.

11 *Figaro* (quoted by June Teufel, "China's Future in Africa," in FEER, 5 December 1963, p. 518).

12 See *Sunday Telegraph,* London, 3 July 1961; CQ 11, 1962, p. 210; and Adie, *op. cit.* (footnote 10 *supra*), pp. 17–8.

13 See Daniel Wolfstone, "Sino-African Economics," in FEER, 13 February 1964, p. 349.

14 See W. A. C. Adie, "China, Russia, and the Third World," in CQ 11, 1962, p. 212.

15 *Cotonou Radio,* 8 January 1965 (quoted in *China Reporting Service,* Hongkong, 30 June 1965).

16 Hamani's statement was in *Fraternité-Matin,* Abidjan, 16 June 1965 (both remarks quoted in *China Reporting Service,* Hongkong, 30 June 1965).

17 Address to the World Assembly of Youth seminar in Dar-es-Salaam, 1961 (published as a pamphlet, *The Second Scramble,* in 1962).

18 Report by Clyde Sanger in the *Guardian,* Manchester, 7 June 1965.

19 *New China News Agency,* Peking, 2 October 1959.

20 Quoted by Anna Louise Strong, *Letter from China,* No. 15, 20 February 1964; and in CQ 18, 1964, p. 183.

21 See Ernst Halperin's "Peking and the Latin American Communists," in CQ 29, 1967, p. 111.

22 *People's Daily,* Peking, 9 August 1963; and *Peking Review,* 16 August 1963.

23 *Letter from China,* No. 18, 15 June 1964.

24 *People's Daily,* Peking, 30 May 1964.

25 *Radio Algiers,* 22 December 1963 (reported in *Hongkong Tiger Standard,* 23 December 1963).

26 *Daily Nation,* Nairobi, 13 March 1962 (report on the Afro-Asian Writer's Conference in Cairo).

27 *Peking Review,* 3 September 1965, p. 9.

28 *Peking Review,* No. 7 of 1964.

29 *New China News Agency,* Peking, 30 December 1964.

30 Alexandra Close, "Aid from the Aidless," in FEER, 29 July 1965, p. 214; W. F. Choa, "China's Economic Aid to Developing Countries," in *The China Mainland Review,* Hongkong, June 1965, p. 13; and the US Congress Joint Economic Committee's

An Economic Profile of Mainland China, Washington, 1967, p. 612.

31 Colin Garratt, "China as a Foreign Aid Donor," in FEER, 19 January 1961, p. 81.

32 Nan Han-chen at the meeting of Afro-Asian Economic Organizations, May 1960 (quoted in FEER, 9 June 1960, p. 1147).

33 Nan Han-chen at Pyongyang Economic Seminar, 20 June 1964 (quoted in FEER, 9 July 1964, p. 42).

34 Dev R. Kumar, "Nepal's Road to China," in FEER, 20 February 1964, p. 419.

35 P. H. M. Jones, "Cambodia's New Factories," in FEER, 9 May 1963, p. 319.

36 Michael Field, *The Prevailing Wind, Witness in Indochina,* London, Methuen, 1965, p. 196.

37 *New China News Agency,* Peking, 30 December 1964.

38 See e.g. CNA 538, 23 October 1964, which suggests that China's messianic complex is a "pathological symptom in one man and his admirers; it is utterly alien to genuine Chinese feeling" (p. 2).

CHAPTER TWENTY: RUSSIA

1 This was said of the Wuhan steelworks: see CNA 229, 23 May 1958. On the other hand, the *People's Daily* reported with apparent pride on 7 November 1959, "Russia gave a 3,500-ton huge pressing machine which was the first result of a new experimental production in the Soviet Union." A donee always complains if an experimental gift fails, accepts it if it works: just as a patient regards the experiment of a surgeon.

2 *People's Daily,* Peking, 31 August 1956.

3 Shen Yu-chang, writing in *Scientific Journal,* Peking, September 1956 (quoted in CNA 155, 2 November 1956).

4 *Kuang Ming Daily,* Peking, 17 June 1956.

5 See Donald S. Zagoria, *The Sino-Soviet Conflict 1956–61* (London, Oxford University Press, 1962), pp. 154 *et seq.*

6 Yu Chao-li in *Peking Review,* 18 August 1959.

7 Zagoria, *op. cit.* (footnote 5), pp. 206–17.

8 Report of 14 February 1964, published in *Pravda,* 3 April 1964, and in *New Times* (Moscow), 15 April 1964.

9 "The Chinese Government solemnly declares that at no time and in no circumstances will China be the first to use nuclear weapons" (Chinese letter to all Heads of Government proposing a world summit conference to ban nuclear weapons, 17 October 1964, *Peking Review,* 23 October 1964).

10 This is an extension, in fact, of the earlier Soviet argument

that as the Second World War allowed many countries to escape from capitalism, so the Third World War would, in the words of a Russian article in the *Kuang Ming Daily*, Peking, on 11 November 1954, "result in the collapse of the whole world capitalist system." Only under Khrushchev did the Russian Government come round to the view that "the nuclear bomb does not adhere to the class principle—it destroys everything" (Soviet Party letter to Peking of 14 July 1963).

11 Report of M. A. Suslov to the Soviet Central Committee, 14 February 1964 (see footnote 8 *supra*).

12 Zagoria, *op. cit.* (footnote 5, *supra*), p. 365.

13 *People's Daily*, Peking, 19 November 1963.

14 Quoted by David Binder in *Chicago Daily News*, 24 March 1954; and by Zagoria, *op. cit.* (footnote 5), p. 106.

15 *People's Daily*, Peking, 9 March 1965.

16 *People's Daily*, Peking, 23 March 1965, editorial.

17 *Peking Review*, 12 November 1965, p. 19.

18 Interview with Japanese socialists, 10 July 1964 (*Seikai Siuho*, Tokyo, 11 August 1964; *Pravda*, 2 September 1964; CQ 20, 1964, pp. 180–1).

19 Soviet Party letter to Peking, 29 November 1963 (the Russians in the second sentence presumably refer to Sinkiang and Tibet); and Chinese letter to Moscow of 29 February 1964. Anna Louise Strong says (*Letter from China*, No. 17, 20 May 1964), "China has written those [territories given to Russia] off, though she would like it on the record that they were taken from her by 'unequal treaties.' "

20 Chinese letter to Moscow of 29 February 1964. David Floyd (*Mao against Khrushchev*, Praeger, London, 1964) argues that the Russians used their aid programme in Stalin's day to gain information about the Chinese military and economic set-up (pp. 13–14). See also *The Chinese Model*, edited by Werner Klatt (Hongkong University Press, 1965), chapter 8.

21 See e.g. the Yugoslav reports on this cited in Zagoria, *op. cit*, (footnote 5), in footnote 2 to chapter 10, p. 433.

22 *People's Daily*, Peking, 1 March 1965.

23 *The Observer*, London, 14 February 1960.

CHAPTER 21: THE WORLD

1 8 September 1961 (quoted in CNA 390, 22 September 1961).

2 Interview with Walter Cole, *Reuters*, Peking, 11 October 1961.

3 Michael Field, *The Prevailing Wind* (London, Methuen, 1965), p. 201.

4 Remark of Tsao Po-han in December 1950 (quoted in CQ 5, 1961, pp. 132–3).

5 Quoted in Hudson, p. 203. Voltaire declared that the Chinese "have perfected moral science," and that "the organization of their empire is in truth the best that the world has ever seen," while Leibnitz wrote that Europe deserved Chinese missionaries in natural theology just as it despatched to China its own missionaries in revealed religion (see citations in Hudson, pp. 318–22).

6 China donated just over $7 million worth of commodities to the Hungarian Government during its 1956 crisis, and extended a credit of about $48 million (half in free currency) to Budapest in 1957. These helped to soften the pressure on Budapest from Moscow. Peking made a $2¼ million gift to Albania in 1954, and lent a further $12½ million over the period 1955–60: this credit was doubled in 1959. (See FEER, 19 January 1961, pp. 84–5.) Albania, that "glorious giant" of socialism, as the Chinese call her, was conducting sixty per cent of her trade with China by 1962.

7 *Letter from China*, No. 8, 15 May 1963. In the same letter another American resident in Peking describes how "our cook lets our potatoes scorch on the stove while he masters Togliatti's structural reform and Italian constitution." Miss Strong comments: "Chinese . . . work harder at Marxism than any people I know. . . . Chinese intend to qualify for the Great Debate."

8 21 March 1963. Chiang Kai-shek wrote in his *China's Destiny* (London, Dennis Dobson, 1947, p. 29) that China was then fighting "an unprecedented war . . . for the freedom and liberation of mankind."

9 P. 420 (London, 1946 edition).

10 See Luke T. C. Lee's *Towards an Understanding of Law in Communist China*, in Szczepanik, p. 335. The Confucian preference for conciliation affects modern Japanese law: Dan Fenno Henderson, *Conciliation and Japanese Law* (Seattle, 1965).

11 Chinese Government statement of 31 July 1963 (see *Peking Review*, 2 August 1963; and Morton H. Halperin, *China and the Bomb*, London, Pall Mall, 1965, pp. 62–70).

12 *People's Daily*, Peking, 18 September 1957.

13 Keesing, pp. 12519, 12567 and 12618.

14 Keesing, pp. 13733, 13889 and 13933. For earlier examples of Chinese misunderstanding of Western legal processes see C. P. Fitzgerald, *The Birth of Communist China*, London, Penguin, 1964, p. 61 (Shanghai incident of 30 May 1925) and p. 91 (procedure of the 1945 surrender in north China).

15 19 April (Keesing, p. 11470).

16 See e.g. Dulles' speech in San Francisco on 28 June 1957 (Keesing, p. 15667).

17 28 January 1955 (Keesing, p. 16388).

18 10 September 1963.

19 The series began on 30 August 1963.

20 Fitzgerald, *op. cit.*, footnote 14 above, p. 270.

21 Peake urged in a letter to the editor of the *New York Times* on 17 October 1963, that the West or the USSR or both should "make it unmistakably clear to the Chinese Communists that . . . aid would be forthcoming if they appropriately modify their foreign policies and enter into disarmament negotiations," wording which betrays remarkable ignorance of Chinese psychology. Haekkerup's plea was made in October 1963.

CONCLUSION

1 Maj.-Gen. David Barr (head of the joint US Military Advisory Group in China), report dated 16 November 1948 (Keesing, p. 10205).

2 Statement of 11 March 1950 (Keesing, p. 10930). General Li returned to China in 1965, after fifteen years exile in the USA.

3 Quoted in *People's Daily*, Peking, 11 February 1963.

4 Quoted in CNA 151, 5 October 1956.

5 In a letter to a friend written in 1951 and published in the *People's Daily*, Peking, 10 June 1955, as part of the evidence for his condemnation as a "rightist."

6 20 September 1964: address to National People's Congress (Keesing, p. 14051).

7 San Francisco speech of 28 June 1957 (Keesing, p. 15668).

8 See A. S. Chen, "The Ideal Party Secretary and the 'Model' Man," in CQ 17, 1964, p. 238.

9 See CNA 133, 25 May 1956. Western authors who are translated and published in China nowadays include Zola, Maupassant, Balzac, Hugo, Rousseau, Diderot, Turgot, Hegel, Shakespeare, Adam Smith, Thomas More, Dickens, Twain, London, Goethe and Heine: virtually no modern or contemporary writers are so honoured. The Shakespeare quatercentenary was mentioned only once in the *People's Daily* (12 March 1964), in connection with the Western commercialization of Shakespeare. The *People's Daily* on 22 March 1964 gave a full-page criticism of Rolland's *Jean-Christophe*, rebutting the Soviet praise for this hero as a revolutionary humanist and categorizing him as actually an individualist: "We believe that what the bourgeois class and modern revisionism appreciate must be rejected by us." In view of this most benighted policy it is encouraging to learn that at Peking University in 1961–2, "in secret the teaching staff discuss such forbidden books as C. P. Snow's *The New Men*" (Sven Lindquist, *China in Crisis*, London, Faber, 1965, pp. 48–9).

10 27 December 1959.

11 September 1956 (quoted in CNA 155, 2 November 1956). The respective destinies of the capitalist and socialist economies are usually compared with "the setting and the rising of the sun."

12 10 December 1954 (Keesing, p. 14037).

13 Quoted in Hudson, p. 263.

14 See CNA 318, 1 April 1960; and 428, 13 July 1962.

15 Quoted in CNA 366, 7 April 1961.

16 *People's Daily*, Peking, 22 November 1953.

17 *Red Flag*, Peking, No. 15 of 1964.

18 Translation of Michael Bullock and Jerome Ch'en, quoted from Jerome Ch'en, *Mao and the Chinese Revolution*, London, Oxford University Press, 1965, p. 360.

19 "Introducing a Cooperative," in *Red Flag*, Peking, 1 June 1958, and *New China News Agency*, Peking, 31 May 1958.

20 *San Min Chu*, Vol. 1, p. 98 (quoted in H. G. Creel, *Chinese Thought*, London, Methuen, 1962, p. 254).

21 Po I-po, interviewed by Anna Louise Strong, *Letter from China*, No. 13, 30 December 1963.

22 *People's Daily*, Peking, 10 December 1961.

23 Yu Chao-li, in *Red Flag*, Peking, 16 August 1958 (quoted in CQ 5, 1961, p. 102).

24 The case of Dr Samuel Rosen: see Daniel Tretiak, "Sino-American Impasse," in FEER, 7 January 1965, p. 14.

25 Quoted in Hudson, p. 249. For Mao's youthful self-toughening, see Edgar Snow, *Red Star Over China* (London, Gollancz, 1937), p. 86.

26 Snow, *op. cit.* (footnote 25 *supra*), p. 102.

27 From Mao's speech at the Yenan Forum on Literature and Art in 1942.

28 Remark at a Hongkong press conference, 2 September 1954 (Keesing, p. 13800).

29 Sven Lindquist, *op. cit.* (footnote 9 *supra*), p. 27.

APPENDIX

1 See CNA 185, 21 June 1957; and CNA 407, 2 February 1962.

2 13 January 1961.

3 *Literature*, Peking, 30 November 1954 (quoted in CNA 68, 21 January 1955).

4 See CNA 313, 26 February 1960, p. 5; CNA 473, 21 June 1963, p. 1; and CNA 570, 2 July 1965 (an illuminating exposition of what can and cannot be gleaned from Chinese newspapers).

5 CQ 15, 1963, p. 59.

6 Quoted in CNA 384, 11 August 1961.

7 Keesing, p. 14182.

8 The story was told in the *Peking Daily,* and retailed by David Chipp, the *Reuters* Correspondent there, in a despatch of 23 May 1957.

9 See CNA 142, 3 August 1956.

10 See CQ 8, 1961, p. 65.

11 The most enlightenment comes from writers who have actually lived in China for a time, such as Mu Fu-sheng (*The Wilting of the Hundred Flowers,* London, Heinemann, 1962), Mikhail Klochko (*Soviet Scientist in China,* London, Hollis & Carter, 1965) and Sven Lindquist (*China in Crisis,* London, Faber, 1965).

12 *Report of the Indian Delegation to China on Agricultural Planning and Techniques,* July–August 1956 (Government of India, Ministry of Food and Agriculture, Delhi, 1956): see quotations, in Li, p. 21.

13 *People's Daily,* Peking, 29 March 1956.

14 See Choh-ming Li, "Statistics and Planning at the Hsien Level in Communist China," in CQ 9, 1962, p. 112; and his *The Statistical System of Communist China,* Berkeley, University of California Press, 1962.

15 John Lossing Buck, in *Food and Agriculture in Communist China* (New York, Praeger, 1966); see also *Current Scene,* Vol. 3, No. 14, 1 March 1965. Peking makes much of the percentage increases in production since 1949, but in that year, as Colin Clark says, "the country was so disorganised that a substantial improvement in productivity was to have been expected as soon as any stable government was established" (CQ 21, 1965, p. 148).

16 *People's Daily,* Peking, 7 April 1959.

17 Professor Chen Yu-sung, in *Wen Hui Pao,* Shanghai, 30 April 1957 (quoted in CNA 182, 24 May 1957).

18 Professor Lo Chih-ju, in *Statistical Work,* Peking, No. 12, of 1957 (quoted in CNA 196, 13 September 1957).

19 Hsueh Mu-chiao, quoted in CNA 196, 13 September 1957.

20 Chia Chi-yun, speaking at October–November 1959 Conference of Statisticians, reported in *Planning and Statistics,* Peking, 23 November 1959 (quoted in CNA 324, 20 May 1960).

21 *Statistical Work,* Peking, 1957 (quoted in CNA 196, 13 September 1957).

22 *People's Daily,* Peking, 22 November 1961.

23 When a Russian book on the trade of the Soviet bloc was translated into Chinese and published in Peking in 1957, the chapter giving data about China's trade was omitted (see CNA 419, 4 May 1962, p. 3).

24 See Li, Chapter 7; see also Alexander Eckstein's *Communist China's Economic Growth and Foreign Trade* (New York, McGraw-Hill, 1966), Appendix B.

A SELECTED BIBLIOGRAPHY

HISTORICAL AND GENERAL

The three best introductory books in China's past and culture are C. P. Fitzgerald, *China: A Short Cultural History* (Cresset Press, 1961); H. G. Creel, *Chinese Thought* (Methuen University Paperback, 1962); and K. S. Latourette, *A History of Modern China* (Penguin, 1954). Chang-tu Hu *et al.*, *China: Its People, Its Society, Its Culture* (Mayflower, 1961) is the most reliable and informative general book on all aspects of China.

EVENTS LEADING UP TO COMMUNIST RULE

C. P. Fitzgerald, *The Birth of Communist China* (Penguin, 1964) is the best short account. Han Suyin's *The Crippled Tree, A Mortal Flower* and *Birdless Summer* (all London, Cape, 1965, 1966 and 1968) give a more personal, semi-fictional insight, and there are novels which illuminate. André Malraux's *Man's Destiny*, Mao Tun's *Midnight* and Lu Hsun's *The True Story of Ah Q* are recommended.

CONTEMPORARY CHINA

The works of Mao Tse-tung are both readable and enlightening. A selection of them has been published in English in Peking and London (Lawrence and Wishart) in four volumes. The best single work to read is Mao's *On the Correct Handling of Contradictions among the People* (Peking, Foreign Languages Press, 1957).

Stuart R. Schram, *The Political Thought of Mao Tse-tung* (Pall Mall, 1963) gives a manageable set of excerpts with commentary, and his biography *Mao Tse-tung* (Penguin, 1968) is the best yet. The best books on the Chinese economy are Yuan-li Wu, *The Economy of Communist China* (New York, Praeger, 1965) and Audrey Donnithorne, *China's Economic System* (London, Allen L. Unwin, 1967). See also Franz Schurmann, *Ideology and Organisation in Communist China* (Berkeley, University of California Press, 1966) and Harold C. Hinton, *Communist China in World Politics* (London, Macmillan, 1966).

Among visitors' books, Edgar Snow, *The Other Side of the River* (Gollancz, 1963) is outstanding: Snow knew pre-Communist China and speaks Chinese, and he has packed this book with information and considered impressions. Mu Fu-sheng, *The Wilting of the Hundred Flowers* (Heinemann, 1962) gives a good account of a returned scientist's view. Sven Lindqvist, *China in Crisis* (Faber and Faber, 1963) is a perceptive and evocative report by a foreign student at Peking University.

INDEX

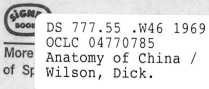

DS 777.55 .W46 1969
OCLC 04770785
Anatomy of China /
Wilson, Dick.

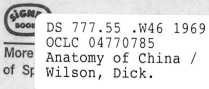

DATE DUE

PRINTED IN U.S.A.

SIGNET
BOOK

More
of Sp

☐ **RUSSIA AND THE WEST** by George F. Kennan. An illuminating review of Soviet-Western

☐

☐

☐

☐

THE
Statio

Please
above
no cu
to cov
Other
taxes.

Name

Addres

City